THE RELIGIOUS CULTURE OF
MARIAN ENGLAND

RELIGIOUS CULTURES IN THE EARLY MODERN WORLD

Series Editors: *Fernando Cervantes*
Peter Marshall
Philip Soergel

TITLES IN THIS SERIES

www.pickeringchatto.com/religious

THE RELIGIOUS CULTURE OF MARIAN ENGLAND

BY

David Loades

MUNDUS
INTELLECTUALIS

LONDON
PICKERING & CHATTO
2010

Published by Pickering & Chatto (Publishers) Limited
21 Bloomsbury Way, London WC1A 2TH

2252 Ridge Road, Brookfield, Vermont 05036-9704, USA

www.pickeringchatto.com

BRITISH LIBRARY CATALOGUING IN PUBLICATION DATA

Loades, D. M.
The religious culture of Marian England. – (Religious cultures in the early modern world)
1. Mary I, Queen of England, 1516–1558 – Religion. 2. England – Church history – 16th century. 3. Christian life – England – History – 16th century. 4. Catholic Church – England – History – 16th century.
I. Title II. Series
274.2'06-dc22

ISBN-13: 9781851969210
e: 9781851965984

This publication is printed on acid-free paper that conforms to the American National Standard for the Permanence of Paper for Printed Library Materials.

Typeset by Pickering & Chatto (Publishers) Limited
Printed in Great Britain by the MPG Books Group, Bodmin and King's Lynn

CONTENTS

PREFACE

This book has been too long in the writing. It arose originally out of two circum-stances. The first was my involvement with the John Foxe Project, which was a British Academy sponsored project for the publication of an online edition of all four versions of the *Acts and Monuments* for which Foxe was personally responsible (1563, 1570, 1576, 1583). I put this idea to the Academy in 1992, and was its director from 1993 to 2004, when Professor Mark Greengrass took over that responsibility. It was completed in 2008. The second circumstance was a perception that existing histories of the persecution had all been written from an elite point of view, and that in any case much was happening in the Marian Church which had nothing to do with the persecution. These were points which I desired to emphasize.

The most obviously elite studies are Professor Mayer's numerous works on Reginald Pole. It is no criticism of Professor Mayer to point out that these are predominantly about the running of the Church, and to some extent about its spiritual direction. They tell us a great deal about policy and how it was imple-mented, but nothing very much about what was going on at the parish level. Cardinal Pole was a grandee, with a very keen theological perception and no time at all for 'superstition'. It was just that his definition of the latter differed from that of his opponents. In so far as he dealt with the laity, it was at the high-est political level, where, on the whole, men told him what he wanted to hear. His relationships with the Queen and with King Philip were essential to his role, and his understanding of Mary was profound, but his grasp of the religious mentality of the English was at best imperfect. It was not that they did not take their faith seriously, but that faith tended to be basic and they had been much confused by the different instructions which had been, and were being, issued in God's name. This confusion he understood in an intellectual sense, but never empathized with. The same is true in a sense of Thomas Watson, the subject of an admirable study by Professor William Wizeman. Watson was less exalted than Pole, but he was equally an intellectual and a leader, who saw his role as a preacher and writer in defence of the establishment. He fought heretics with their own weapons of biblical exegesis, and used tight rational arguments, but he never showed any sign of understanding the un-intellectual (and even anti-intellectual) attitude of the ordinary believer. The same accusation could not be levelled against Professor Eamon Duffy, whose *Fires of Faith* appeared while this book was in gestation. Professor Duffy does understand the man in the pew, but is not mainly concerned with him. He believes that the persecution was justified, indeed inevitable by the standards of the time, and expends a great deal of scholarly energy explaining how, and why, it came about. He is therefore very much concerned with inquisitors and inquisitorial practices, and with the responses which articulate heretics made to them, but is not particularly interested in what happened out of that selective spotlight.

My justification for writing is therefore partly that the time is opportune, with the online Foxe having just been released and an upsurge of interest in the subject manifest in a number of learned (and some less learned) articles and papers. It is also partly that there is a tendency to see the Marian period in isolation, so that although the Henrician and Edwardian roots of heresy are usually acknowledged, the equally interesting origins of conformist faith are usually ignored. It is my contention that the Marian Church can only be properly understood in its contemporary context, as an aspect of the ongoing history of English religion in what is usually called 'the reformation period'. In that respect what happened under Elizabeth is just as relevant as what happened under Edward VI, and central figures in the story are the conformists – those who did as they were told – who are nobody's idea of heroes and who do not feature in the hagiography of either side.

The work is based partly on my own research, going back over many years, and partly on the work of other scholars, most notably that of Professor Duffy, with whom I had the privilege of collaborating in the publication of *The Church of Mary Tudor* in 2006. I do not necessarily agree with Professor Duffy, particularly in *Fires of Faith*, but am much indebted to his pioneering efforts. I am also indebted to the work of numerous colleagues who have worked on the Foxe Project, most notably Professor Patrick Collinson and Dr Tom Freeman, without whose insights much of what follows could not have been written. The series editor, Professor Peter Marshall, has been indulgent of my delays, and to him I would also like to offer grateful thanks.

This study is not the definitive history of the Marian Church, for which historians have been clamouring, but it is, I hope, another piece in that most interesting jigsaw. The people of England in Mary's reign were the same people who had been there under Edward and were to be there again under Elizabeth. The elite pressures which were brought to bear upon them were only a part of the story, and I hope that I have been able to show that it is worth probing below that surface to establish the essential social continuities.

David Loades
Oxford, April 2010

INTRODUCTION

The alliance between ecclesiastical and secular authority is almost as old as Christianity itself. What started as a purely spiritual commitment to a vision of Jesus Christ as the Son of God, had become by the fourth century inextricably entangled with the politics of the Empire. The support of Constantine and his successors converted bishops into imperial administrators, and the prayers of the faithful recognized and upheld the imperial authority.[1] When the Empire in the West collapsed, the Church survived, and carried the concept of *romanitas* forward into a world of successor kingdoms, which often enough showed little political continuity, but were ambitious to preserve the ideal. The Pope was the Bishop of Rome, and based his claim to authority on that fact, an authority which was allowed to transcend that of the secular kingdoms and lordships because of what it symbolized.[2] What these kingdoms sought above all else was authenticity, a validity which transcended the exploits of warlords and conferred upon their kings some echo of the imperial authority. It was this that the Church conferred. In creating dioceses and founding monasteries, rulers were entering into a compact with the Church, which in return for this material superstructure, recognized their power and interceded for them with God. The doctrine that this world is a mere antechamber to the next gave the Church an unchallenged cultural ascendancy which more than compensated for its lack of military muscle. Priests did not fight, they prayed, and prayer was as potent as the sword.[3] As the Church expanded into hitherto pagan lands beyond the reach of the Empire, it was usually with the assistance of temporal lords who recognized the benefits which this alliance could confer upon themselves. It was by such means that the Roman Church embraced Anglo-Saxon England in the sixth and seventh centuries.[4]

After the Norman conquest, relations between Rome and the Crown of England had fluctuated, but the one thing which no king could afford to do to the Church was to ignore it. Because of its Latin heritage, the Church had a virtual monopoly of literacy, at least in northern Europe, and the clerks who staffed the king's Chancery and his Exchequer were nearly all in holy orders. The colleges which provided higher education were ecclesiastical foundations, which doubled as chantries, offering prayers for the souls of their founders and their kin.[5] In so far as aristocratic education extended beyond the martial arts and 'courtesy', it was a clerical monopoly. How far this cultural grip extended down the social scale is a matter for some speculation, because the written records, as far as they exist, were either produced in the service of the Crown or for the information of educated monks and priests. The chronicles reflect everyday life only at second hand. By the thirteenth century the parish system covered the whole of England, and every adult was supposed in theory to worship in his or her parish church, to be baptized and to receive the sacraments. Most probably did so, but with what degree of understanding it is difficult to say.[6] The Church had long since learned to compromise with the deeply rooted customs of the rural year – so the winter solstice became Christmas and the spring festival of re-birth became Easter. This did not mean that the faith which they expressed was any less genuine, but the conformity of the ecclesiastical calendar to existing patterns undoubtedly made the transition to Christianity easier. By 1300 paganism was residual, even in the more remote parts of the country, and the Church's projection of its own intercessory role was generally accepted. Even those with very little in the way of worldly goods would bestow what they could on the well-being of their souls in the afterlife, and the rituals performed by the priest were accepted as the gateway to salvation. The more elaborate the ritual, the more effective it was perceived to be, and the Church flourished both culturally and materially on this acceptance of its indispensable intercessory function.[7]

Human nature being what it is, however, dissent was never totally absent. No doubt at first there were sullen pagans whose conformity to the newly established order was purely nominal, and there had been more or less sophisticated heresies in the Church from its very early days.[8] Doubts were expressed about the cosiness of the relationship between the Church and the feudal hierarchy. Should bishops and abbots really double as temporal lords? What was the justification for tithe? Should the clergy really enjoy so much jurisdiction on the pretext of their spiritual functions? Heretical groups sprang up, even at the height of the Church's power. The Waldensians questioned ecclesiastical wealth and the extent to which it claimed moral jurisdiction.[9] The Albigensians or Cathars were Gnostics, who questioned the whole foundation of the faith, and other smaller groups cast doubt on particular teachings; on the efficacy of penance, for example, or the Church's extremely negative attitude to sexuality.[10] As far as England was concerned, these doubts were conveniently focused in the teachings of one man – John Wycliffe, the eccentric Oxford don. His followers, and others whose dissent owed little to his teachings, were collectively and contemptuously dubbed 'Lollards', and were persecuted in the early fifteenth century.[11]

None of this would have had very much to do with the Crown if it had not been for the vagaries of English politics. This was the time of the papal schism, with Urban VI and Boniface IX in Rome squaring up to Clement VII and Benedict XIII in Avignon. Richard II inevitably supported Boniface against the French backed Benedict, and hoped to gain some autonomy for the English Church in consequence. Benedict, however, was under other pressures and would not concede. The result was the statutes of Provisors and Praemunire, culminating in 1393. This made it unlawful for the Pope to provide to any benefice in England without the king's licence, or for any ecclesiastical jurisdiction to be exercised without his consent.[12] In principle this Act could have made the English Church completely independent, but it was never understood in that sense, either at the time or after. There was no intention of withholding the royal licence under normal circumstances, but it was intended as a warning to Rome that the kings of England reserved their rights when it came to dealings with the Church. That was why successive popes pressed unsuccessfully for many years to have it repealed. At first it did not matter very much, because in 1399 Richard was deposed in questionable circumstances by his cousin Henry Bolingbroke, and Henry thereafter needed all the support that he could get. Both he and his son, Henry V, were conspicuous for their conventional piety and generous patrons of religious establishments. They persecuted Lollards and supported papal jubilees.[13] Good relations with Rome were restored – but the Act of Praemunire remained on the statute book – unused but still a potential threat.

In spite of the Lollards, traditional piety flourished in fifteenth-century England. This may have been partly due to the devastation which had been wrought, and was still being wrought, by bubonic plague. Between about 1340 and 1420 the population collapsed from nearly six million to a little over two million. This had all sorts of consequences which do not concern us here, but one result was an acute awareness of the presence of death and of the need for strategies to cope with it. Purgatory became something of an obsession and intercessory prayer rose in importance.[14] At the same time the Church's teaching on good works became increasingly emphasized. The two things went together, because the more works a person had performed in their lifetime, the easier the task of the intercessors became. A kind of calculus developed, not among theologians but in the popular mind. Every person must render account for their lives, and this came to be taken literally – so many good deeds on the credit side of the ledger, so many sins on the debit side – and the prayers of friends and kindred to tip the balance.[15] Under the impact of this preoccupation, fashions in piety changed. The monasteries, which had offered the *opus dei* on behalf of all Christian souls, became seen as distant – almost irrelevant, and even the great houses struggled to recover from the effects of plague.[16] The benefactions of the faithful became increasingly channelled into schools, colleges and almshouses, which constituted social benefits with intercessory overtones – good for the souls and bodies of all concerned. Numerous straightforward chantries were endowed, a significant number of them in perpetuity, and the friars, those famously 'hands on' preachers and healers, did particularly well, taking up many of the vocations which in a previous generation would have gone to the monasteries.[17] Never had the sacramental functions of the clergy seemed to be more relevant, or urgent, and the mass in particular developed a huge variety of exotic forms, some of purely local significance.[18] This piety both Edward IV and Henry VII were happy to exploit, and their relations with the Holy See benefited in consequence. Edward revived the Order of the Garter as the symbol of his Christian chivalry and Henry supported the Pope to such good purpose that he was able to abolish most of the Church's rights of sanctuary without protest.[19] Meanwhile the Act of Praemunire remained unrepealed.

Nevertheless behind this façade of enthusiastic unity, dissent increasingly lurked. Lollardy, driven underground by the persecution of the earlier part of the century, resurfaced about the beginning of Henry VIII's reign. Concerted episcopal investigations in 1511 revealed a disturbing number of individuals infected with one or other of these heresies. Statistically they may have been insignificant, but in some areas, such as the Cotswolds, they formed a measurable fraction of the population.[20] For the most part they recanted, and the Church's grip on popular piety was not seriously challenged, but they were a worrying sign to the perceptive. More importantly, at a sophisticated educational level, questions were being asked with which the Church was not well equipped to deal. Humanist scholarship had originated in Italy, in a renewed interest in the writings of the pagan Greeks and Latins. This not only raised the curtain on a world view which antedated the appearance of Christianity, it also awakened linguistic curiosity. Behind St Jerome's Latin Vulgate Bible were original documents in Greek and Hebrew, which represented the authentic voice of the Holy Spirit. How accurately had that voice been rendered?[21] The papacy had at first welcomed these questionings, because they appeared to lend authenticity to the Church's message. However, conservative voices were soon pointing out that if the Church conceded errors in the Vulgate text, it cast doubt upon its whole claim to infallible leadership. If the Universal Church, as represented by its General Councils, could have been mistaken about an issue so fundamental to the faith, where did its sacramental authority lie?[22] For the most part the humanists had no desire to challenge that authority, but they were very committed to the authentic text of the scriptures and some began to claim that all Christians had a right of access to the Bible in their own tongue. Henry VIII was brought up in this humanist tradition and, although that did not at first affect his somewhat unreflective piety, it sowed the seeds for a dramatic shift of emphasis in later life.

The jolts which derailed Henry's acceptance of the Church's claims and pretensions were political rather than theological, but their impact was to be profound. The first warning shot had been fired in 1514, when, in the untidy

aftermath of the death of Richard Hunne, he had declared that he did not recognize any superior authority on earth.[23] This did not represent a considered
position and was interpreted at the time as a rejection of papal claims to feudal
suzerainty – claims which went back to the rather desperate attempts of King
John to escape interdict. In any case, Pope Leo X was looking the other way and
Anglo-papal relations continued to be good. When the King 'ghosted' the *Assertio Septem Sacramentorum* against Luther in 1521, he was rewarded with the
title *Defensor Fidei*. What disrupted this amicable situation, and transformed
Henry's relations with the Church, was his obstinate insistence on annulling his
first marriage. In nearly twenty years of cohabitation, Catherine had given him
no son, and since this could not possibly be any reflection upon him, it followed
that their union was displeasing to God.[24] There had been doubts about it from
the beginning and these could now be seen to have been well founded. Being
Bible-learned he knew (or thought that he knew) that the Book of Leviticus for-
bade such marriages.[25] When Pope Clement VII refused to accept his arguments,
he became obstinate and pertinacious. Catherine's defence of her marriage, and
Henry's infatuation with Anne Boleyn, hardened attitudes on both sides, and by
1533 an impasse had been reached. This the King broke in the only way which
was open to him. He used his own legislature – the parliament – first to prohibit
appeals to the Holy See, and then to declare him to be 'the only supreme head
in earth of the Church of England, called the *Anglicana Ecclesia*'.[26] He set aside
Catherine, married Anne and proceeded to adjust the practices of the Church
to suit his own tastes.

He had sworn in his coronation oath to uphold its liberties, and was soon
being reminded that his current proceedings were not quite what the clergy had
had in mind. Nevertheless the King's need for a son was real and urgent. He had
a daughter, but there had never been a Queen Regnant in England and if (or
when) she married a foreign king was in prospect. Such a thought was abhorrent,
not only to Henry but to most of his subjects as well.[27] Consequently, although
the country became bitterly divided, the King gained more support than the
religious profile of England in 1534 might have suggested. Attempts were made
to disguise the radical nature of what had happened. The parliament had not
(of course) created the Royal Supremacy, but recognized an existing authority,
reinforcing it to 'repress and extirp all errors, heresies and other enormities and
abuses hereto fore used'. Henry was a loyal son of the Church; it was the Pope
who had gone astray, claiming and usurping a jurisdiction which did not properly belong to his office.[28] How far anyone was convinced by these arguments we
do not know, but the King got his own way. High-profile dissidents like John
Fisher and Thomas More were executed for treason, and that powerful but mud-
dled and self-contradictory movement known as the Pilgrimage of Grace was
defeated.[29] At the same time doctrinal orthodoxy was upheld, and heretics like

Robert Barnes and John Lambert went to the stake – the latter on the King's personal insistence. There was much grumbling, particularly among the conservative clergy, and especially when the King authorized an English translation of the Bible, but the way in which this grumbling was denounced reveals a substantial body of support for Henry's idiosyncratic policies.[30]

The English Bible provides a useful test. The reformers, of course, welcomed it, and the underground remnants of the Lollards rejoiced. The King insisted on its use, but in fact it seems to have been far more widely accepted than one might imagine given the prevailing climate of religious conservatism.[31] This was partly because there had been a steep increase in lay literacy over the previous half century, thanks to the founding of many new schools and the availability of books created by the printing press. But it was also partly because intelligent laymen were aware that Christianity was a religion of the book and they wanted to access it for themselves. This did not necessarily express any hostility to the clergy, but more people were asking questions, and expecting answers. Conservative clergy (who had probably received very little education themselves) might be appalled at this prospect, but the more alert welcomed it as tending to the strengthening of the faith.[32] Henry certainly did not see it as encouraging heresy – rather the reverse. By the end of Henry's reign a *modus vivendi* had been found. Most of his subjects had not cared much about the Pope anyway. He was part of the furniture, but his interventions were few and had little impact on the regular routines of worship. It was not difficult to represent him as an interfering foreigner rather than a father in God. For centuries kings had claimed a special place in the divinely ordained hierarchy. Coronations had made them the Lord's Annointed, and God's approval, or disapproval, was reflected in their well-being. They had largely endowed the Church and continued to control such things as the bishops' temporalities. It was therefore relatively easy, within the existing religious culture, to think of Henry as Supreme Head of the Church of England. This was particularly the case when he continued to be the most strenuous upholder of the sacraments and to persecute anyone who could be accused of holding Lutheran or sacramentarian views.[33]

There was dismay in some quarters when the King used his authority to dissolve the monasteries. They had existed for a thousand years, and were a comfortable feature of the religious landscape. However, the fashion for the *opus dei* had long since departed and when measured against contemporary standards of usefulness they did not score highly. Moreover their lands were immense and their disappearance opened the way for the greatest shake up which the property market had seen since the Conquest.[34] Nostalgia, or even piety, could not compete with this appetite, which reached far down the social scale to the yeoman farmer wishing to round off a modest estate. The monks were pensioned, and many were rapidly absorbed into the parochial system. The servants mostly stayed put to serve new masters and consciences, if they became officious, were easily pacified. The King took the monasteries' valuables, and the cultural vandalism represented by the destruction of their libraries was lamented by few.[35] The piety of the vast majority focused on their parish churches, where the regular orders impinged but seldom, even when they were the patrons. It made little difference to the churchwardens, or even to the incumbent, whether their advowson belonged to the local Benedictines or to the gentleman who had purchased the rights.

'Religion as King Henry left it' seemed a sensible compromise, and in any case, if the King had got it wrong with God, that was his affair. His subjects were absolved of responsibility by the divinely enjoined duty of obedience. Not everyone, of course, shared this comfortable vision. There were still quite a lot of clergy (and many ex-religious) who hankered after the security of the Universal Church, from which Henry had been unceremoniously expelled, although they were wise enough to keep their opinions to themselves. At the same time there were evangelicals, particularly among the educated laity, who believed that the King had been guilty of half measures. These were men and women who shared the King's humanist credentials, his enthusiasm for the English Bible and his aversion to the regular orders, but were not repelled by Lutheran teachings such as justification by faith alone. They were Henry's natural allies against both the Pope and the monasteries, but were sceptical of the *potestas ordinis* and unhappy with many aspects of the prevailing religious culture. They were strong in the court and in close proximity to the King, but they were also circumspect about making their views known.[36] At the time of Henry's death the official Church was an idiosyncratic blend which reflected nothing but the King's personal preferences. The Act of Six Articles, which had been only slackly enforced since 1543, was strictly orthodox and anyone who defied its teachings on the mass, as Anne Askew did, was liable to meet an unpleasant fate. The King's Book was much less conventional, setting aside such popular teaching as that on purgatory, and opening the door to dissent on the sacrament of penance.[37] At the same time, for reasons which had nothing to do with doctrine, but a great deal to do with the King's suspicious nature, the most important conservatives in the court were disgraced. Stephen Gardiner, the Bishop of Winchester, was rusticated and excluded from the number of the King's executors, while the Duke of Norfolk was imprisoned, tried for treason and condemned to death.[38]

In the last months of his life, Henry's main concerns were to protect the Royal Supremacy, to defend Boulogne and to finish his business with Scotland. The first presented the most difficult problem, because it was obvious that his son and heir would succeed as a minor. Edward was only nine, and there was no way the King was going to live another nine years. In spite of its parliamentary endorsement, the Supremacy was personal to the King, and so Henry had conceived it from the start. To sustain it in the hands of a child therefore presented problems, and

Henry felt that he could trust only the most committed anti-papalists to achieve that.[39] This meant that he placed Edward's education in the hands of evangelicals such as John Cheke and Richard Cox, and promoted like-minded courtiers such as the Earl of Hertford and Viscount Lisle to the leading positions among his executors. Above all, he trusted his Archbishop of Canterbury, Thomas Cranmer, about whose unorthodox views he was already well informed.[40] It may well be that he deceived himself about the extent to which some of these men had already crossed the shadowy divide which separated evangelicalism from Protestantism. Cranmer, at any rate, was still orthodox on the mass, which was central to the King's spirituality, and that may have been sufficient. However, it was as a result of these dispositions, made by Henry at the end of his life, that the Church of England was to become Protestant in the two years after his death. Without the Royal Supremacy there would have been no Protestant settlement, because although Protestants (of a sort) were in a majority among the King's executors and strong in the court, they were a tiny minority in the country as a whole.[41] There were quite a few among the better-educated clergy and among the urban elites of towns such as London, Bristol and Norwich. They even controlled some parishes, and in London a few churchwardens rushed headlong into reform as soon as news of the old King's death was confirmed.[42] But the prevailing religious culture was conservative, particularly in its devotion to the sacraments. Both the mass and penance retained their pre-eminence, and with them the mystique of the *potestas ordinis* – the unique intercessory function of priesthood. However, it soon transpired that the strongest cult of all was that of obedience to the Crown. It was to be argued later that parliament had been coerced into endorsing the Royal Supremacy, but the Lord Protector was in no position to apply such pressure in 1548/9. Nevertheless chantries and obits were abolished in 1547, the clergy were permitted to marry and the First Prayer Book was introduced in 1549, all by statute.[43] The Act against chantries was a much more severe blow against popular piety than either the abolition of the papacy or the dissolution of the abbeys. Unlike those earlier measures, this came right inside the parish church, abolishing those small pieties which had (apparently) meant so much to so many. Endowments of a few shillings to pay a mass priest for month's minds; a cow, the sale of whose milk was to pay for prayers; and the funds of those modest associations known as fraternities, which paid for the funerals of indigent brethren; all were confiscated by the Crown.[44] Intercessory prayer was dubbed superstitious and disappeared from the new vernacular liturgy.

Given the radical nature of these changes, and the level at which they operated, the lack of overt resistance is remarkable. Many parishes adopted strategies to cope. Some urban parishes bought back their endowments and converted them to the use of a school or almshouses with no 'superstitious' overtones.[45] Some resorted to concealment, often unsuccessfully. Most grumbled, but the

council seems to have had no difficulty in recruiting the commissioners necessary to enforce the changes, and it is natural to suppose that a fair proportion of
the profits stuck to their fingers. In the summer of 1549, there was resistance in
the context of a general discontent with the Protector's policies. In some places,
notably in Oxfordshire and Devon, religion was high on the malcontents' agenda.
In both places conservative clergy were prominent among the leaders, and in the
south-west they drew up the lists of the rebels' demands.[46] Conservative parishes,
like Morebath, sent small contingents to join the rebel forces, but the scale of the
problem had more to do with the government's hesitant response than with the
actual power or numbers of the rebels.[47] The biggest disturbances took place in
East Anglia and had nothing to do with either the Prayer Book or the chantries.
No doubt in parishes with a strong conservative consensus, and that would have
embraced the majority, especially in the north and west, conformity was kept to
a minimum. The Communion Service in the 1549 Prayer Book could be made
to look, and sound, very much like the mass if the rubric about a 'loud and distinct voice' was ignored, and it was relatively easy to disguise intercessory prayer.
However, such duplicity depended upon consent. A few humble dissidents
might lack the confidence to denounce their incumbent or might have other
reasons for keeping quiet. However, it only needed a few Protestants among the
richer members of the community to ensure that the attention of the authorities
was attracted.[48] Such quarrels within parishes became frequent and it would be
safe to say that the government's policies were deeply divisive. At the level of
national politics, some may have hoped that these divisions would cease with the
fall of the Protector in October 1549, but the Earl of Warwick, who took over
his role (although not his title) had other ideas. He knew that the King, now
aged twelve, had convictions of his own and showed clear signs of growing into a
zealous, not to say bigoted, reformer. Warwick had every intention of serving the
adult King in a few years' time, and knew what that would require.[49]

So the Protestant reformation remained on track. Cranmer revised the Prayer
Book, removing conservative ambiguities, and drew up a confession of faith similar to the Lutheran Confession of Augsburg.[50] Images were removed from parish
churches on the grounds of 'superstitious abuse' and in 1552 commissions were
sent out to inventory and confiscate 'superfluous' church plate, vestments and
other ornaments which were no longer required by the minimal liturgies of the
second Prayer Book.[51] Again there seems to have been no difficulty in recruiting gentlemen to serve on these commissions and, although there was a great
deal of grumbling and concealment, there was no concerted resistance. In some
places there was sullen defiance, and in others scuffles broke out, but by and large
the council imposed its will successfully. All of which raises fundamental questions about what was going on. At the higher political level, voices were raised
protesting against this misuse of the Royal Supremacy during a royal minority.

Both Bishop Stephen Gardiner and the Princess Mary argued forcibly that the Supremacy was personal to the King, and could only be exercised in an administrative capacity while Edward was a child.[52] Gardiner seems to have taken the view that Henry VIII's settlement was definitive and should not be altered in any circumstances, but Mary professed herself willing to obey her brother in all things – when he came of age. These were dangerous arguments, because they could cast doubt upon other aspects of the minority government. Could the King's consent to legislation be taken seriously while he was a minor? Or did all such laws as were passed need to be ratified once Edward had reached the age of eighteen – and if so, were they valid in the meantime?[53] Quite apart from its ideological preoccupations, it is not surprising that the council rejected all such arguments and pressed ahead with its legislative programme. Protestantism became a touchstone of the legitimacy of the minority government. At a lower level, there are signs of similar arguments, particularly among the better-educated conservatives, but they do not feature among the Articles of the south-western rebellion. These were all about demanding a return to the old ways, and not at all about the legitimacy of the changes.[54] They amounted to a complete rejection of the whole reforming programme but did not anywhere question the King's authority except by implication. Grass-roots conservatives faced a dilemma which they did not want to recognize. They had accepted the Royal Supremacy as being consistent with the law of God, but they did not like the way in which it was being used. Should they argue that the old faith was the only true one – and if they did, where did that leave King Henry VIII? No one knew that Edward was going to die at the age of fifteen, so they were not waiting for better times. On the whole they accepted that the King's will took priority over any other consideration, even if he was a child. No doubt many of them hoped and prayed that he would change his mind when he came to man's estate.[55]

Obedience was thus a prime feature of the popular culture of mid-sixteenth-century England. In a sense there was nothing new about this, because a duty to observe the king's laws had been recognized in subjects since well before the Norman Conquest. However, law had slowly changed its nature. Firstly Pleas of the Crown had become recognized as distinct, and to be pleaded only in the king's courts, except where that jurisdiction was delegated to the holder of a defined franchise or liberty.[56] Those laws which dealt with most aspects of everyday life, such as land use and straying beasts, were dubbed customary and were dealt with in the lords' courts of manor and honour. Other aspects of human behaviour, such as sexuality, matrimony and probate; or anything which involved oaths (such as contract) were designated as spiritual and were dealt with by the Church courts.[57] If you lived in a corporate town, much of your life was controlled by the mayor and council, who exercised jurisdiction by the terms of their charters. If you were a member of a guild or livery company, then you were expected to obey its rules. Obedience was expected, the procedures of the courts were well understood and the laws which they enforced were (or were supposed to be) congruent. You would not get into trouble with the king's courts by observing the custom of the manor, nor with the spiritual courts by observing the laws of the king. The fact that all these laws were regularly broken, and penalties imposed, did not affect the general culture of allegiance. Traditionally, where problems had arisen, these had involved loyalty rather than the law. If a lord summoned his affinity in arms, it was a part of their obligation to obey; but suppose he summoned them in defiance of the king? It was high treason to obey, and petty treason to refuse.[58] Suppose the king himself was accused of breaking the law? Did the subject's allegiance lie with the king's laws, or the king's person? Such problems had arisen in the reigns of John, Edward II and Richard II, and the solution in each case had been political rather than legal.[59]

However, the reign of Henry VIII had seen new problems arise, which had centred on the authority of parliament. It was generally recognized that an Act which had been duly processed and had received the consent of King, Lords and Commons had the force of law; but suppose that Act contravened law which had been accepted for centuries, but did not have a recognized legislative basis? It was blandly assumed that the law of statute and the law of God were consistent, but that was not how it appeared to everyone.[60] In purely temporal matters, like the abolition of franchises, it was no contest, because it had always been recognized that those liberties were royal creations; it was just that no law hitherto had provided for their removal. Even in quasi-temporal matters, such as the dissolution of the monasteries, the authority of statute was accepted.[61] But over purely spiritual issues, like the Act of Supremacy or the Act of Six Articles, there was more room for dispute. As we have seen, the King won; partly by coercion, partly by force of habit, but mostly because his chosen course was acceptable to most of his subjects. The Church which King Henry created was, broadly speaking, a popular church, and the more so because it was an identifiable aspect of the realm of England. The Englishman knew that he was not French, or German, or Scottish, and he was proud of that fact. He was proud of his distinctive laws and customs, even if he had no means of comparing them with other lands, and he was proud of his king for having defied a whole raft of beastly foreigners, Francis I, Charles V and even the Pope.[62] Very few understood, or cared about, the implications of this declaration of independence. The fact that Henry had also defied Martin Luther was not wasted upon some of his subjects either. Opposition to the 'King's proceedings' had been strong as long as Anne Boleyn was alive, but had faltered thereafter. This was partly because of what she stood for in terms of marital infidelity, and partly out of loyalty to Catherine. It did not come to a head because Thomas Cromwell was diligent to frustrate it, but also because it was assumed that it represented a passing mood. Once Catherine and

Anne were both dead, it was widely assumed that Henry would renegotiate his relations with the papacy and effectively start again. Both Paul III and Charles V believed this, and there was little point in running the appalling risks of high treason to resist a temporary aberration.[63] Once it had become clear that the King believed his own propaganda, it was too late to turn the clock back – a fact which the fate of the Pilgrimage of Grace made clear.

So the Royal Supremacy was the will of the King; but it was also the will of God. There were, of course, those who resisted any such suggestion, but most of them, like Reginald Pole, had taken refuge in exile, and it should not be assumed that they spoke for a large constituency. The popular culture of the Church in England was Henrician, and that was not simply 'Catholicism without the Pope'. Not only were there no regular orders in England, but the calendar of the Church had been extensively modified, many traditional saint's days having been removed and the consequent holidays abrogated. The English Bible was set up in every church, along with Erasmus's *Paraphrases* for the benefit of the better educated, and doubts had been cast upon the doctrine of purgatory.[64] The clergy were under the authority of the King, and the highest ecclesiastical court was that of the Archbishop of Canterbury. The Pope's name was omitted from the standard franchises, and every schoolboy knew that the Roman jurisdiction was usurped. On the other hand the traditional sacraments were strenuously defended, particularly the mass, and intercessory prayer continued to be enjoined. The role of the clergy in this latter practice was not in any way diminished, and the role of good works in the attaining of salvation was vigorously maintained. Such Lutheran doctrines as justification by faith alone, and the more radical Swiss notions about the presence of Christ in the Eucharist, were heresy and still carried the full penalties. The statute *De Haeretico Comburendo* remained in force, and Anne Askew was tortured and burned alive as late as 1546.[65] This was not the result of any confusion in the King's mind. He knew exactly what he wanted his Church to believe and had even laid quite a lot of it down by statute. Unfortunately, it did not correspond exactly to anyone else's agenda. Among the conservatives there were those who hankered after the security of the Universal Church, and on the evangelical side were many who believed that the King's defence of the sacraments was simply wrong. However, it should be emphasized that the majority, even among the educated elite, did not share these doubts. Their comfort lay in the presence of their redeemer in the host, and in the timeless rituals of Easter, Pentecost, Corpus Christi and Michaelmas. They said their prayers, paid their dues, went through the rites of passage and provided for their souls in the afterlife. Those who disagreed with them – if there were any – and who tended to 'the new ways', were regarded with deep suspicion and probably ostracized.[66] They did not much care who ran the

Church. Their king was a Christian prince, was he not? The faith was just as safe in his hands as in those of some distant foreigner.

However, precisely because it was such an idiosyncratic balance, Henry's Church was unsustainable. The reasons why it was tipped in a Protestant direction under the minority council were purely political and had nothing to do with religious consensus. Thinking to strengthen their position, the council virtually abandoned censorship of the press, and the predictable result was a spate of radical literature, including ribald attacks upon the mass.[67] Those who produced such works must have been expecting to make a profit from their sale, because that was the nature of the printing business, and that in turn raises an interesting point about the strength of conformity. These works would have been deeply offensive to anyone of a conservative mentality, and yet the market was deemed to be big enough to justify the risk. The answer probably lies in the unusual ideological balance of London. London had a population of about 150,000 at this stage, ten times the size of any other city in England, and embraced religious views of all kinds.[68] Some parishes had certainly accepted radical ideas by this time, and were waiting for the end of Henry's repressive regime to express themselves. In some places this was due to Continental influences, in some to survivals of radical Lollardy and in others to the convictions of individual clergy. Neighbouring parishes might at the same time be deeply conservative, but on balance the climate of London was sympathetic to reform, and that was where the majority of the market lay. Thousands of copies of these leaflets must have been shifted in the first eighteen months of the reign, and the Bishop of London, Edmund Bonner, was deeply perturbed. The issue became one of discipline. The council had every intention of reforming the liturgy, but realized that due process would be essential to its chances of preserving order. If it did not check the freelance radicals, they would destabilize the whole process, at least in London. A statute was therefore passed in November 1547 prohibiting disputes on the Eucharist, and that was followed up at the end of December with a proclamation of enforcement.[69] Some parishes which had abandoned the mass were made to restore it, 'until further order be taken'.

The law was clearly very important in what followed. There is very little sign of enthusiasm for the first Prayer Book of 1549. Conservatives derided it as 'a Christmas game', and radicals were disappointed at its moderation, but it was validated by statute, and that meant that it represented the will of King, Lords and Commons. Where it was rejected, as it was by some in Devon and Cornwall, it was in the context of open rebellion.[70] More typical was the reaction of Henry Machyn, a wealthy and conservative citizen of London who began to keep a journal during these years. Machyn rejoiced in all the ceremonies of the old faith, but passed without comment over the reforming measures which he found distasteful. There is no suggestion that he objected more forcibly, because he was a good citizen and knew his duty.[71] When the council ordered a royal visitation in the summer of 1547, the clergy were specifically instructed to 'preach and declare that the King's majesty's power, authority and pre-eminence is, within this realm and the dominions of the same, the most supreme and highest under God'.[72] This was strictly in accordance with recent precedent, but it made a meaningful statement about the minority government, to which Bishops Gardiner and Bonner objected. They were sent to the Fleet, and other objections were not articulated. The will of the King as Supreme Head was paraded, but what mattered during the minority was the will of parliament, and every religious change of any consequence was authorized by statute. In other words it became a part of the law of England, and recruited all the habits of obedience which that implied. The minority government of Edward VI did command the services of modest numbers of German and Spanish mercenaries, but they would have been powerless if the levies and the retinues of the aristocracy had not supported the established order. We know from what happened subsequently that many nobles were deeply suspicious of the reformers and their practices, but upholding the Church order had become a seamless part of maintaining social and political discipline – and that took priority over any other consideration.[73]

Wills are notoriously unreliable guides to the convictions of testators, but the uncertainties introduced first by Henry's changes and then by the legislated reformation did have an impact upon preambles. First bequests to religious orders disappeared; references to 'the Virgin Mary and the whole company of heaven' became less frequent; and the establishment of obits and lights with an intercessory intention almost disappeared.[74] Purgatory had become an uncertain hypothesis well before the Chantries Act of 1548. Before 1547, it was a brave (or foolish) man who used the typically Protestant formula of expressing exclusive faith in the saving grace of Christ; probation might have been refused. However, by 1549 such expressions were not uncommon, especially among the urban elite. They still represented only a tiny fraction of the wills proved, but they are an indication, like the actions of radical London churchwardens, that the policies of Edward's government were not without support.[75] Protestant Bishops like John Hooper despaired at their failure to make better progress in converting their flocks, but even Hooper faced no violent resistance; and when Nicholas Ridley set out to remove altars and images from the parish churches of his diocese in 1550, he encountered little overt opposition.[76] We should probably conclude that 'religion as King Henry left it' was the popular cry, but also that there was also a general tendency to tarry for the magistrate, and if King Edward had lived a natural span, England would have become a genuinely reformed country within twenty years.

However, he died on 6 July 1553, without ever achieving his majority, and what happened thereafter provides a good test of the religious and political culture which prevailed. The King's half-sister, Mary, had resisted his Protestant reformation to the best of her ability, every step of the way. She had done this not on the grounds of defending the true faith but because it broke her father's settlement. This, she claimed, the council was not entitled to do while the King was a child, and in this she received strong diplomatic support from the Emperor.[77] Charles was not interested in Henry's settlement, but he was interested in embarrassing and obstructing a heretical government. Within England, Mary's intransigence achieved two things. It convinced the conservative majority that her heart was in the right place, and it persuaded the King that she must not succeed to the throne. When he was convinced that he was terminally ill, Edward insisted on an instrument being drawn up settling the succession on his Protestant cousin, Jane Dudley.[78] In this he was strongly supported by the Duke of Northumberland (who was Jane's father-in-law) and by a minority of his fellow councillors. Most, however, obeyed his orders very reluctantly, because although Mary was only Henry VIII's illegitimate daughter, she had been placed after Edward in the King's last succession Act, and in his will which that Act validated. In other words, she was the lawful heir unless or until that Act was repealed, something which the rapid advance of Edward's illness made it impossible to achieve in time.[79] Mary may have been secretly convinced that she was legitimate, but she had long since accepted her father's judgement on that point, and when she proclaimed herself Queen on 8 or 9 July, she did so on the basis of the law. When her proclamation was repeated on 19 July, it spoke of her 'just and lawful' possession of the Crown, and made no reference to Henry.[80] What had happened in the meantime baffled foreign observers and has fascinated historians ever since. When it came to the point, the Duke of Northumberland's resources simply disappeared. His men deserted and the ships which he had sent to the east coast to intercept any possible flight to the Continent defected.[81] Those with an affinity to Mary had immediately rallied to her, and perhaps that was to be expected, but others flocked to join her who had no previous association. Most remarkably of all, the Protestants divided. Some, like Nicholas Ridley and (more reluctantly) Thomas Cranmer, recognized Jane, but others, including the outstandingly godly John Hooper, openly supported Mary as the lawful heir, irrespective of her known religious conservatism.[82] As this situation rapidly unfolded, between 10 and 19 July, the council similarly divided. The majority made haste to Mary's headquarters at Framlingham and those who were too slow, or too deeply compromised, found themselves isolated. Within ten days, Mary had won a total and bloodless victory. Simon Renard, the spokesman for the imperial ambassadors, watched these events in disbelief. As late as 10 July he had believed that Northumberland would win, because of his established position and command of resources, and had withheld any advice from Mary in accordance with his instructions.[83] The outcome, he declared, was nothing short of a miracle.

What these events demonstrated was not the rightness, or otherwise, of Mary's religious convictions, but the culture of obedience to the law. Edward had not been a king in the full sense, and his will was not therefore pitted against the statute. If it had been the outcome might have been different, but that we do not know. When Northumberland and his associates were put on trial, they were not accused of any offence committed before 6 July, because it was tacitly accepted that it could not be high treason to obey the commands of a living king, even if he was a child, and even if his commands were unlawful.[84] That was an issue which would not be resolved for almost another century. Meanwhile, England had a lawful Queen; a *femme seul* in possession of her private lordship, and a champion, it was believed, of her father's Church. On 18 August she issued a proclamation confirming her allegiance to the old faith and promising to refrain from any coercion until further order was taken, which everyone (rightly) assumed to refer to parliament.[85] What her loving subjects, and even her council, did not know was that she had committed herself to the restoration of the papal jurisdiction and that she was seriously thinking of marrying a Spaniard. When her first parliament, in its second session, repealed Edward's religious legislation, abrogating the Prayer Book and restoring the mass, there was a general sense of relief. It no longer had to be pretended that Protestantism represented the law of God. But where did that leave the similar legislation of King Henry VIII?[86] For the time being Mary continued to act as Supreme Head of the Church, but by the time that her marriage to Philip was settled in January 1554, there were many who were wondering how much longer that would last. There was an obvious case for the Queen to use the Ecclesiastical Supremacy as her father and brother had used it, to extend and support her temporal authority – to recruit God onto her council. However, there was another way to achieve that goal, and one which was better recognized outside England, and that was to settle with the papacy and re-enter the Universal Church. That had not been an option for Edward, but it had been for Henry and was again for his daughter. As a ruling Queen, the extra support would be welcome, and might settle any lingering doubts about her rights when she became *femme couvert*.[87] It was also an obvious course for the daughter-in-law of the Holy Roman Emperor. The drawback was that it blurred the distinction between heresy and political opposition until the two became indistinguishable. No heretic could be a loyal subject, and that, as John Hooper had demonstrated, did not correspond to reality.

1 THE STRUCTURE OF COERCION

The Church was well placed to coerce dissidents, both because of the legal structure of which it was a part and because of the pervasive culture of conformity. To some extent these forces had been pulling in different directions under Edward. The law required obedience to a magisterial form of Protestantism but most clergy, and most congregations, preferred something a great deal more conservative. These laws, of course, dated only from 1549, but the expectation that all parishioners would attend their parish church, and receive such sacraments as were available to them, went back to the origins of the parochial system in the eighth century.[1] It was, first and foremost, the responsibility of the incumbent to see that this happened, and his eyes and ears in this respect were the churchwardens. However the sanctions available to him were limited. If the offender yielded to exhortation and reprimand, and came to confess his or her faults, then a suitable penance could be imposed. However, if any person failed to appear at all, or declined to submit to penance, then the incumbent had little option but to refer him to a higher jurisdiction, and that would mean the court of the archdeacon.[2]

The archdeacon was a ubiquitous presence in late medieval society. He exercised the bishop's authority by delegation and intruded into every situation where the canon law reached. Matrimonial problems, illicit sexual relationships and the closely related issues of defamation and slander all came before him. Matters arising out of disputed wills and the prosecution of those who meddled with dead men's goods were equally his concern. He pursued the non-payment of tithes and other Church dues, and punished those who showed the slightest desire to question the teachings of the Church. His visitation was one of the most predictable features of Church life, and one of the few ways in which disputes between incumbents and their flocks could be resolved. In fact most of the business of the archdeacon's court was not to do with litigation or correction, but with the thousand and one matters of routine administration which arose in the running of the most sophisticated institution which then existed.[3] The scribes of the court spent most of their time on the admission of clergy, validation of process and authorizations of various kinds, the approval of wills and the issue of licences and dispensations. For all this work the relevant parties paid fees, which could not be guaranteed in the case of litigation, defendants being particularly reluctant to pay the costs of actions brought against them.

These were courts of the canon law, but the parameters of their activities were laid down by the common law and by parliament. They were not, for example, permitted to deal with any cases touching real property, even where the Church was a party, because such cases were reserved to the king's courts. Nevertheless, boundary disputes between the two jurisdictions were endemic, and a lot depended upon the policy being pursued by the Crown at the time. Edward IV had been indulgent and allowed the Church courts to adjudicate upon all sorts of issues of 'broken faith', including breaches of contract, which had long since been regarded as temporal by the royal judges.[4] The result had been a great (and profitable) extension of the work of the Church courts and corresponding resentment among the common lawyers. Henry VII, on the other hand, interpreted the statutes of praemunire more rigorously, and cases involving breach of faith fell away dramatically after 1492. He also made extensive use of writs of prohibition to forbid the Church courts from dealing in certain specific issues – usually where some kind of property right could be construed. Henry's relations with Rome were amicable and the canon lawyers therefore had very little leverage to use against him in their own defence. The foundation of Doctors' Commons in the 1490s was probably intended to protect the professional status of canon and civil lawyers against the encroachments of royal policy, but it seems to have had little effect.[5] This provoked considerable disquiet, particularly among conservative bishops, and one confided at some time towards the end of Henry VII's reign that he would like to accuse those responsible of heresy. However, since the King himself was largely responsible for the flexible use of praemunire, this was scarcely a realistic option. It was to surface later in the case of Richard Hunne, but the King was not a party to that.[6]

The archdeacons' courts were thus workhorses of Tudor administration, and only a small proportion of their cases had anything to do with recognizable religious dissidence. Some of those who abstained from church attendance did so for conscientious reasons and remained obstinate, but the majority were probably just careless and submitted readily once a touch of the law had been applied. There were several normal ways of finding oneself in the archdeacon's court. The first was through an offence or other issue which had arisen in the course of a visitation; these were office cases in which the accuser was effectively one of the archdeacon's officials. The second was when an incumbent or churchwarden denounced an offender, and the third was when one party sued another, neither having any official standing. This third type was probably the commonest, where the court was used as an arbitrator in some testamentary or similar case, and less formal systems of arbitration had not worked.[7] Religious dissent was not very often detected during a visitation, where the archdeacon's main concern was usually with the fabric of the church and whether the incumbent was resident and kept hospitality. The most common way for an issue of dissent, which might or might not turn out to be heresy, to appear was through denunciation. The records of these cases are extremely patchy, but the offenders were often drunk and sometimes simple-minded, so that the normal outcome was submission and penance, or occasionally a fine and a spell in the bishop's prison. Only rarely does an offender seem to have acted out of some genuine objection to the Church's practice or teaching, and these cases were invariably referred to the jurisdiction of the bishop's consistory court.[8] The courts of canon law did not follow the common law practice of using juries to determine matters of fact, and the archdeacon alone was the arbiter of the fate of those who appeared before him, although he had the advice of skilled lawyers for the trickier issues.

The next step up in the hierarchy of Church courts was the bishop's consistory. The relationship between the archdeacon's court and the bishop's was flexible, and often vague. Practice seems to have varied, not only from one diocese to another, but even from one archdeaconry to another within the same diocese.[9] Sometimes matters which appeared to be serious were brought direct to the bishop, who had first instance jurisdiction in such cases. He also had appellate jurisdiction from the archdeacon's court, and wealthy or obstreperous litigants would often take this route, particularly over party issues. The bishop could summon such officials or others as he might deem appropriate to sit with him as judges in consistory, and his authority extended as far as the obstinate heretic who might end up by being condemned to death. The bishop could not, of course, inflict such a penalty himself. Since the days when the clergy had first been forbidden to shed blood, it had been the business of the secular magistrate to implement this sentence. The judgement of the ecclesiastical court was sufficient in such cases, and no further judicial process was involved, but no execution was supposed to take place without a writ *de haeretico comburendo*, which was issued out of Chancery.[10] This had been laid down by statute in the early part of Henry IV's reign (2 Henry IV, c. 15), and although that act had been repealed by Edward VI, it had been reinstated early in 1555 (1 & 2 Philip and Mary, c. 6). It was invariably the sheriff who was responsible for receiving the person so convicted, and arranging for the sentence to be carried out.

Above the bishop's court was the court of the archbishop – in the case of Canterbury the Court of Arches – and above that again appeal to Rome. The Court of Arches was kept busy with normal ecclesiastical litigation and very seldom heard appeals on issues of heresy. This was not because the victims were content with the bishop's sentence, but because they normally lacked either the contacts or the means to pursue the matter further. The appeals system as it existed before 1533 was only open to the wealthy, because of the high level of fees charged at the Curia and because notaries who knew how to put together such appeals did not come cheap either. From 1518 to 1529 Cardinal Wolsey could exercise that appellate jurisdiction as Legate *de Latere* on the Pope's behalf, but those who were sufficiently exalted to consider pursuing such a course did not usually trust the lord chancellor and preferred to go direct to the centre.[11] From 1533 to 1555 appeals to Rome were forbidden by statute, and during those years the only appeal from the Court of Arches lay to the Crown in Council, or to such special commissioners as the Crown should choose to appoint. From 1555 the old channels were reopened, but Reginald Pole as Legate exercised the Pope's jurisdiction and handled the great majority of such appeals as arose before his Legateship was withdrawn in 1557. Thereafter such appeals as still subsisted had perforce to go to Rome, but they received scant attention, as Sir Edward Carne frequently complained.[12]

Whether topped by the Crown or by the Pope, such ecclesiastical courts should have constituted a self-sufficient system, which was well capable of dealing with religious misdemeanours, but from the early fifteenth century the lay magistrates had been intimately involved in order to show the commitment of the Crown to the cause of religious orthodoxy. Statutes of Henry IV and Henry V empowered justices of the peace to receive accusations of heresy and to imprison those so accused. They were then supposed to hand them over to the bishop's officers for trial in the consistory court.[13] This represented a new departure, because hitherto no secular officer would have taken cognisance of such a charge, but it did not affect the judicial process. This measure was aimed against the Lollards, whose views were reckoned to be socially subversive as well as heretical, a position which was reinforced by Sir John Oldcastle's rebellion in 1414. During the drive against Lollardy in 1511, it became normal for process against offenders to be initiated through denunciation to the justices, and they were often arrested by the constables or other similar officers rather than by the bishop's apparators.[14]

The statute of 1533 (25 Henry VIII, c. 14), however, brought about a significant change. Heresy, as distinct from other ecclesiastical offences, now required either the testimony of two witnesses to initiate a case or an indictment under the common law. The two witnesses could testify directly to an ecclesiastical court, but an indictment required an appearance at the quarter sessions. This formalized the role of the justices of the peace, who had hitherto been able only to receive and transmit accusations, and made them the court of first instance for a religious offence. Once an indictment had been found, it would go directly to the bishop's consistory, and made the quarter sessions a parallel jurisdiction to the archdeacon's court

From 1535 to 1540 the King's ecclesiastical authority was exercised by Thomas Cromwell as Viceregent in Spirituals. He carried out visitations on the King's behalf, and suspended the bishop's and archbishop's ordinary jurisdiction while he did so.[15] He also issued commissions for ecclesiastical causes in the King's name, usually for administrative or investigative purposes. Such commissions used the canon law in the same way as secular commissions used the common law, and their terms of reference were specified in the commissions themselves. From Cromwell's fall to the end of the reign in 1547 there was no Viceregent in Spirituals, and Henry exercised such authority directly.

It was therefore possible in theory for a heretic to be denounced to the commissioners, rather than to the ordinary magistrates or the bishop's officials, and to be tried and condemned by them without passing through any other court.[16] It would have been futile for a person so accused to appeal to his ordinary, because the King's jurisdiction took precedence. It was an ecclesiastical as well as a statutory offence to be a heretic, and the related crime of refusing the oath of supremacy was made treason by Act of Parliament in 1534, so it was a secular court which tried Sir Thomas More. It was, however, extremely rare for a case of heresy to be tried by commission. If such persons were brought to their attention, the normal reaction of the commissioners would be to refer it to the bishop's court. Even more rarely, the King intervened personally in such a case, as he did with John Lambert in 1538. Lambert had been condemned by the normal process of canon law when he was brought to dispute before the King, and when he appealed to the King as Supreme Head against his conviction, Henry brushed his appeal aside.[17] A royal pardon was regularly offered to the condemned person, but that was a pardon for life only, and did not alter his status as a convicted heretic. Had any such pardon been accepted, the result would have been a lifetime in an ecclesiastical prison. Presumably the King had the power to pardon the offence as well, but given Henry's well-known hostility to heretics, that was extremely unlikely to happen.

The main change during Henry VIII's reign was brought about by the Act of Six Articles of 1539. Unlike the Act of Supremacy or the dissolution of the monasteries, this intruded the King's authority into the field of spiritualities by defining certain theological positions as heretical.[18] It also decreed that anyone refusing to receive the sacrament at the normal times was to be fined and imprisoned by the council, a second offence being felony and therefore (presumably) triable by the normal secular courts. The statute also declared that enforcement was committed to special commissions of bishops and archbishops which were to be appointed from time to time, as well as to the ordinary ecclesiastical courts. Justices of the peace were authorized to make enquiries, and presumably to take indictments, but were then expected to refer such cases either to the commissioners or to the bishops' courts. There were, therefore, a considerable number of ways in which offenders could be dealt with, and no very clear guidance as to which was to be preferred. The ultimate penalty prescribed was death by burning, and a number of executions in fact took place as a consequence of the Act.[19]

When Henry died, the Royal Supremacy was deemed to have reverted to the council, along with all the other prerogative powers of the Crown. This was not acceptable to those conservatives who opposed the direction of government policy in religious matters, and both Stephen Gardiner, the Bishop of Winchester, and the Princess Mary objected strongly.[20] Gardiner was imprisoned and eventually deprived of his see, while Mary's objections made her the subject of a prolonged game of cat and mouse with the Emperor's ambassadors. The first parliament of the new reign had meanwhile repealed the Act of Six Articles, and the miscellaneous early fifteenth-century laws which had empowered the justices of the peace and prescribed death by burning for the unrepentant heretic. This in a sense left the Royal Supremacy in no-man's land, without the support of the normal secular courts, except for the option of indictment at quarter sessions. But of course the Church courts were just as much the King's courts as any other, and the canon law (or what was left of it once the Pope had been excised) was the King's law. In any case, heresy was not much of an issue for the duration of Edward's reign. Calling the King a heretic was quickly restored to the category of treason, and for the rest the normal Church courts were adequate.[21] It was difficult enough to enforce the most minimal standards of conformity to the new order and many bishops did not try very hard. Only two Anabaptists were burned during the reign, and they were executed in accordance with ancient custom rather than for infringing any specific law.[22] When it came to the judicial business of depriving bishops, however, the Crown was more careful, appointing special commissions to hear and determine each case. This was a perfectly proper way to proceed, as the law then stood, and the decision taken by the council in Mary's reign that these commissions had acted *ultra vires* was political rather than legal.

For two years, from 1547 to 1549, the Church of England had no defined standard of doctrine, either by statute or in any other way. This was then remedied by the first Act of Uniformity, prescribing the use of the English Prayer Book and laying down a graded scale of penalties for non-compliance. These ranged from a £10 fine to life imprisonment, and it was expected that they would be imposed by the church courts. However, when the Second Act of Uniformity was passed in 1552, this was obviously found to have been inadequate, because enforcement was transferred to the 'justices of assize, justices of oyer and terminer, justices of the peace in their sessions, or any of them'. Nonconformity thus became a statutory offence, specifically to be imposed by the secular courts.[23] This restored a function to the Royal Supremacy, but the Act was only in force for about a year, and its impact on actual judicial practice is hard to assess.

Then Edward died, and the whole question of religious conformity went into the melting pot. For several months the law remained unchanged, but anyone who tried to enforce the Edwardian Act against the mass ran a serious risk, as James Hales discovered to his discomfort when he was confronted by Lord Chancellor Gardiner with the (legally quite improper) injunction that he should pay attention to the Queen's proceedings rather than to the law.[24] It was not until 20 December 1553 that the repeal of the Act of Uniformity took effect, but in the meantime churches up and down the country – including the Chapel Royal – were restoring the mass in defiance of the law. This could have been legitimated by the issue of a general dispensation under the Royal Supremacy, but that does not seem to have been done. For upwards of a year Mary was Supreme Head of the Church, and although she did not use the title after 20 December, resorting to an enigmatic 'etc.', she certainly exercised the power. Her first proclamation, issued on 18 August, declared her own allegiance to 'that religion which God and the world knoweth she hath ever professed from her infancy hitherto', expressing the hope that the same would be 'quietly and charitably embraced' by her subjects. There was to be no coercion until 'further order by common consent' had been taken, but the moving of sedition or the 'stirring of unquietness' on the grounds of religion was strictly forbidden, and all unlicensed preaching was prohibited.[25]

Enforcement was entrusted to the justices of the peace and other secular law officers, and the ecclesiastical courts were not mentioned. It was under the provisions of this proclamation that Thomas Cranmer and others who spoke up for their Protestant faith were arrested and committed to prison. Cranmer was eventually tried for his part in Northumberland's abortive coup of the summer, but the chances are that he would have been left in peace if he had not made a strong declaration against the mass in September. On 29 August a special commission was issued to Lord Chancellor Stephen Gardiner to license preachers, and that was as effective a way as any to silence the opposition because it was for unlicensed preaching that the majority of arrests were made.[26] When Mary's official title was proclaimed at her coronation, she was described as 'the most high, most puissant and most excellent Princess Mary the First, by the grace of God Queen of England, France and Ireland, defender of the faith, and of the Church of England and Ireland Supreme Head'.[27]

Although the Queen was probably already committed to the restoration of the papal authority, in the opening months of her reign all appeals made were to the precedents of Henry VIII's last years, and her efforts were concentrated on restoring the canon law as it had been administered at that time. These efforts focused particularly on the restoration of the traditional liturgy and ceremonies, and the removal or re-ordination of those clergy who had been ordained under the revised ordinal of 1550. Above all, those priests who had availed themselves of the 1549 Act permitting them to marry were, now that the Act had been repealed, required either to renounce their wives or face deprivation. In spite of the enthusiasm with which the mass and other traditional usages had been restored, there seems to have been a marked reluctance to deal with the disciplinary aspects of the return to the old canon law, and on 4 March 1554 Mary decided to give the sluggish ecclesiastical authorities a hefty nudge by conducting a royal visitation.[28] Letters were sent to all incumbent bishops and to *sede vacante* officials of vacant dioceses to visit their cures and administer the Articles which were sent under cover of the letters, not using their own authority as ordinaries, but that of the Crown. These Articles were mostly concerned with the discipline of the clergy and the observance of traditional rites, but two were of particular significance in respect of the Supremacy itself. It had been required by law under Edward that each newly incumbent bishop should be issued with a commission under the Crown, signifying that he derived his authority not from his orders, but from his appointment. That law had been repealed and Mary abandoned the practice, instructing that no bishop was henceforth to endorse his formal proceedings *Regia auctoritate fulcitus*. Article 3 likewise instructed that no ecclesiastical promotion was to require any oath 'touching the primacy or succession, as of late in few years past hath been accustomed and used'.[29] These oaths had been required by an Act of Parliament of the first year of King Edward VI, but the oath of the supremacy went back to 1534 and the statute requiring it was still in force. Of course the monarch as Supreme Head could dispense with this requirement, and that seems to be the implication here.[30]

No bishop was deprived as a direct result of this visitation, because the visitors were not commissioned to administer such a penalty. Special powers were required for that purpose, and on 13 March 1554 Gardiner, Tunstall, Bonner and three other bishops were commissioned to summon Robert Holgate, Archbishop of York, Robert Farrer, Bishop of St Davids, John Bird, Bishop of Chester and Paul Bush, Bishop of Bristol, 'who have contracted marriage with certain women'. As a result Holgate, Bird and Farrer were deprived and Bush resigned. Two days later the same group was issued with a further commission to summon John Hooper, Bishop of Worcester, John Harley, Bishop of Hereford and John Taylor, Bishop of Lincoln. The main charge was again marriage, but Hooper was also accused of holding unorthodox opinions concerning the Eucharist.[31] He had been imprisoned since the previous September and was a marked man, famous for his radical views. All those summoned were in custody and the proceedings took only a few days. The deprivations were decreed on the 17 March. Holgate submitted and vainly sought rehabilitation, but Hooper and Farrer were eventually burned.[32] On 29 March a third commission was issued to Gardiner to summon the canons of Westminster and also to deprive any of them that were found to have married, 'without any noise or figure of judgement', although given that the deprivations were to take place under the canon law and by exercise of the Royal Supremacy, it is difficult to see how some judicial form could have been avoided.[33] Finally, a further commission was sent to George Dowdall, the Archbishop of Armagh, authorizing him to deprive any married clergy found within the kingdom of Ireland, a task which he presumably discharged through agents, since he could hardly have covered the whole island himself. Protestant-ism was only skin deep in Ireland, and confined mostly to the English settlers of the Pale, so it is unlikely that he found many victims. In the remoter parts of tribal Ireland the ancient Celtic tradition of clerical marriage still persisted, but these would not have been within reach of the Primate's visitors – and the Supreme Head's injunction was not aimed at them in any case.[34]

In the summer of 1554, as Mary awaited the arrival of Philip of Spain, whom she was contracted to marry, the realm was still therefore firmly in schism. An attempt to remedy this situation was made by Lord Chancellor Gardiner in the April parliament of 1554, with the Queen's backing. However, it was inad-equately prepared and ran into such determined opposition in the House of Lords that it had to be abandoned.[35] Meanwhile Cardinal Reginald Pole, who had been hopefully named Legate to England the previous August, was stuck in Bavaria awaiting the Emperor's permission to proceed. This had been with-held partly because Pole had been opposed to the marriage of Philip and Mary in the first place, partly because Charles V was misled by his representatives in England about Protestant strength, and feared a rebellion, and partly because he wanted his son to secure the credit for the reconciliation with Rome, which he knew was high on the Queen's agenda. When they came to be married in July 1554 the ceremony was conducted with all the ancient rites and ceremonies, and Philip blandly ignored the fact that the presiding Bishop Gardiner was still an unreconciled schismatic.[36] Within a few weeks he had made the first moves in Rome which were to lead to the recall of Cardinal Pole in November and to the formal submission and acceptance of the English Church, which was completed in the following January with the second Act of Repeal. This Act repealed all of Henry VIII's ecclesiastical legislation going back to 1529, except the dissolution of the monasteries, and restored the situation as it had been in the twentieth year of his reign. The Royal Supremacy was thus formally abolished and ecclesiastical jurisdiction reverted to its medieval format.[37] As we have seen, a separate statute resurrected the heresy laws of Henry IV and Henry V, so that the jurisdiction of the Church and its relation to the secular power were re-established in the form which had existed from 1416 to 1533.

After January 1555 the Crown had in theory no role in the management of the Church's affairs, while the secular magistrates were confined to the receiving and passing on of religious accusations, and carrying out the death penalty when prescribed by an ecclesiastical court. The Pope was the head of the Church, and Cardinal Pole as his Legate carried out those duties on his behalf. However, this was not altogether the reality of the situation. In the first place, many justices of the peace took their duties in this respect with great seriousness. Not only did they receive accusations, they deliberately sought them out, often using their own servants as promoters.[38] The reason for this may well have been the close connection which was perceived to exist between heresy and sedition, a connection which government propaganda was keen to emphasize, particularly after the Wyatt rebellion.[39] It was also partly to establish their credentials with the council. A reputation as a zealous supporter of the Queen's most cherished policy would not do a justice any harm if there were grants or other favours to be won. Sir John Tyrell in Essex is an obvious case in point. Some councillors took a similar line, seeking to ingratiate themselves with a Queen whose disposition was only too well known. Some, like Robert Rochester, had been appointed mainly for their known orthodoxy in the first place, others, like Richard, Lord Rich, had dubious pasts to live down.[40] The one thing that every lay official, whether councillor or justice of the peace, knew perfectly well was that zeal against heresy would be equated with enthusiastic support for the regime, and if heretics were not particularly numerous in your home area, it was always possible to invent a few.

There was consequently a good deal of cooperation between parish officers and local magistrates at that level. The case of George Marsh is a good example. Detected by 'certain adversaries', who were probably not the churchwardens, he was arrested by the constable and imprisoned in the bishop's house in Chester. From there he was brought before the Earl of Derby and 'certain of his counsel'.[41] Derby had no ecclesiastical authority and his position was that of a local magnate. He had no particular commission and his councillors were probably not justices of the peace, but he was known to be a keen supporter of traditional religion. Having satisfied himself that Marsh was indeed a heretic, Derby then committed him to the bishop, who proceeded against him by his ordinary authority. Once he had been condemned, he was handed over to the sheriff of Cheshire for execution. The great majority of the 284 victims of the persecution were dealt with in a similar fashion, being presented either from their parishes or from the place where the alleged offence took place and being tried in the consistory court of the relevant bishop.[42] Only the distinctive circumstances in Cheshire make the role of the Earl of Derby noteworthy, although he was a member of the Privy Council and was probably acting under the general authority of the commission of the peace. Protestants were not numerous in Cheshire, but in Essex, where there were a great many, Richard, Lord Rich, was similarly involved in a number of inquisitions.

Such process was not, however, adequate for the trial of former bishops. Although in most cases their episcopal orders were not recognized, they were tried under special commissions issued by Pole as Cardinal Legate. The first such commission was issued on 28 January 1555 to Stephen Gardiner, and to several other bishops who had already been individually reconciled to Rome by the Legate. This was for the trial of John Hooper, John Rogers, Rowland Taylor, Robert Farrer and Laurence Saunders, and was intended to be a showpiece event.[43] Only Hooper and Farrer had actually been bishops, but the others were leading preachers and evangelists, and the intention was to force high-profile submissions. It did not work because only Farrer recanted, and that temporarily. Ridley and Latimer were similarly dealt with by a Legatine commission addressed to James Brooks, the Bishop of Gloucester, White of Lincoln and Holyman of Bristol, and the trial was held in Oxford in September 1555.[44] Thomas Cranmer, however, presented a problem, because he had been papally confirmed in 1533, and although he had sacrificed his temporalities through his conviction for treason two years earlier and was a dead man by English law, he was still by the canon law Archbishop of Canterbury. He was consequently *Legatus natus*, and therefore technically Pole's equal, who could not be tried by his normal jurisdiction. Pope Paul IV had delegated his case to Inquisitor General Jacopo Puteo, who had in turn referred it by commission to James Brooks. Brooks was therefore operating by virtue of two separate commissions, one from Pole for the trial of Ridley and Latimer, and the other from Puteo to investigate the case of Cranmer.[45] On 7 September the Archbishop, who had been a prisoner in Bocardo (the town jail of Oxford) since the spring of 1554, was summoned to Rome. This was a pure formality and it was clear that his appearance before Brooks would constitute the only trial he was likely to get. Brooks duly reported his findings to Rome and on that basis, as well as his technical contumacy for non-appearance, Cranmer was condemned and sentenced early in the following year.

Although Mary could in theory have issued commissions herself under the Royal Supremacy for the trial of heresy, or permitted her bishops to exercise their ordinary jurisdiction, she chose not to do so. Although her newly appointed bishops had actually been reconciled to Rome by Pole while he was still awaiting entry to the country, she seems not to have regarded their authority as complete until the realm itself had been received back into the Roman communion. The reason for this may have been that if any appeal had been lodged against a bishop's sentence, she would have had to deal with it herself, and she saw her role as Supreme Head as that of a housekeeper rather than a proprietor.[46] This attitude was well demonstrated by a statute of her first parliament against disturbers of divine service (by which she meant the mass). Such offenders were to be arrested by the churchwardens, and could be imprisoned by a single justice of the peace. Within six days they were to be interviewed by at least two justices, who were empowered to jail them for up to three months, or until they repented and gave assurances at the quarter sessions. Although the enforcement of this Act was specifically entrusted to the justices of the peace, it was emphasized that this did not in any way impugn the normal ecclesiastical jurisdiction.[47] Presumably (although this was not stated) at the end of three months the recalcitrant offender was to be committed to the archdeacons' or the bishops' court. Similarly in the next session of the same parliament, certain parish churches were 're-edified' by the repeal of Edwardian Acts, and the Queen was authorized to issue constitutions for the government of cathedral churches under the Great Seal – a provision which was realized in the case of Durham in 1557.[48]

After the restoration of papal authority, Mary retreated somewhat, but remained keen to demonstrate her supportive role. In 1556, and on the petition of the surviving monks, she refounded the abbey of Westminster with an endowment of over £2,000 a year, and by a statute of 1555 abolished the payment of First Fruits, restoring the Tenths of spiritual and ecclesiastical promotions to the Church in the person of Cardinal Pole for the purpose of discharging the payment of pensions to such former monks as were still in receipt of them.[49] In a similar helpful vein, on 25 April 1556 she issued a commission to Henry, Lord Abergavenny, George, Lord Cobham, and five others both clergy and laity, but including no diocesan bishop, 'to enquire concerning all heresies, heretical and seditious books, and all conspiracies against the King and Queen'.[50] This seems to have been inspired by the near panic which had followed the discovery of the Dudley plot in February of that year, and covered only the diocese of Canterbury, but it is indicative of just where the government saw the boundary between secular and ecclesiastical jurisdiction to lie. Conspiracies against the Crown were of course purely secular concerns, and were to be referred to the council or to the assizes, but the production of books which were seditious only in so far as they were also heretical was more marginal, and heresy proper was a spiritual matter. Nevertheless the commissioners were instructed to search out those who refused to be confessed, to receive the sacraments or to come to mass, and to refer them to the 'proper ecclesiastical courts'. In other words they were to assume in a more proactive manner, the function which already belonged to the justices of the peace. Any cases of difficulty were to be referred to the newly installed Archbishop, Cardinal Pole, who presumably had the last word in deciding which jurisdiction a case belonged to.[51] It is interesting that he should have been granted by Royal Commission an authority which he would probably have regarded as his right *ex officio*.

This particular commission was headed by lay councillors and was only dubiously an infringement of the Church's rights, but other similar authority was at the same time conferred on several bishops, instructing them to commit offenders to ward and to certify the fact into Chancery. Matters of importance or difficulty were to be referred in this case not to the Archbishop but to the Bishop of London, 'who has a larger commission from the crown'. This looks like a clear infringement of Pole's authority as Legate. Why should a bishop require the authority of a royal commission to investigate cases of heresy? And why should imprisoned offenders be notified to Chancery? Above all, why should Bishop Bonner of London have a commission from the Crown to adjudicate issues which should have been entirely within the jurisdiction of the Cardinal Legate?[52] Pole and Mary shared a common objective, and it seems that these border skirmishes did not generate any tension between them, but they are indicative of the extent to which Mary – or perhaps her councillors – hung on to some of the traditional powers of the Royal Supremacy.

The most conspicuous example of this attitude, however, came in a commission issued on 8 February 1557. This was addressed again to Edmund, Bishop of London, Thomas (Thirlby), Bishop of Ely and twenty-one others, both laymen and clergy. In addition to enquiring concerning seditious books and conspiracies, they were instructed to 'hear and determine all misdemeanours and negligences committed in any church or chapel ... to search out all such as refuse to go to church, take holy water, go in procession, or in any other way misconduct themselves.'[53] This apparently authorized them to act as an ecclesiastical court of first instance, because it is only persistent offenders who are to be referred to the ordinary to be dealt with by canon law. Clearly an overlap of jurisdictions is created by this commission, because anyone wishing to draw attention to nonconformity may chose either to being such cases to the commissioners or to their ordinary, either the archdeacon or the bishop. The commissioners would presumably have been administering statute law, because unless they received a second commission from the Legate, they would not have been authorized to use the ecclesiastical law.[54] In June 1557 Pole's Legatine authority was withdrawn, but this did not lead to any fresh royal commissions. For all practical purposes, the government ignored this action and carried on as before. Pole was anguished by the Pope's decision and wished to obey the summons to return to Rome. However Philip and Mary declined to allow him to go, and Pole instead lodged a formal appeal. Although it seems certain that the Cardinal recognized the fact that his authority had been revoked, many of his servants took the view that, pending his appeal, they should simply carry on – and they did so.[55] Mary rejected Paul's attempt to replace Pole with the aged Observant friar William Peto, and the Cardinal continued to run the English Church as before, using his status as *Legatus natus*, which he had acquired with the Archbishopric of Canterbury, to which he had been appointed in March 1556. It was believed in some quarters in Rome that the English schism had been renewed, but it never came to that and relations stumbled on to the end of the reign.

Early in 1558 a further commission of a somewhat marginal nature was issued to Bonner and to Henry Cole, who was Pole's chancellor. Ironically in view of the state of Anglo-papal relations at that point, the Bishop of London was instructed to enquire of all registrars and other officers holding records, for any 'books, scrolls, or other writings' against the Pope, and to confiscate them and burn them. This was clearly an attempt to 'tidy away' the years of schism and heresy, but why it should have been seen as a proper concern of the secular authorities remains obscure.[56] At the highest level the two jurisdictions were working so closely together that it is often difficult to distinguish between them. The trial of heresy was a matter for the bishops, or for the Legatine commissioners, but how those offenders got into court and what happened to them afterwards were matters for the secular magistrates. There are clear indications that some of the bishops were proceeding very reluctantly and were unwilling to bring offenders to trial if the outcome was likely to be condemnation and death. Edmund Bonner, because of the nature of his position, had more burnings on his conscience than most, but even he had to be prodded into action occasionally by the council, and is on record as having said that if a flogging would induce conformity and save a man from the stake, then he would administer it with a good will.[57] Pole was not squeamish about burning heretics, whom he loathed with a whole heart, and issued quite a number of commissions to investigate and try particular cases. These were often high-profile issues, and the efforts made to induce the victims to recant were often prodigious. John Philpot underwent fifteen separate examinations before he was finally condemned.[58] However, the driving force seems to have come from certain members of the council, particularly those close to the Queen, and it was her own sense of duty which was motivating her.

At the grass-roots level there were a number of different ways of getting into trouble. The commonest was probably presentation by the incumbent or churchwardens to the archdeacon's officials, with a resultant appearance in his court. The great majority of such cases resulted in submission and penance, a process which can only be traced where the court records survive, and which subsequently ceased to be of much interest to anyone. Some of those presented were, or had been, Protestants, but the majority were probably just ribald or careless. Frivolous remarks made in an ale house could well be sufficient if overheard by the wrong person. In theory it was an ecclesiastical police state, but much depended upon the zeal of the (often self-appointed) promoters and informers.[59] There seems to have been, as one might expect, a great deal of settling of private scores, because no penalty was imposed for false accusations and it was risk free method of harassing a personal opponent. If the charge was the more serious one of heresy, or if the accuser was actually the incumbent, then there was a greater likelihood that the first move would be to involve the justices. The statute of 1533 had been repealed in 1555, so there was no need for a formal process of indictment, but the magistrates would have been more likely to demand two witnesses, which was by this time standard common law requirement, before committing a case to the bishop. In taking cognisance of such cases, they would have been acting under the revived statute of 1416.

Once past the justices, a case could be routed in a number of different ways. The commonest was direct to the bishop's consistory, but they might chose to send the offender first to the King and Queen's commissioners, if such a body was sitting in their area. This was likely to happen if the charges were less than firmly established, or if for any reason they wished to shed the responsibility.

The royal commissioners had power only to investigate, but if they chose either to refer the case to the diocesan or to the Legatine commissioners then it was they who had established the presumption of guilt rather than the magistrates. Finally, they could chose to send the accused straight to Pole's commissioners. Such bodies were not always available, but they had full power to deal with cases of heresy without reference to the ordinary, and this might be a preferred method if the ordinary was thought to be reluctant. As we have seen, several of the 'front-line' bishops were unwilling to have blood on their hands.[60] The machinery of enforcement was thus multi-layered, and stretched from the parish to the Lord Legate in clearly marked stages, but, except in cases like William Flower who drew attention to himself by striking the celebrant at mass over the head with a wood cleaver, the initiative nearly always lay in the parish.[61] Religious conformity was a cultural phenomenon and was enforced at a popular level as much by the weight of public opinion as by coercive officials. In some places there was a counter-culture of dissent, and the number of denunciations may well have reflected the balance between these two forces in any particular place. However, there was also an inquisitorial process, and that reflected less the interface between popular cultures than the impact of official policy. This study is not concerned with the high-profile cases, such as those of John Rogers or John Bradford, where steel-tipped Protestant consciences were in conflict with the Catholic Church and its political supporters. Rather it is interested in the way in which inquisitorial process was supported in the local communities, and in what inspired neighbours, workmates and even family members to denounce each other for not taking the Easter communion or for persistently absenting themselves from the mass. Such accusations often resulted in charges of heresy as Edwardian conformists became the targets of their conservative fellows and those who had so warmly welcomed the Queen's proceedings came to terms with the demand of the Papal Legate. They probably did not like having a foreign king, and were largely indifferent to a distant papacy, but they knew what the Queen wanted, and that corresponded well enough with their own tastes.

2 ELITE RELIGION

As the Reformation developed, the Protestant churches began to split apart, giving their Catholic opponents many polemical opportunities. Lutherans disagreed with Zwinglians over the Eucharist, and both were derided by radical sects which were given a new lease of life by the disputes.

The Catholic publicist Miles Huggarde commented 'if these good fellows will needs be of Christ's church, as arrogantly they presume by their own confession, they must needs have one unity of doctrine as the church hath, which surely they have not', adding that punishments were not so various in hell as were the doctrines of these same Protestants.[1] However, the unity of the Catholic position was more established in Huggarde's imagination than it was in reality. Admittedly there were not the same rather obvious disagreements over the Eucharistic presence as divided Protestants, but the transmission of grace was almost equally contentious and the strictly Pauline position taken by Cardinal Pole caused him to be regarded in conservative circles as a crypto-Lutheran.[2] It was this dispute, going back nearly twenty years, which prompted Pope Paul IV to regard the Cardinal as a heretic, and led to his summons to return to Rome for 'investigation'.

It was the business of a General Council to resolve such issues, and such a council had met at Trent in 1545–7 and again in 1552–3. However, its decrees remained in draft, having never been confirmed, and it had not in any case approached the issue of the transmission of grace. What it had done was to repudiate most of the biblical scholarship of the last hundred years, and reaffirmed the sanctity of the Vulgate (Jerome) Bible, which was declared to be the only authentic text. This was a decision with which Pole was in profound disagreement, but as the decree was unratified, it did not greatly affect his mission.[3] What was relevant was the Cardinal's attitude towards the English Bible which he found still installed in many parish churches. This was based on humanist and Protestant scholarship of the 1520s and 1530s, and was, from a Catholic point of view, seriously flawed. Many conservative English clergy, including several bishops, wanted it to be banned. Bishop James Turberville of Exeter, for example, ordered parishes in his diocese to stop using it, collecting up and destroying copies where he could find them.[4] Occasionally, as we shall see, reading the Bible in English was taken as evidence of heresy, but it was never officially withdrawn. Pole was perfectly well aware that Archbishop Arundel's Constitutions had banned only unauthorized translations (that is the Lollard Bible) and this version, the Great Bible, had been fully authorized. Unfortunately the authorizer had been a schismatic prince, and that left the whole issue in limbo.[5] The legatine synod of 1556 promised a fully Catholic translation, but that could not be delivered in the time available. No new edition of the Great Bible was published during Mary's reign for obvious reasons, and its use was widely discouraged, but it remained as a bone of contention within the Catholic establishment, because both Pole and Mary thought that it was better than nothing. Neither of them, however, felt able to come out openly in support of it.

There were also what might be broadly described as evangelical issues. Pole's alleged aversion to preaching has been recently exposed as a myth, but his enthusiasm was tinged with caution.[6] Good sermons were fine, and necessary, but there had been far too much 'gadding to sermons' recently, particularly in London. Preaching needed to be carefully geared to its expected audience and contentious issues should be avoided. A sermon should be an edifying experience and, as the Cardinal was only too aware, the majority of conservative clergy were quite incapable of preparing and delivering such an exhortation. Unless or until properly educated clergy could be provided to deliver sound and inspiring sermons, it was better to stick with the sacramental discipline which was already in place when the Cardinal returned to England.[7] Training also was a potentially contentious matter. As Legate, Pole was very concerned that the universities should return to being preparation places for well-educated priests, who would be able to defend the faith with logic and learning. His Legatine Synod also decreed the establishment of diocesan seminaries for the training of more 'ordinary' priests, whose vocation had up until that time been left to a hit-and-miss system of apprenticeship. Pole's refusal of the offer of help from Ignatius Loyola, which the Count of Feria attributed to lukewarmness, and has been thought to reflect an aversion to the Jesuit discipline, is more likely to have been caused by a cool appraisal of their teaching methods.[8] In any case direct help would have been out of the question as none of the members of the order at that time spoke a word of English. The ongoing feuds between the Dominicans and the Franciscans over the immaculate conception of the Virgin Mary did not much affect the situation in England, but they did affect perceptions of the unity of the Catholic faith. Above all, strategic arguments about how to confront the menace of heresy divided the Curia, and it was the hard line taken by Pope Paul IV which caused the Council of Trent to remain in suspension and led to the arrest and imprisonment of Cardinal Morone. Although an aggressive counter-attack against Protestantism had already begun in Rome, the Catholic Church in 1555 was not altogether at ease with itself.[9]

This was not immediately apparent because, whatever her ultimate intentions may have been, the 'old faith' which Mary re-established immediately after coming to the throne was not internally contentious. The first Act of Repeal decreed that after 20 December, 'all such divine service and administration of the sacraments as were most commonly used in the realm of England in the last year of the reign of our late sovereign Lord King Henry the Eighth, shall be ... used and frequented'.[10] However the Act of Six Articles was not reinstated and, although its standard of orthodoxy was clearly implied, the punishments decreed by that Act were not reinstated either. What happened in the Chapel Royal, and in showcase churches such as St Paul's, was that the mass and other elements of the traditional liturgy were re-established, processions and other ceremonies began again. Theological controversy was confined to disputes with such zealous Protestants as still dared to show themselves, and the issues which divided the Roman Church on the Continent did not appear. Some awareness of these contentions must have come in with such educated exiles as Richard Smyth, who returned to Oxford almost immediately upon Mary's accession, but they did not surface in the religious dialectic of the period.[11]

The elite religion of the first twelve months of the reign was very much dictated by the Queen, who imposed her will upon the court with a firm hand. She forced her reluctant sister Elizabeth to attend mass and appointed her chaplains, and subsequently her bishops, for their known Catholicism. She imported chrism from the Low Countries for her coronation, being unwilling to use that which Cranmer had contaminated through Edward's anointing six years earlier. The ceremony itself on 1 October was celebrated with the full traditional rites, including the same oath that her father had used in 1509. Only the revels were subdued, no one knowing quite what to make of a ruling Queen, and there was no coronation tournament.[12] For several months there was nothing to show that Mary intended to go back beyond her father's settlement, as that had finally stabilized in 1539. Her personal history also pointed in the same direction. She had defended the papal primacy stoutly before 1536, but that had been largely out of loyalty to her mother and hostility to Anne Boleyn. After surrendering to cruel pressure from Henry in the summer of 1536, she had never looked back. The dissolution of the monasteries and the revisions made to the calendar passed without any recorded comment from her, and she fitted comfortably into the semi-evangelical circle that surrounded Henry's last Queen, Catherine Parr.[13] She even undertook to translate Erasmus's paraphrase on the Gospel of St John into English, and although the work remained incomplete, that was because she was ill, rather than reluctant. When Nicholas Udall published the first volume of the Paraphrases in 1548, he went out of his way to praise Mary

who in the midst of courtly delights ... hath by her own choice and election so vir-
tuously and fruitfully passed her tender youth that ... she doth now confer unto
[England] the inestimable benefits of furthering both us and our posterity in the
knowledge of God's word[14]

She had been a resolute opponent of the Protestant policies of Edward's council, but always in defence of her father's settlement and, whatever she may have
thought privately, she never made any public allusion either to the Pope or to
what was happening in the wider Catholic Church. She was regularly in touch
with the imperial ambassadors, who supported her stand with the weight of the
Emperor's diplomacy, but if they ever discussed theology, it was not recorded.
Yet something, or someone, converted her from this insular way of thinking,
and caused her within a week or two of securing the Crown to confide to her
council that she not only intended to restore the Church, but also the Pope's
authority.[15] She may have been dissembling since 1536, which is what she suggested to Gian Francesco Commendone when he visited her as an emissary
from Julius III during August, or she may have had a 'conversion experience' as a
result of the circumstances of her success against the Duke of Northumberland.
That triumph the imperial ambassadors had hailed as 'a miracle', and Mary may
have shared that view.[16] It may also have been in her mind that although the
Royal Supremacy featured among her official titles, it was an authority which no
woman could wield. However it came about, the Queen's mind was turned outwards from her own realm in various ways in the opening months of her reign.
Outwards as she searched for a satisfactory marriage and began to negotiate for
the hand of Philip of Spain, but outwards also as she corresponded with Reginald Pole, who was appointed as Legate to her court, and with the Pope whose
emissary he would be. Mary's world was about to widen dramatically.

The principal agent of that widening was, of course, Philip. He had not
much wanted to marry Mary, who was a spinster eleven years older than himself, but he bowed to his father's wishes. He had not much wanted to come
to England either, but that was an inevitable part of the plan.[17] The courtiers
who had insisted on coming with him were not very happy either. England had
two images in the Spanish mind; either it was the Arthurian realm of mist and
romantic chivalry or it was a wet and miserable hole, full of heretics and barbar-
ians. Philip himself was courteously, even generously received, but his courtiers
were soon at daggers drawn with their reluctant hosts and most of them quickly
retreated to the Low Countries.[18] The exceptions were his clergy, a distinguished
team of theologians, led by Pedro de Soto, Juan de Villagarcia and Bartolomé
Carranza. The friars in his entourage were received with hostility by the people
of London and did not in any case speak any English, but these theologians confined themselves to the court and the universities, where their Latin made them
readily understood. They preached, not only to Philip and his advisers but to the

court at large, and they talked; to Stephen Gardiner, the Lord Chancellor, to Mary's chaplains and confessors, and to the Queen herself. Carranza in particular was thoroughly conversant with the proceedings which had so far transpired at Trent and was entirely familiar with the latest developments in Catholic spirituality.[19] There can be no doubt that during the three years which he spent in England, Carranza brought the Queen up to speed with what was happening in the wider Church. Whether that made much difference to the faith which was actually practised at the English court is another matter. The most conspicuous display of Spanish piety was made on Corpus Christi day, 9 June 1555, when a liturgical procession was staged at Kingston upon Thames. The blessed sacrament was borne to the church by Cristobel Becerra, one of Philip's chaplains, supported by numerous Spanish knights and noblemen. The whole ceremony was organized by Bartolomé Carranza, and some members of the English court also attended.[20] Although they were at nearby Hampton Court, the King and Queen did not take part and the impact of this sumptuous demonstration is hard to assess. To John Foxe it was just another bit of popish frippery, but he was many miles away at the time, and is in any case not an unbiased witness. The example was followed, although in a somewhat lower key, when in the following year Bishop Bonner bore the sacrament at Fulham. A few days after the feast, on 7 June 1556, Carranza himself bore the host in a similar procession at Whitehall, when, according to later testimony

> many English people ... with great haste and excitement came to see the same procession, and when the said most Reverend [Carranza] raised the most Holy Sacrament in his hands [this witness] saw many English people kneeling upon their knees, weeping and giving thanks to God because they were seeing such a good thing, and calling down blessings on those who had been the cause of it.[21]

Becerra, who was certainly present, may have misunderstood the nature of this reaction, but perhaps he was right and the piety of the assembled Londoners outweighed their hostility to all things Spanish. That, certainly, was what Carranza was aiming for when he introduced this new style procession to the English Church. Pole seems to have followed his example at Canterbury, but using English ministers and English music.

As far back as 1547 it had been noted that Mary might attend as many as four masses a day and there is no evidence that her practice had changed since. These were, of course, low masses and the Queen did not communicate, but there is no sign of the services of special intent which might have been expected to appear after July 1555.[22] They had become fashionable and there is no doubt that Philip's Capilla Real used them, but there is no indication that the usage spread to the Chapel Royal proper. Perhaps it did, but nobody thought to comment on it. Nor is there any sign of the typically Counter Reformation cults, such as that of the Holy Blood, to which some of Philip's clergy were devoted. It might be expected that the Queen would have shown a special devotion to the Blessed Virgin, but that seems not to have been the case either. In fact the saints were strangely neglected.[23] Of all the great pilgrimage shrines which Henry VIII had destroyed, only that of Edward the Confessor at Westminster was re-erected, and that was done by the monks after their reintroduction. St Cuthbert at Durham, St Thomas Becket at Canterbury, Our Lady at Walsingham and dozens of others remained desolate throughout the Catholic restoration. True to her Erasmian upbringing, Mary undertook no pilgrimage throughout her reign; and Philip, who knew little of English saints, did not venture without her. A few chantries were founded by devout gentlemen, but when the Queen wished to give thanks for her victories over the Duke of Northumberland and Sir Thomas Wyatt, she gave money to the universities to found scholarships for poor students.[24] A small number of monasteries and friaries were founded and endowed by the Crown, but Westminster, which was by far the largest, was erected on the petition of the former monks of the old foundation, not on the initiative of the Queen. Carranza is thought to have been behind that petition, in which case he was working in close collaboration with Cardinal Pole, if not as his agent.

The other, and more obvious connection with the Universal Church was provided, both symbolically and really, by Reginald Pole himself. Pole was an intellectual, a remote kinsman of the Queen, and was thoroughly steeped in the thinking, and the controversies, of the Counter Reformation. As a leader of the *spirtuali* in the 1530s he had favoured negotiations with the Lutherans, but he had no sympathy with heretics as such.[25] His theology was subtle and sophisticated, which caused his position to be frequently misunderstood, and very little of it was published in his lifetime, but he was an immensely influential figure. His impact on the English Church was administrative and jurisdictional rather than theological, but his commitment to the Pope whom he represented was real and important. He sent Stephen Gardiner a copy of his unpublished treatise on the papal authority, 'De Summo Pontifico', which he had written during the conclave of 1550, at which he had himself come within a single vote of being elected.[26] As Legate, Pole worked closely with Carranza and encouraged him to write his *Comentarios sobre el Catechismo christiano*, which was published in Antwerp in 1558. In spite of being written in Spanish this was apparently aimed at an English clerical readership, although in the absence of a translation into either English or Latin, its effect must have been almost zero.[27] Pole received over 300 appeals to his jurisdiction as Legate, some of them actually before his return when he had by English law no right to receive them. This indicates, Professor Mayer has argued, 'a pent up demand for papal justice', which may be correct, but only on a small scale.[28] The whole question of Pole's exercise of his Legatine jurisdiction before it was legally approved is a murky one, because there was obviously a good deal of connivance, not least by Mary, who judged that certain business could not wait.[29] His leadership of elite religion was partly institutional, partly by example, and partly also through the informal conversations which he had with the King, the Queen and with leading courtiers. These conversations are necessarily elusive, because no one kept a record of them, but they surface repeatedly in the Cardinal's voluminous correspondence, and occasionally in the comments of diplomats.[30]

The academic world was international and, as a renowned scholar, Pole was well positioned to take an initiative in clerical education. This was a priority for him and his task was aided by the fact that Cambridge elected him chancellor after Gardiner's death in November 1555, while Oxford followed suit after Sir John Mason's resignation in 1556.[31] Both universities had been forced to become Protestant strongholds under Edward VI, Oxford more reluctantly than Cambridge. Peter Martyr's tenure of the chair of divinity in the former had been more than usually contentious because it had followed the dismissal of Richard Smyth, and several Oxford divines had followed Smyth into exile. Cambridge had welcomed Martin Bucer and Paul Fagius with more enthusiasm, and during his brief occupancy of the chair the former had acquired a numerous following. However, Mary's accession changed the politics of the situation dramatically. Bucer was dead by that time, but between 1553 and 1555 over seventy Cambridge theologians fled overseas and all the key positions were soon occupied by Catholics. In conservative Oxford the turnaround was both swifter and more complete; between fifty and sixty scholars fled, although on the whole they lacked the status of their Cambridge colleagues.[32] In both universities the gaps were quickly filled with conservative appointments, some of whom had previously been ousted to make way for the reformers. Yet each for the time being continued to operate under their Edwardian constitutions, which induced a tension between the theory and the practice which was not good for discipline.

In 1556 the Cardinal decided to rectify these anomalies by conducting visitations, and began with Oxford in the summer. A commission was issued to James Brooks, Bishop of Gloucester, Pole's secretary Nicholas Ormanet and several Oxford doctors, who were instructed to administer thirty articles designed to remove all traces of heresy, to expose any 'novelties' which had been introduced since 1533 and to remedy remaining deficiencies in the teaching methods being employed.[33] On 20 July the visitors formally opened their campaign with a public meeting in St Mary's church. They then proceeded to each college, punishing any scholars still in possession of Protestant books, and burning the same books, together with any English Bibles they could find. They even exhumed the bones of Peter Martyr's first wife from her grave in Christ Church cathedral and cast them on a dunghill. So far their work had been almost entirely negative, but Pole followed up the visitation in November with a new set of statutes, which covered all aspects of university life. Again all unorthodox teaching was censured, but this time the observance of good and Catholic customs was decreed and a pious lifestyle enjoined.[34] What was required in doctrinal terms was not so much stated as implied. A year before Pedro de Soto, previously a confessor to the Emperor Charles V, had been installed in the Regius chair of divinity, where he was supported by his fellow Dominican, Juan de Villagarcia, by Antonio Rescius, and probably for a while by Carranza. It was they who set the standard of orthodoxy which was now demanded, just as Peter Martyr had set the standard under the previous regime.[35] The teaching at Oxford was thus firmly locked into the latest Dominican mode, which was another reason why Pole did not want to upset this arrangement by introducing the rather different methods of Loyola. He had no intention of allowing the Dominican model to be challenged, which was why all Protestant books were destroyed rather than being publicly refuted. Any future graduate of Oxford proceeding to the priesthood would have known only one mode of thought, and that was the mode laid down by De Soto.

Having thus arranged one university, Pole proceeded to the other, and in December 1556 issued a similar commission for the visitation of Cambridge. The commissioners on this occasion were John Christopherson, who was both Bishop of Chichester and master of Trinity College, Thomas Watson the Bishop of Lincoln, Nicholas Ormanet and several Cambridge doctors.[36] As in Oxford, they started their proceedings with a public meeting in St Mary the Great on 11 January, having first heard mass at King's College, which is just opposite. There was a sermon 'inveighing against heresies and heretics, as Bilney, Latimer, Cranmer, Ridley etc.' after which the Cardinal's commission was read out. In the afternoon the commissioners examined the university's statutes, and then spent two days trying and condemning the deceased Bucer for heresy.[37] On 14 January they began their round of the colleges, carefully hearing mass in each chapel before getting down to business. Rather surprisingly, they found little amiss, although they confiscated a large number of books, being no more minded than their colleagues in Oxford to allow anything in the way of disputation to take place. On 29 January they required the vice chancellor, the heads of houses and the representatives of the town parishes to supply written lists of all their books, and on 6 February a magnificent bonfire was held in the marketplace to consume them. In the same fire were also burned the mortal remains of Martin Bucer and Paul Fagius, whose doctrines had been formally repudiated by the congregation of the university on 15 January, and which had been exhumed from their burial place in St Mary's church for the purpose.[38] The church was then re-consecrated because it had accorded them Christian burial. The visitation came to an end on 16 February with the delivery to the vice chancellor of a new set of statutes, ordering the teaching of the university to conform to the Oxford model and making further specific provisions for the preservation of orthodoxy.

In one sense these visitations were purely administrative, designed to tidy away the relics of twenty years of schism and heresy. In another sense they were a part of the general campaign against dissent which embraced all institutions and all levels of society. However, they were also intended to secure the grip of the Church on elite education, and in that they were remarkably successful. So successful, indeed, that when Protestantism returned under Elizabeth it found the universities to be hostile territory, or, more accurately, Oxford was hostile and Cambridge reluctant. Only the most malleable and compliant accepted the new changes and the exodus from both was on a greater scale that it had been at the beginning of Mary's reign.[39] Former Oxford fellows, like Thomas Harding, Nicholas Sander and William Allen, kept up a running theological fire upon the Elizabethan Church, and their determined rearguard action constituted one of the most important legacies which Cardinal Pole left to his native land.[40]

With the exception of Richard Smyth, academics in post were not among the leading defenders of Catholic doctrine during Mary's reign, nor were the Spanish divines who came with Philip, influential though they may have been in other ways. The elite theologians who most effectively explained to their fellow countrymen where the Catholic Church had got to in its evolving spirituality, and the reasons why they should now be obedient to the Pope, were nearly all working clergy, and their writings formed the backbone of their mission. These books were the interface between the religion of the learned and that of the people at large, because in fact there were two constituencies to be addressed. The first was that of those who were literate in English, and it was this group which had been most affected by the Protestant propaganda of the previous decade. As Pole put it, 'people have been corrupted here even more by books than by the spoken word, so they must be recalled to life through the written word'.[40]

They were important because, although a minority, they were the natural leaders of society; merchants, gentlemen and yeomen. Those whose families had sufficient means to send them to school but who had no ambition to pursue a learned profession. By this time it was normal for a justice of the peace to have studied for a year or two at university and to have proceeded to an Inn of Court, but there were many gentlemen below that level, the so-called 'parish gentry', who were the leaders of their local communities. In this group also were to be found the churchwardens and petty constables, whose cooperation was essential if the laws were to be effectively enforced.[41] These were not, on the whole, people with ideas of their own, but they were accessible to print, were buyers of books and were extremely important as the mediators of learned ideas.

The second sort, the illiterate majority, were not directly accessible, except to the spoken word, but it should not be assumed that they were indifferent to books. It was the normal practice for those who were literate to read aloud for the benefit of those who were not, and this practice had been assiduously encouraged under the previous regime. Consequently there were Protestants even at the lowest social levels, and these needed to be redeemed no less than their betters.[42] Manuals, primers and guidebooks, sometimes of a very basic nature, were therefore produced in large numbers, in which the learned set out for the benefit of both these constituencies what it meant to be a Catholic. Basic liturgical instruction was provided – for example how a layman should conduct himself when attending mass. Because such piety had been under assault in recent years, the underlying conservatism of the people was not thought to be sufficient. The old ways needed stiffening with understanding, and that could only be provided by those who were well versed in the new ways of Catholic Europe.[43]

The learned wrote comparatively little for each other. A second edition of Cuthbert Tunstall's *De Veritate Corporis Domini* was published in 1554, and of Stephen Gardiner's *Confutatio Cavillationum* at Louvain in the same year. Philip's chaplain Alonso di Castro produced two works against heresy, *Adversus Omnes Haereses* and *De Iusta Hereticorum Punitione*, the first in Antwerp and the second in Lyons, both in 1556.[44] Neither of these was aimed specifically at England, although their relevance would have been obvious, and Carranza's work on the catechism, which was aimed at England, appeared only in Spanish. The great majority of the Catholic polemical and devotional works were published in English and ranged from ballads of a popular nature, such as Leonard Stopes's *An Ave Maria in Commendation of our Most Vertuous Queene* (1553) to Thomas Watson's *Holsome and Catholyke Doctryne concerninge the Seven Sacraments* (1558).[45] They expressed contemporary Catholic concerns but were often inspired by, and modelled on, the works of earlier defenders of the faith, particularly John Fisher and Thomas More. More's *Dialoge of Comfort* was reissued in 1553 and a collected edition of his complete English works, edited by his son-in-law William Rastell, appeared in 1557.[46] Several of the other works purported to be, and perhaps actually were, individual sermons or collections of sermons. Two of Bonner's sermons were printed, presumably with his consent, one edited by Hugh Glasier in 1555 and another by John Harpesfield in 1556. James Brooks and Thomas Watson also published sermons, and no doubt many others circulated in manuscript.[47]

Before 1555 the emphasis of most of this writing was upon the number and validity of the sacraments, particularly the mass and confession, both of which had been targets of Protestant ridicule. There were also various celebrations of Mary's remarkable victories over the Duke of Northumberland and Sir Thomas Wyatt, including John Gwynneth's *A Brief Declaration of the Notable Victory geven of God*, and John Proctor's *Historie of Wiatts Rebellion*, both emphasizing the role of religion on either side in those conflicts.[48] John Christopherson's

Exhortation to all Men to take Heed against Rebellion was written in a similar vein, drawing attention to the presumed relationship between heresy and sedition. Against the Queen's godly proceedings all heretics were potential rebels.[49] No sooner was it clear, however, that the papacy was returning than the issues of Catholic unity and the authority of Rome began to be handled in these instructional writings. John Fisher had defended the papal primacy with force and eloquence in 1521, while it was still safe to do so, and his sermon was reprinted to coincide with the issuing of the papal absolution on 30 November 1554. John Standish's *The Triall of the Supremacy* (1556) was devoted entirely to refuting the 'blasphemous objections' raised by heretics against the Pope in the 'late miserable years'.[50] Standish may have been more focused upon the issue than others, but his approach was well-nigh universal among the later writers. Carranza, for example, treated the papacy in the context of the article on the Church in the Apostle's creed. Richard Smyth, Martin Edgeworth and John Churchson all discussed the papal power in positive terms, as did the anonymous authors of *A Treatise concernynge the Masse* and *An Exclamation upon Heresy*.[51] Below the surface, however, there was a conciliarist current running through these educated writers. In his apology to Paul IV (which he never sent), Reginald Pole stressed the role of the bishops in governing the Church. Martin and Watson expressed similar views. While not denying the overall authority of the papacy, they saw the Church as essentially collegiate rather than monarchical, and this no doubt helped them to cope with the eccentric (and to most of them unacceptable) behaviour of Paul IV in and after 1557.[52]

The most widely read and most influential of all these works, however, did not venture into these dangerous waters at all. Bonner's *Profitable and Necessarye Doctryne* was published, along with a revised set of homilies, in 1555.[53] These homilies made all the right noises, about the seven sacraments, about justification, about the use of images and prayers for the dead. About the papacy he wrote

> forasmuch as this catholike militaunte church ... hath for the preservation of the unitie thereof, by the ordinaunce and appointment of our Saviour Christ, one principal head or chief gouvernoure here upon earth, whiche being the chief vycar and substitute of Chryste in his sayde church, doth and ought, with other ministers under hym, attende and geve heede to the good order and rule of the sayde militant churche. (S. Peter the Apostle beynge the fyrste generall vicar and gouvernoure therein, and having to hym, and to al his lawful successors in the apostolique sea, the gouvernaunce, rule and charge thereof, chieflye committed and geven ... by the continuall helpe and assistaunce of the holye spyryte of God ...)[54]

This is carefully worded to avoid any conciliarist overtones. Peter was the head shepherd and his successors continue to have 'the rule of the whole church'. His support comes from the Holy Spirit rather than from the bishops. According to Leonard Pollard's supporting homily the Pope was 'the next head under Chryste', and it was this rather over-simplified view which was presented to the laity. General Councils were of special authority, but they had to be convened by popes in order to be valid.[55] The most authoritative pronouncement of which the Church was capable was that issued by the Pope with the support of a General Council, but such a council depended for its authority upon the occupant of St Peter's chair, rather than the other way round. The *Profitable and Necessarye Doctryne* also kept to safe ground in its advocacy of the priestly function, which had been heavily devalued by the Protestant abolition of the mass. Without the special powers derived from his ability to convert the Eucharistic elements into Christ's body and blood, the priest became just a minister, whose right to absolve sinners after confession and penance was also removed. Orders had ceased to be a sacrament under the reformers' dispensation, so that no one ordained under the 1550 ordinal could be deemed to be a priest at all.[56] Worse still in some ways, had been the statute of 1549 which permitted clerical marriage, because sex (even when lawful) was especially polluting. When the Act was repealed in 1553, many clergy were proceeded against for 'concubinage', and that had also weakened the clerical image. Having renounced their women, a number were inducted into other benefices, but a doubt still hung over the lawfulness of their sacraments. A visceral hatred of clerical marriage was one of the bonds which held together the elite and popular religions of the period.[57] Bonner made it clear that no such doubts should affect the status of those who had been reconciled by the authority vested in the Lord Legate, and that all Christians should 'esteme the right priesthode now brought home again'.[58]

The main function of the priest was to administer the sacraments, but both Watson and Bonner advocated the importance of preaching, both for instruction in the Catholic truth and also for the advocacy of godly living. Knowing the limitations of the average parish priest, Watson published a series of model sermons in the hope and expectation that congregational trust would be re-established in those who read them aloud. Although not in their own words, such clerics were 'teachynge holesome and catholyke doctrine, and the imitation of the lyfe of our Saviour'.[59] Wholesome doctrine included reverence for the priesthood. The leaders of the Marian Church were under no illusions about the importance, and the difficulty, of instilling Christian habits into the lifestyle of the masses. They deceived themselves into believing that selfishness and lax morality were the result of schism and heresy, but whereas Protestant abuse of the clergy and the sacraments had probably encouraged a ribald carelessness in some quarters, what they were really dealing with was human nature. Writers urged their audiences not only to Christian reverence for the officers and functions of the Church, but to charity, meekness and humility. Some even went so far as to adopt (without acknowledgement) the Lutheran doctrine of the priesthood of all believers, urging them to work and pray in imitation of the disciples, so that 'the gates of hell, that is to say tyrannye, schisms and heresy shall never prevail against it'.[60] The elite vision of the Church may have been clerically dominated, but it was sufficiently informed about current shifts in opinion to realize that its ultimate objective of a healthy spirituality at all levels could only be achieved by a regeneration from below, and to that regeneration simple conservatism formed almost as serious an obstacle as the carelessness and scepticism induced by years of heresy and schism.

The *Profitable and Necessarye Doctryne* was based on the *Necessary Doctryne* of 1543 and was a deliberate attempt to preserve some level of continuity, because as Bonner was well placed to recognize, the 'new Catholicism' would stand a better chance of acceptance if it were seen as the reform of traditionally well-liked practices.[61] It consequently went out of its way to emphasize that there could be no salvation outside the Church and that membership of the Church was signalled by full and regular participation in the sacraments. It also explained such recently controversial doctrines as that of purgatory, newly re-established, and the papal primacy, which was now an article of faith. New material was also covered, such as the cults of the saints, although these seem to have been little heeded. Together with his *Honest Instruction for Children* (1556),[62] the *Profitable and Necessarye Doctryne* served as an official doctrinal text for London clergy and schoolmasters. Pole's Legatine Synod called for a new catechism, which explains Carranza's work of two years later, but in the meantime Bonner's book was to be used in all parishes and not merely in London. It was, for all practical purposes, the doctrinal handbook of the Marian Church, and was recognized as such in the large number of times it was reprinted. It would have been axiomatic that an orthodox Catholic Church had no need of any equivalent of the Forty Two Articles, which had belatedly defined Edwardian Protestantism, but it was also recognized that no one under the age of thirty would have been exposed to orthodox teaching as it was developing in the outside world. In spite of the questionable antecedents of its author, Bonner's catechism fulfilled the requirement well enough.

At the same time, Pole was more concerned with the clergy than he was with the laity. Not only was it sensible to approach congregations through their parish priests, it was also necessary in so sacerdotally organized an institution. Although many of them were poorly educated and less articulate than some of their parishioners, they were in principal part of the ecclesiastical elite and as such were directly subject to the authority of their bishops. When Bonner visited his diocese in 1555, all the clergy summoned were instructed 'to diligently study the book and treatise entitled A profitable and necessary doctrine ... And the contents thereof they shall declare to the people in their parish churches.'[63] They were furthermore required to declare and set forth the meaning of a long list of ecclesiastical ceremonies, including the use of candles on Candlemas day and the practice of creeping to the cross on Good Friday. No parson or vicar was to be absent from his benefice without providing a 'sufficient, honest and able priest' to serve his cure. No priest was to visit ale-houses or other suspect places, nor permit any unlicensed preacher to occupy his pulpit. Interestingly, although all clergy were required to observe the laws, statutes and commandments which had been issued since the coronation of the Queen, there was no specific require-ment for them either to acknowledge the papal primacy or to make any allusion to it in their exhortations to their flocks.[64] Presumably obedience to the Legate in the Pope's name was deemed to be sufficient. Only in the section devoted to the archdeacons was there a requirement that the Pope's name should be restored in all intercessions, along with that of St Thomas of Canterbury and 'all other that heretofore have been … used'.[65]

When James Brooks visited his diocese of Gloucester in 1556 he did so as deputy for the Cardinal Archbishop, who was conducting a metropolitan visita-tion of the whole country, but even so there was no requirement that the clergy acknowledge the papal supremacy. The first article related to the necessity of preaching and drew attention to the decree of the recent Legatine Synod in that respect, while the second required readings from the *Profitable and Necessarye Doctryne* when no sermon was offered. All parsons, vicars and curates were to diligently teach the Pater Noster, the Creed and Commandments in English at the time of divine service, and were to exhort their parishioners to teach their children the same at home.[66] The haunting of ale houses and resort to women were roundly condemned, and every parish priest was instructed that within a week of Easter he should make certificate in writing to the bishop or archdeacon of eve-ryone who had not been to confession in Lent, or received the sacrament on the feast day itself. Each year, upon St Andrews day, special masses were to be said of thanksgiving for the Church's reconciliation with Rome, and care was to be taken that the Pope's name had been restored to the franchises.[67] This oblique recogni-tion, which appears in a number of sets of articles, seems to have been the only acknowledgement that was required. Perhaps it was thought better to take the papal primacy for granted, although that was not a view shared by either Pole or the elite writers of the restoration. Thomas Goldwell's injunctions for the diocese of St Asaph repeat many of the same requirements, but are uniquely hard on sex-ual misconduct. Article 3 lays down that 'no man or woman, having at their death time a paramour, contrary to the laws of God and holy Church, shall be buried in Christian burial' and that the sacrament was to be refused to any such person, even in extremis.[68] It is not at all clear why Goldwell was so severe and explicit against this sin. It may have been that the people of north Wales were particularly prone to such offences, or perhaps the fact that Goldwell was also a chaplain to Reginald Pole is sufficient explanation. The Cardinal was known to have been keen on cleri-cal celibacy, but why ordinary laypeople should have been cast out of the Church and effectively damned for eternity as a result of such a common misdemeanour is hard to understand. It serves as an example to warn us that elite thinking on moral and religious issues, which is reflected in all the writings which we have surveyed, was not necessarily shared by ordinary people. They were accustomed to being led, taught and bullied by their social and intellectual superiors, but they did not always respond to expectation, either in behaviour or beliefs.

A good example of the way in which the clerical leadership sought to take advantage of old habits and customs to get their message across comes in the sermons delivered by the boy bishops. The election of such children upon St Andrew's day was an ancient custom in most cathedral chapters, and the high point of his incumbency was the delivery of a sermon on Holy Innocents' day, 28 December.[69] The point of this ritual had originally been to celebrate St Nicholas's day on 6 December, and the child sometimes appeared disguised as the saint. There was often more than a hint of carnival about such performances, which were used as a focus for fundraising collections, and such activities had been banned by proclamation in July 1541.

> And whereas heretofore divers and many superstitious and childish observations have been used, and yet to this day are observed and kept in many and sundry parts of the realm, as upon St. Nicholas, St. Catherine, St. Clement, the Holy Innocents and such like, children be strangely decked and apparelled to counterfeit priests, bishops and women, and so to be led with songs and dances from house to house, blessing the people and gathering of money, and boys do sing mass and preach in the pulpit

All such things were to be 'left and clearly extinguished'.[70] However, the opportunities presented by these 'counterfeitings' were too good to be missed, and Bishop Bonner permitted St Nicholas to return in the traditional style in November 1554.[71] Two years later the custom was firmly re-established. In 1555 the Childermass day sermon was apparently devoted to a panegyric of the Queen, comparing her to Judith, Hester and the Blessed Virgin, but the texts very seldom survive. One which does was that delivered by John Stubbs, chorister, at Gloucester on 28 December 1558, before any attempt had been made by the new government to interfere with such celebrations. Stubbs's sermon was prepared by Richard Ramsey, the almoner of the cathedral, and was childish only in the most formal sense.[72] Preaching on the text 'Except you will be converted and made like little children, you shall not enter into the kingdom of heaven', Stubbs proceeded to give a highly sophisticated interpretation of the innocence of childhood. In spite of the uncertainties which must by then have been clouding the future of the Church, he stuck determinedly to the benefits of the Catholic faith.

> I report me to you how many witless childer and childish people were in the realm of late years, and yet are in many places, which wavered in their faith and were carried hither and thither, from one opinion to another, as children are carried with an apple, or with a puff of wind

He quoted the scriptures frequently, both in English and in Latin, and generally gave such a mature performance that the fictitious nature of the occasion cannot have been wasted upon his audience. He observed sagely that 'the shunning of evil belongs to the innocent; [while] the doing of good belongs to the just man', and proceeded to a thoroughly adult exposition on the rearing of the young, centred on the adage 'he who spares the rod, spoils the child'.[73] It was a perfectly proper sermon to deliver on Holy Innocents' day, but was entirely devoid of humour, and was clearly regarded by the cathedral establishment as an opportunity to deliver several orthodox messages at a time when a large crowd must have been assembled.

Such festivities were not always either solemn or purposeful, in fact mobs of children appear to have accompanied 'St Nicholas' on his rounds, in the manner of the modern 'trick or treat' on Halloween. It is probable that Mrs Crockhay was not alone in turning such revellers from her door in London in 1556, a rejection of which, according to John Foxe, the Archdeacon was unable to take advantage because so many perfectly orthodox households felt the same.[74] As a device for re-engaging the faithful with the Catholic Church, the boy bishop appears to have been a rather questionable move, and perhaps that is why it was not discussed by any of the elite writers we have noticed. The introduction of a new Catholicism was a serious matter and did not necessarily benefit from a revival of old ways. This was to be one of the most serious problems confronting the restored Church.

3 POPULAR RELIGION

There is plenty of evidence for the faith of the laity in the century or so before the reformation, but most of it relates to the literate minority. Only those with property to bequeath left wills, and although the mystery plays were aimed at a wide audience, those who wrote them were, by definition, educated. Also, because of the way in which this evidence is slanted, it gives the impression of an obsession with death. The *danse macabre* was a pervasive image after it had been imported from France to St Paul's in the 1440s, and representations of death were commonplace in the ballad literature of the period. 'With drede we dwellen, With drede we wenden' as one writer put it.[1] Life was short, medicine expensive (when obtainable at all) and death frequently sudden or unexpected. The *Ars moriendi*, or skill of dying, was thus a strategy designed to cope with this natural and inevitable anxiety, and designed, with its emphasis upon extreme unction, to cement the authority of the Church as the custodian of that grim portal. Stories of edifying deaths were numerous and circulated both in writing and by word of mouth, but always the outline of the story was the same: the sufferer, with the aid of the priest, coming to repentance and receiving the sacrament, thus baffling the army of fiends who lay in wait for the unwary or unrepentant soul.[2] The deathbed struggle was a trope, in which saints, particularly the Blessed Virgin, and guardian angels figured prominently. This reality was eased by the Church in two ways. First by the concept of purgatory, that intermediate place where the redeemed but still sin-stained soul endured the punishments which would prepare it to enter heaven. Purgatory was accessible to the prayers and intercessions of the living, who were encouraged to help the deceased by shortening their stay.[3] This led to the second palliative, the communion of the living with the dead. The Church was the community of all the saints, and that sense of fellowship was heightened by the teaching that commemoration was efficacious and that even the humblest offering was acceptable to God.

The simple believer was thus locked in to an ecclesiastical structure, where every stage of his life was monitored with care; from baptism, through confirmation, penance and the regular reception of the Eucharist, to extreme unction and the afterlife of the soul. There is little sign of any theoretical objection to this dependence. The Lollard might argue that the efficacy of a priest's sacraments depended upon the quality of his life rather than the validity of his orders, but he would not deny the need for such sacraments.[4] In practice, however, there was a good deal of backsliding, not necessarily from lack of faith but rather from the natural waywardness of human nature. The records of the Church courts are full of sexual misadventures, abusive behaviour, carelessness and refusal to pay tithes. In fact the humbler the offender, the more likely he, or she, was to find himself in trouble, because he would lack the social defences of the well-to-do. The usual result was a penance or a small fine, and if that was not sufficient to cure the problem, it normally had the appearance of doing so. Of anticlericalism in the institutional sense there is very little evidence in England.[5] Quarrels involving individual clergy were frequent, arising often from personal antipathy or from disputes over money, but objections to clerical authority as such seem to have been very rare. If the expectation that the dying believer would leave at least a few pence or a beast to support some function of his parish church was found oppressive in any way, this did not appear in recorded resentment.

At the same time, there was an exploitative aspect to this ascendancy, and it only required a slight shift of emphasis for that to appear clearly. So much of the Church's authority was based on the concept of 'works salvation', that is that the destiny of the individual soul depended heavily upon its deeds in this life. This could easily lead to a calculated approach to piety; so many 'credits' for a gift to the poor, so much for the refurbishment of the church; so much merit for paying tithes on time, so much for attending mass and confession. These would be set against the sins of which the accountant was only too well aware; so much debit for that undetected spot of adultery, so much for cheating his neighbour out of a cow; the object being at the end of the day to emerge with more on the credit side than the debit, with a deathbed profession of repentance and the offices of the Church to tip the balance, should that be needed.[6] This sounds more cold blooded than it really was, but it set a great premium upon the offices of the Church, which did nothing to discourage it. It was, after all, the 'magical' element in the miracle of the mass which gave the priest's other sacraments, and his intercessory authority, their power. It was not in the interests of the Church to discourage a belief that gifts and bequests had merit, or that attendance at mass should be seen as a 'good work'. However, if the believer's point of view shifted and he became convinced that faith alone carried the secret of salvation, then the whole business of 'works' became a confidence trick, designed to extract money from the gullible. Purgatory became a myth, because the faith (or lack of it) of the deceased was a given fact, and intercessory prayer became an illusion. The money invested in such prayer – everything from the perpetual chantry to the humble obit – was thus being spent on fat priests, whose function should have been pastoral rather than sacramental.[7] So radical a shift came (when it came at all) mainly among the educated, but was passed on through sermons and vernacular writings. It is not surprising that the clergy took fright at the appearance of such notions and quickly resorted to persecution. They affected only a small minority, but the appeal of their simplicity was obvious, and the Church had no means of knowing how many were infected.

Just as the *ars moriendi* depended for its appeal upon its very realistic images of the process of death, so the everyday life of the Church relied heavily upon the tangible and visible. This preoccupation was focused in and upon the saints. Images proliferated in parish churches, where lights burned before them, and most parishes had subordinate altars, where special masses were sung in their honour.[8] There were several reasons for this. In the first place every church had a rood, a crucifix supported by St John and the Blessed Virgin, which usually sat on top of the screen dividing the chancel from the nave. There it formed the focus of an orchestrated representation of the Kingdom of Heaven, in relation to which the array of saints, both carved and painted, were organized. This was why so many rood screens contained panel portraits of the saints, their identity varying from parish to parish according to taste. The fact that some of these screens survive, without the focal rood, makes the original iconography hard to reconstruct.[9] Secondly, most saints were deemed to have some special protective or patronage function, and the images were very often given and maintained by guilds of the relevant craftsmen. St Loy, for example, was the patron saint of blacksmiths, and no one could expect to get his horse shod upon that saint's feast day. Very often the choice of saints represented would depend upon the individual donor, as was the case of Alice Chester, giving images to All Saints, Bristol, in 1483, who specified 'of the which images be 3 principal, a trinity in the middle, a Christopher on the north side, and a Michael upon the south side'.[10] It was quite normal also for benefactors to present their name saints, or those to whom they felt particularly grateful for having solved some crisis in their own lives. Very often the Apostles were specified, and sometimes a cult might carry political implications, as did Lancastrian devotions to Henry VI (who had not even been canonized).

All this says a great deal about the religious tastes of the well-to-do, who no doubt often consulted the clergy before making their choices, but it says little about the equivalent tastes of the poor, who could not hope to donate an image, let alone an altar or a stained-glass window. However, the evidence suggests that they followed willingly where their betters led. It was often the very humble who kept the lights burning, just as it was the humble who cleaned the church and kept the graveyard tidy. It was perhaps their tastes, as much as those of the rich, which gave regional differences to the choice of saints; so that St Richard was much favoured in Chichester, Etheldreda in East Anglia and St Kevern in Cornwall.[11] A saint was a comfortable creature; one who had shared the woes and small joys of this mortal life, and who would understand. Doctors of the church, like Augustine and Ambrose, might feature on rood screens, but they were for the learned. Ordinary worshippers preferred a saint who had borne the burden and heat of the day and who was remarkable, not for intellect or royal status, but for the extraordinary nature of his, or her, piety. In other words, a saint was an approachable intercessor, the kind of person that the suppliant could identify with, and as such they performed a very important function. As Professor Duffy has pointed out, the late fifteenth and early sixteenth centuries was a very flourishing period for devotion to the saints and many churches were embellished, not merely with images, but with chapels dedicated to them, and with towers and steeples erected in their honour.[12] The saints were a major industry and those churches fortunate enough to possess (or unscrupulous enough to invent) relics of these same ancient martyrs were keen to encourage pilgrimages to, and offerings at, their shrines. St Thomas Becket at Canterbury was doing particularly well in that respect, but the shrines of Our Lady at Walsingham and Caversham also attracted royal visitors, with all the extra support that such visits involved.[13]

This popularity caused problems, not for the majority of clergy who happily benefited from the windfalls which all this attention involved, but for the educated elite. They were uncomfortably aware that in its most unthinking form, this devotion had pantheistic overtones. It was not right that the people should be seeking St Blaise or St Uncumber to resolve problems, or to make intercessions, which should have been referred to Christ the Redeemer. In seeking the intervention of the saints, it was all too easy to forget that they had no redemptive power of themselves. Even the Apostles could only be effective by taking issues to Him who was uniquely both God and Man. This was particularly worrying in the case of the Blessed Virgin, who, for all her unique status, was a woman like any other.[14] It was often believed that she had a special access to the Godhead, bypassing her Son, and that, to the learned, bordered on blasphemy. In other words there was a general failure to distinguish *latria* – that worship which is due to God alone, and to Christ as his son – from *dulia*, the reverence which is due to human holiness. Those brought up in the humanist tradition, and that included most of the leading prelates of the early sixteenth century, to say nothing of the King himself, were particularly worried about what they saw as a failure to make adequate distinctions in the life of the Church. This was a failure which, as they were quick to appreciate, left it exposed to the attacks of heretics, for whom the whole business of intercessory prayer was a fraud.[15]

When Henry took over the responsibility for the English Church in 1533, the Curia had been too busy condemning Luther to pay serious attention to the validity of some of his charges, and it was that mistake which Paul III was seeking to remedy when he set up his commission in 1536.[16] The King, however, had no cause to wait for the cumbersome workings of Roman bureaucracy to come up with a solution, and he tackled this issue both in the Ten Articles of 1536 and in his royal injunctions of the same year. Both were concerned to make the essential distinction between honour and worship. Denouncing the 'superstition and hypocrisy crept into divers men's hearts', the latter went on to instruct the clergy that 'they shall not set forth or extol any images, relics or miracles for any superstition or lucre, nor allure the people by any enticements to the pilgrimage of any saint otherwise than is permitted'.[17]

Exactly what was 'permitted' at this stage is not clear, because the Ten Articles make no mention of pilgrimages. However they do instruct preachers to tell the people how the images of saints were to be used, as

> representors of virtue and good example, that they may also be by occasion the kindlers and stirrers of men hearts, and make men oft to remember their sins and offences, especially the images of Christ and Our Lady, and therefore it is meet that they should stand in the churches[18]

In other words images had a didactic function, as reminders of that condition to which mere mortals may aspire, but that is not how they were perceived by the majority of worshippers. The saints were comforters in distress and sharers in the toils and troubles of life. They were far more real than the awesome person of Christ the King, and the fact that they had no share in the Godhead continued to be forgotten despite the best efforts of the learned. It was no doubt awareness of this fact which caused the official line to stiffen, and the 1538 injunctions introduced the sinister word 'idolatry' into its regulation for the clergy, which ran

> Item. That such feigned images as ye know of in any of your cures to be so abused with pilgrimages or offerings of anything made thereunto, ye shall, for the avoiding of that most detestable sin of idolatry, forthwith take down and delay, and shall suffer from henceforth no candles, tapers or images of wax to be set afore any image or picture.[19]

The only exceptions being the light on the rood loft, and that set before the reserved sacrament, both of these being considered proper objects of veneration. Although repeated in various other episcopal injunctions over the next few years, this rule obviously met with great difficulties of enforcement, not least because it depended ultimately on a subjective definition of abuse. When Bishop Stephen Gardiner of Winchester endeavoured to defend the continued use of images in 1547, against Archbishop Cranmer's campaign to remove them altogether, he found himself caught in this subtle trap.[20] As they moved towards an increasingly defined Protestant position between 1547 and 1549, Edward's council instructed his bishops to destroy or deface all images, whether of saints or members of the Holy Family, and by 1553 the interiors of parish churches should have presented an aspect of altogether unprecedented austerity. In many places the images were taken down and stored, but a great many were in fact destroyed by the zeal of the reformers. In this campaign, something of the Old Faith was lost for ever, because although Mary instructed that such images were to be restored, it was with her father's reservations. The comfortable luxuriance of the saints, which had been the fashion before 1530, did not return, because Pole and his colleagues were extremely sensitive to the charges of idolatry which, they were only too well aware, had been justly launched against the pre-Reformation church. Mary's royal injunctions of 1554 ordered the restoration of processions 'after the old order', and of 'good and laudable ceremonies', but said nothing about images of the saints.[21] It was with a somewhat uneasy conscience that that the restored Catholic Church retraced its steps, and the official manuals of instruction were careful to explain that the purpose of such images was as aids to devotion, not as objects to be venerated in their own right.

What should be venerated in and for itself was the sacrament of the altar – the host consecrated by the priest in the celebration of the mass. Since the formulation of the doctrine of transubstantiation in the early thirteenth century, the consecrated host had been unique, because it was deemed to be the physical body of Christ into which the elements were mystically transformed.[22] Popular culture was full of stories of heretics, doubters and Jews who had been converted to the orthodox faith by glimpsing the bleeding flesh momentarily present in the priest's hands. In one fifteenth-century Corpus Christi play, a Jew who witnesses the communion sees a beautiful child being devoured by the congregation, and it is pointed out that this is a sign of God's wrath against his people.

> And thy kun made hym dye,
> Therefore al blodi thou hym seye

Inevitably, the Jew seeks immediate baptism, exclaiming

> Help that I were a Cristene mon;
> For levere ichave cristned ben
> Then evere seo such a siht ayen[23]

Participation in the communion was thus a very solemn action, and one which required a great deal of preparation. Only the extremely pious – or those with no other gainful employment – could communicate weekly, or even monthly. Margery Kemp, who tried to receive once a week, was a virtually full-time mystic, and was regarded as a saint by her contemporaries, while Margaret Beaufort, who communicated once a month, was looked on with awe for her piety.[24] Normally the layman received only once a year, at Easter, and was supposed to have undergone the rigorous fast of Lent, and to have confessed at least once to his parish priest in preparation. This was known as 'taking your rights', and could raise extremely sensitive issues. Every recipient was supposed to be in love and charity with his neighbours, and this could lead to a good deal of jockeying for position, as rivals sought to extract the first apology which would lead to reconciliation. The communion was a social as well as an individual occasion, and the priest might well refuse the host to anyone whom he suspected of insincerity. By thus preserving the integrity of the sacrament, the celebrant might well make the underlying situation worse, as a consuming sense of grievance would be added to the original dispute.[25] In such circumstances what was intended to be a bonding exercise could end up by dividing the community, so it is not surprising that incumbents were often wary of such scrupulosity.

The normal function of the mass was the 'showing' of the host, whereby the celebrant elevated the bread at the moment of consecration, and the congregation was invited to worship it. The proximity of the people to this showing varied a good deal with the circumstances. If the mass was at the high altar, where it would have been celebrated at least once a day, then the attendants would be at some distance, in the body of the church beyond the rood screen. In that case they would have been unable to hear (let alone understand) the words of the liturgy, and would have been dependent entirely upon the sight of the elevated host to attract the attention which they had been supposedly giving to their own devotions. If, however, the mass was at a side altar, or in a guild chapel, then the proximity would have been much greater, and in extreme cases the priest would need the protection of his servers or assistants to keep him from the jostling crowd.[26] It was by no means uncommon for the layman (or woman) who wanted to impress the neighbours to declare that he could not bear to let a day go by in which he did not 'see his saviour'. Given the close proximity of most places of work to the parish church, and the relative brevity of a low mass, this was usually a realizable ambition. So although every mass was in a sense a piece of clerical exhibitionism, the laity did not normally feel excluded. This was particularly the case with the well-to-do, who might very well have set up the relevant side altar themselves, or been members of the responsible fraternity. Such people might, or might not, receive more frequently than once a year, but they would have assumed a right to be present, and close to the celebrant at the mystic moment of the 'showing'.[27] Small gifts and bequests were often given to the high altar of any given church, but these might well be outnumbered by the obits and lights which constituted the typical offerings of the poor, and which were usually offered to 'the Jesus' altar, or the altar of St Thomas or St Winifrid.

A mass might take various forms, and the late medieval period was one of rich variety in this respect, but masses collectively formed the core of the worship of every church and were the focal point of many people's lives. A great deal of spectacle focused on the moment of consecration, quite apart from the 'showing' at the mass itself. In Croxton (Norfolk) a play of the sacraments was presented in which the figure of Christ appeared as the Man of Sorrows, 'all bloody', to awaken in the spectators a sense of guilt and the need for repentance, in a direct echo of the sacrament of the altar.[28] The imagery of blood was pervasive. As John Fisher explained, the virtue of all the sacraments rested in the fact that 'it is to be byleved [that] they are sprencled with the droppes of the same moost holy blode'.[29]

But the iconography of the mass was special, as is revealed by the 'mass of Pope Gregory', whose bending figure is set against the image of Christ emerging from his tomb and displaying his wounds, which appears above the altar, symbolizing the unity of Christ's suffering with the daily sacrifice performed in every parish church.[30] To the orthodox the mass was a re-enactment of the sacrifice of Calvary and was thus a channel of divine grace even to those who did not receive the elements. Everyone could participate in the penitential act which it represented. In spite of his excommunication, the mass remained central to the personal piety of King Henry VIII, and transubstantiation formed the core of the Act of Six Articles. Consequently there was no threat to this devotion as long as the King lived, and the idea that the celebration required a communion of the people in order to be valid was robustly rejected. The 'private mass', which was already coming under attack by the reformers, was positively asserted, and when the King came to make his will, many hundreds of masses for the repose of his soul were decreed.[31] Somewhat illogically, having questioned the doctrine of purgatory, Henry never ceased to believe in the efficacy of prayers for the dead, and masses for that purpose continued to be a feature of the Henrician Church. Nor did it cease to be believed that it was the punishment of the unrepentant sinner to be unable to see the sacrament when it was raised, or when it was borne in procession. Hence the eagerness to 'gaze', which was a way of reassuring oneself that no sins had been forgotten in confession.

At an elite level, transubstantiation was a difficult doctrine, because it not only defied common sense, it also defied those concepts of the nature of matter which were beginning to emerge with the Renaissance. A physical body could only be in one place at a time, and the risen body of Christ was, according to the best biblical evidence, in heaven at the right hand of God. It was impossible that it should be present even in one Eucharist, let alone the thousands of celebrations which were taking place all over the world. Thomas Cranmer was openly contemptuous of such superstition.

> What made the people to run from their seats to the altar, and then from altar to altar ... peeping, tooting and gazing at that thing which the priest held up in his hands, if they thought not to honour that thing which they saw? ... What was the cause of all these, and that as well the priest and people so devoutly did knock and kneel at every sight of the sacrament, but that they worshipped that visible thing which they saw with their eyes and took it for very God?[32]

He was not alone, but at the parish level such scepticism was unusual, and the thing which the people missed most acutely when the Protestant order of service was introduced in 1549 was the mass. They were not concerned with subtleties of interpretation. As far as they were concerned the host was the body of God – a mystery, perhaps, but one which they could accept as part of the greater mystery of the incarnation. The world could only be understood in terms of divine intervention, and this led to a natural pantheism. The host was God, just as the image of the Blessed Virgin was the mother of God, and the fact that the one was bread and the other carven alabaster presented no difficulties to the believing spirit. This was the 'white magic' of the Church, which was powerful enough to overcome the 'black magic' of the devil or the magus.[33] There was no natural science to explain the thunderstorm or the outbreak of plague, so divine or diabolical explanations were universally accepted, and this acceptance infused the whole attitude of the laity towards the Church. For those out of reach of philosophy, there was no alternative. The fact that this also supported a structure of clerical power and privilege might be resented by some of the educated, who were in competition with the clergy for wealth and authority, but had little effect at the level of the ordinary parishioner. The Church, and its role in society, was a fact of life which it was pointless, and possibly dangerous, to resent.

The sacraments, upon which the Church rested, were a clerical monopoly, of which the laity were the grateful recipients. The same was true of the sacramentals, consecrated bread and water which were distributed on given occasions, the palms on Palm Sunday and the ashes on Ash Wednesday, all of which were symbols of penance and of the due order of things.[34] Nevertheless the Church was the community of the faithful and, although the clergy did not always admit it, it existed for the benefit of the unconsecrated people. The bishop and the parish priest might be concerned over the behaviour of their flocks, but at the end of the day this was for their own good. In a Church where every transgression and every good deed were relevant to the soul's immortal health, such concern was simply responsible pastoral care. They might be no more than enthusiastic spectators at the mass, and the anxious receivers of penance and absolution, but the laity in fact played a very positive role in the late medieval Church. As we have seen, they made offerings, both voluntary and involuntary, and without those gifts the churches would have been bare and silent – where they existed at all. They held offices, most notably as churchwardens, but in many lesser capacities also, and without them both the administration and the discipline of the Church would have suffered.[35] There was no 'lay ministry' in the modern sense, but the clergy very often relied upon the good offices of neighbours and kindred to resolve quarrels and to bring sinners to repentance.

Above all, they endowed intercessory prayer, and it was this more than anything else which brought the wealth and energy of the layman to support the functions of the clergy. This was done in a multitude of ways, but most obviously and effectively through the guild or fraternity. These were organizations for mutual help and support which were founded and run by laymen, and although their main objective was usually spiritual, they had many other functions. In some cases that function was to protect the interests of the craft or trade which the guild represented. So the seamen of Ratcliffe had their guild, as did the glovers of Coventry or the haberdashers of Norwich, the main purpose of which was to influence the city council to maintain the monopolistic control of the craftsmen over their own market.[36] Such guilds would normally maintain a chapel or an altar in their local church, and pay for masses on the feast days of their patron saints. They would also guarantee a suitable funeral for a deceased guild member, support for his family (should that be required) and prayers for the repose of his soul. There were, however, many other fraternities which had no such mundane objectives in mind. They are best described as friendly societies; spontaneous associations of men and women, usually dedicated to a particular saint, whose main purpose was intercessory prayer. They had their feast days and patronal festivals as the craft guilds did, but mainly they were chantries, which offered prayers, and usually masses, for the souls of deceased members.[37] They were a way of ensuring that the individuals in question were not forgotten, even if they had no immediate family to remember them, and that their spiritual needs were attended to. All such guilds were bodies corporate, and some were very wealthy. Boston's (Lincolnshire) St Mary guild may have been exceptional, but that had an annual income of over £900 in the mid-1520s, and even the Palmer's guild at Ludlow, not a particularly wealthy place, received about £250 a year.[38] Coventry's Holy Trinity guild employed thirteen full-time priests. Even the guild of St John the Baptist in Shepton Mallet, with an income of £15 13s. 6d., maintained two priests.

Although clergy, and even bishops, were often members of these fraternities, they were financed and run entirely by the laity, and their priests were employees. They formed an autonomous aspect of the worship of nearly every parish church, which was not controlled by the incumbent, and was outside the jurisdiction of the churchwardens. Craft guilds, of course, made their own charitable arrangements. All guilds charged an entry fee for membership, which might be as high as £1 for a married couple, but would not normally recruit enough new members in one year to make this a significant part of their income.[39] The main income was derived from rents, very often of urban property, which had been given or bequeathed to the guild, and even fraternities which had no craft or trade affiliation were active in charitable giving. For instance in 1548, at the time of its dissolution, the guild of Salve Regina at St Magnus church in London was paying 2s. a week to a brother who was in prison, 1s. 2d. a week for life to a blind brother, 1s. a week to a sick sister and 10d. a week each to various other brethren who had fallen on hard times. These were responsibilities which in due course would be taken over by the parish, but at the time the confiscation of the property of the Salve Regina must have left a number of disadvantaged individuals in destitution.[40] Such guilds were very numerous. There were seven in Leicester alone, and even the little town of Godmanchester near Huntingdon had six. There were 120 altogether in Lincolnshire, and they clustered thickly in East Anglia. Some counties, like Sussex and Wiltshire, had relatively few, but there must have been at least 2,000 in England as a whole, and collectively they demonstrate that the lay commitment to the Church and its offices was by no means passive or reluctant.[41]

Nevertheless, the heyday of the guild was the fifteenth century. York's biggest guild had over 70,000 members in the course of its life, which was some 150 years. In most places these fraternities held up well enough until about 1530, but thereafter many were struggling.[42] The craft guilds were not affected by these difficulties, so the question arises as to whether there was some change in religious fashion at about that time. There was no reason why the break with Rome should have affected such piety at all, any more than it was responsible for the undoubted decline in monastic vocations in the first thirty years of the sixteenth century. It is possible that the chantry certificates give a misleading impression, because the compilers were only interested in those foundations which had endowments, not in those which lived off casual revenue. For example only twenty-four were returned for Lincolnshire – about a fifth of those known to have existed – while the certificate for London and Middlesex lists twenty-eight out of over fifty.[43] However, where the records survive, there is persistent evidence of decline in the last twenty years of Henry's reign. The Corpus Christi guild in Boston (a poor relation of the great St Mary's guild), was recruiting about ten members a year in the 1520s, but that had declined to three by 1536, and there were none at all between 1540 and 1542. Significantly, the register peters out in 1543, at least two years before there was any question of suppression.[44] Similar evidence can be cited for the Corpus Christi guild in Coventry, and for the fraternity of the Holy Trinity in Sleaford, which had boomed in the 1520s but slumped badly after 1536. It seems that the well-to-do were turning away from such observances, just as they were turning from the monks to the friars, although whether this had anything to do with the rise of evangelical fashions such as family prayers and Bible reading, there is not enough evidence to be sure.

When the crunch came in 1547, and all these endowed fraternities were dissolved by statute, the major urban guilds simply rolled over. There is very little sign of the type of rearguard action which might have been expected from the evidence of earlier years. More typical was the reaction of the town council in King's Lynn, which petitioned for a grant of the property of the church's major guild on the grounds that its main purpose had been the upkeep of the sea-defences.[45] Fraternities often acted as the guardians of roads and bridges, and that obligation was usually transferred to the new owners of the relevant property. Whether this arrangement proved satisfactory is not usually known, but the volume of complaint generated by this dissolution was much less than might have been expected. There is more than a suspicion, however, that the chief sufferers were the members of those small rural brotherhoods which subsisted on 'offering pennies' and small bequests. These assets did not feature in the certificates, or come within the compass of the Act, but they were confiscated nonetheless, and it was at this level that the main impact upon popular piety was felt. Such foundations had no political leverage, and no voice to speak up for them, unless it were the parish priest, and he had problems enough of his own in adjusting to the new regime without adding to them in such a hopeless cause.[46] There is no evidence of decline amongst these village pieties, but their records (if they ever existed) have not survived and it is hard to be sure. Small bequests for lights and prayers seem to have gone on until both purgatory and prayers for the dead were condemned by the royal injunctions of 1547. Sometimes urban guilds survived, or were re-founded, in a strictly secular disguise, as charitable or educational foundations, or as dining clubs, but their rural equivalents seem simply to have disintegrated when their main *raison d'etre* was removed.

Guilds had begun to reappear with the restoration of Catholicism by Mary, but the spontaneous revival seems to have begun (as might be expected) at the rural level where records are most imperfect. The royal injunctions ordered that all these 'good laudable and ancient customs' were to be respected, and prayer for the dead seems to have begun again almost at once, but such evidence as there is suggests a reluctance to invest in such practices.[47] This was even more true at the urban level, where the recovery of former guild property, long since alienated, was extremely problematical. The Queen's own policy in this respect was very low key, because her intention was to restore rather than to establish anew, and this presented endless problems. This was most obvious in the establishment of religious houses, which could not be restored, partly because of the property deal which had been done with the papacy and partly because the bull *Praeclara* had canonically extinguished all the dissolved houses. Some half dozen new foundations were established, with an endowment from the Crown of about £3,000 a year between them.[48] Similarly a few privately endowed chantries were licensed, but no coherent policy seems to have been followed. The town of Basingstoke petitioned successfully for the restoration of the confraternity of the Holy Ghost, but that was only possible because the town already held most of the property. Mary herself restored Manchester College and the Hospital of the Savoy in London, because that property had remained in the hands of the Crown, but her most significant – and unique – establishment was that of the Jesus guild in St Paul's. This was possible because a neighbouring parish had bought the crypt chapel where the original guild had been based, and was prepared to make it available.[49] However, this was not really a restoration, because the Crown gave the new guild an elaborate constitution, and named all the first office holders, who were predominantly clergy. Exceptionally this foundation, which occurred in July 1556, resembled a Counter Reformation fraternity rather than a medieval one, and perhaps the initiative came from Cardinal Pole rather than from the Queen.

Fraternities were, if anything, bastions of the old faith, not because of their charitable or secular functions, but because they were based on intercessory prayer. They should therefore have sprung into new life as soon as the ban on prayers for the dead was lifted. They do not, however, appear to have done so, and this is something of an enigma. In some places Protestants were sufficiently numerous as to insist at first on obedience to the law. At St Bartholomew's in London on 11 August 1553 a priest who tried to 'jump the gun' by celebrating mass was set upon by the irate crowd and almost lynched.[50] However that cannot have been the case in more remote areas, such as Yorkshire, where all the evidence suggests that the old ways were at once resumed, even before news of Mary's permissive proclamation of 18 August could have reached them. In most places the popular reaction was simply not recorded. Even in London the conservative but extremely cautious Henry Machyn was probably typical. Although he recorded a number of funerals in August 1553, including King Edward's, and described the attendance in some detail, nothing was said about prayers for the soul of the deceased, and the first mention of a mass does not come until 21 August.[51] Whereas in 1547 we can do a reasonable stocktaking of the major fraternities from the chantry certificates, nothing of the kind survives from 1559. Such guilds as were then in existence were quietly discontinued and their assets absorbed into the parish stock. Because there was no question of confiscation, no specific accounts were called for, and it was in the interests of the churchwardens to gloss over such transactions in the presentation of their own reckonings. So, although purgatory was restored and prayers for the dead officially reinstated, we have very little idea of the extent to which fraternities were resurrected in the average parish, rural or urban. Bequests continued to be made, and masses of special intention to be sung, but the institutional framework remains elusive and was probably scrappy in practice.

So what was restored in 1553–4? First and foremost it was the mass, and so eager were conservative clergy to resume this function that they sometimes started singing the service before they were entitled to do so. Most of them had conformed to a heretical regime, and were therefore *ipso facto* excommunicate. They could not in theory celebrate until they had been absolved, and Richard Thornden, the suffragan Bishop of Dover, was probably not alone in committing this offence. He was subsequently reconciled (and reprimanded) by Reginald Pole,[52] and several others sought Pole's jurisdiction long before it was lawful for them to do so. However, Thornden was high profile, and it seems that most priests simply assumed an authority to officiate well ahead of their official reconciliation, which should not have taken place until after January 1555. The return of the mass, moreover, brought a lot of baggage with it, in the shape of the full liturgical practice of the old faith, together with all the equipment which that involved. Parish churches had been stripped bare by the iconoclasm of the Protestant regime, and each needed to be elaborately re-equipped. In some places this was straightforward, because the liturgical books, vestments and ornaments had been secreted or purchased by sympathetic parishioners, who returned them as soon as the ecclesiastical climate changed. The churchwardens of Ashburton in Devon, for example, were able to recover a cope and their vestments in this way, although it required a certain amount of travel to assemble them.[53] In most parishes, however, it was a question of starting again from scratch, and that could be a slow and expensive business, even with the good will which usually seems to have been deployed. As Professor Duffy has pointed out, destroying a rood could be the work of a few moments and cost nothing, whereas replacing it required thought, and a great deal of costly labour.[54]

Out of some 9,000 parishes, only 134 sets of churchwardens' accounts survive from the early part of Mary's reign, so any conclusions about the process of re-equipment can only be tentative. In those which are recorded, however, the process seems to have been fairly uniform. The first thing that was done was to rebuild the high altar, demolished by orders of Edward's council, and to sell off the communion table which had replaced it. This involved not only the purchase of building stone, but also the acquiring of a suitable slab to be consecrated as the altar itself, the original having (usually) been conscientiously smashed. In every case this had been done by the end of 1554, by which time also vestments had been replaced and the basic liturgical books and implements obtained.[55] This stock was progressively added to during the rest of the reign, often culminating in the commissioning of a new rood, some of which were not in place until the early part of 1558. This was the case at Stanford in the Vale in Berkshire, a conservative community which had earlier sent its wardens to Oxford in search of books, and had paid a carpenter 3s. 4d. to make a lockable pyx for the high altar.[56] There is no reason to doubt Stanford's will to conform, but these things took time. Longer, in some cases, than Mary had, because the visitations of 1557 show a number of churches still deficient in equipment, and this was not necessarily the result of reluctance. How spontaneous all this restoration was is a matter of some doubt, and no doubt it varied greatly from place to place. Work which had been carried out before the royal visitation of March 1554 can reasonably be so described, but at that time, and particularly in Edmund Bonner's injunctions which followed, the heavy hand of coercion began to be applied. Bonner not only set out in detail the equipment which every parish was supposed to have, but even urged his clergy to put pressure on the dying to 'remember the great spoil and robbery that hath of late been made' and to make suitable bequests to the church to help it to remedy these deficiencies.[57]

The response to these heavy promptings was usually satisfactory, but took time. This may have been the result of reluctance, but is more probably explained by natural caution. Most people seem to have adopted the Henrician and Edwardian practice of making gifts and bequests to the poor directly, rather than helping to fund parish devotions, and this continued for some time into the Marian restoration. Again there were regional variations. In Northamptonshire such devotional gifts began almost at once, whereas in Sussex they did not recover their vitality until 1557. There is no obvious explanation for this, because there were no more Protestants in Chichester diocese than there were in Peterborough, nor was John Chambers a more zealous bishop than George Day.[58] In Kent, which was religiously very diverse, bequests begin to pick up after 1555, where the removal of Thomas Cranmer from Canterbury may have had the effect of encouraging a return to the old ways. Other bishops followed Bonner's example, although less forcefully. Bishop Brooks's injunctions for Gloucester, for example, placed as much emphasis upon the needs of the poor as of the parish church.[59] Although in many places there was a positive response in time to the devotional priority, gifts never even approached the level of the 1520s where comparable records enable a comparison to be made. In this respect the evangelical pattern of charity seems to have won a more general acceptance than the authorities were altogether happy with. Whereas the restoration of 'massing gear' seems to have been general, rapid and spontaneous, other traditional practices did not recover with the same speed – or at all. The devotions of the saints, and the side altars and images which expressed them, came back only patchily, inspired probably by the attitude of the individual incumbent or of some forceful personality within the parish. Religious guilds and fraternities hardly revived at all, having been for the most part converted into secular friendly societies, and gifts for lights or for other less essential items of equipment came back late and fitfully. This should not be taken to imply a sympathy for Protestantism, the doctrines of which were generally rejected, just as the mass was preferred to the communion, but it does imply a shift in the concept of poor relief. In 1498 John Sothill of Dewsbury willed that 'ye deal for my saull the day of my burial one penny to 50 pore men and women there present', whereas in 1568 Sir Thomas Roe, Mayor of London, gave to the Merchant Taylors 'lands or tenements, out of them to bee geven to ten pore men Clothworkers, Carpentars, Tilars, Plasterers and Armourers, £40 yearly'.[60] In other words the relief of poverty had become a largely secular matter. The first compulsory rate had been decreed by the city authorities of London in 1547, an example followed by Norwich, Bristol and other cities.[61] In due course a poor rate was to be levied by statute, and although the parish continued to be the administrative unit, that was more for convenience than because the distribution was considered to have a spiritual dimension. By then, of course, Protestantism was the established faith, but there is a continuity in this respect going back into Henry VIII's reign which the Marian restoration did not seriously disrupt.

Consequently, although very few ordinary folk would have admitted to believing in justification by faith alone, the culture of giving to the Church had undergone a subtle shift as a result of the Protestant ascendancy. In some ways this was welcome to the hierarchy, because no bishop or serious theologian wished to encourage the notion that a sinner could buy his way into heaven, but the price was paid by the parish churches. This is why there was a discernable reluctance to restore those churches to the full luxuriance of the 1520s. Concern with poverty was mounting in the mid-sixteenth century, for reasons which had nothing to do with the shifts in religious practice. This was demonstrated by the writings of the so-called 'Commonwealth men', many of whom had evangelical antecedents, but whose concerns were entirely secular and social.[62] The targets of their criticism were the gentry and merchants rather than the Church. In this climate of opinion, it is not difficult to see why testators should have remembered their poor neighbours before they thought of beautifying their parish church. Education was another priority which had been encouraged during what the Marian clergy chose to describe as 'the evil years', and that was a tendency which Reginald Pole had no intention of discouraging. When Sir Thomas White, the Lord Mayor of London, and Sir Thomas Pope wished to do their bit for the Church (and for their own souls) they were encouraged and licensed to found the Colleges of St John and of the Holy Trinity in Oxford.[63] A large number of small and unendowed schools had disappeared with the dissolution of the chantries in 1547, but many had been picked up and refounded as secular institutions by town councils or by individual benefactors, and this was also a tendency which continued during Mary's reign.[64] The official purpose of such foundations may have been the provision of educated clergy, and there was certainly an upsurge in those seeking ordination once the old order was restored, but the real objective of the founders was often more mundane – to ensure respectable careers for their own sons. None of this is to deny the general enthusiasm for the restored liturgy and the traditional ceremonies of the Church, or to suggest that there was an antagonism between popular and elite religion, but there had been a cultural shift. Reginald Pole applauded the good work done amongst the Italian poor by the new orders of friars, but there was no equivalent religious initiative in England.[65] The needs of the poor had been significantly detached from the functions of the Church.

4 RELIGION AND DAILY LIFE

Every day brought the ordinary man into contact with God. He lived his life in a liturgical context, which marked the seasons of the year and provided the kind of order and control which he needed, and which could not be provided in any other way.[1] The Church could not control the weather, but it could provide explanations as to why the sunshine, rain and frost behaved in the way that they did. They were fulfilling God's purpose, and if they produced a bumper harvest one year, and dearth the next – that was part of His purpose as well; to reward the virtues or punish the sins of the community. It was all very intimate, and the natural and supernatural interpenetrated each other all the time and in all sorts of ways. The offices of the church, and the building itself, were parts of that context. All sorts of gatherings – sometimes for purposes far from sacred – took place in the church, and rituals such as the offertory reinforced the hierarchy of the community. The wife of Bath resented anyone who ventured to go before her to the offering![2] Young men went there to spy out likely girls (sometimes with unfortunate consequences), and young women used the rituals of St Agnes eve to discover the identities of their future partners. Major pagan festivals, such as the winter solstice and the spring rebirth, had long since been incorporated into the Church's calendar as Christmas and Easter, and several lesser celebrations had been similarly consecrated. The plough ceremonies, for example, which had originally been fertility rites, and which occurred just after the winter solstice, had by the later middle ages been absorbed into the calendar. Many churches kept a 'plough light' burning in front of the rood, and Cawston church in Norfolk even had a 'plough gallery'.[3]

In the same way, Christian commemorations could be colonized by pagan or ribald features. St Nicholas day on 6 December and Holy Innocents' day on the 28th, both being festivals of childhood, were marked by the appearance of the Boy Bishop, but these boys were often vehicles for ribaldry and 'misrule', which offended the strict (and the elite). If such maskings and disguisings appeared to mock a solemn season such as Lent, they might be treated as subversive, as happened in Norwich in January 1443.[4] The popular culture of such seasons as Christmas often steered a delicate course between the Christian message of the Incarnation and the essentially pagan celebration of birth itself, as can be seen in the immensely rich traditions of the nativity carol. Another festival with built-in ambiguity was Candlemas, celebrated on 2 February. Ecclesiastically this commemorated the purification of the Virgin and the presentation of Christ in the temple, but it was also a festival of light. The Candlemas procession was compulsory for all parishioners, who bore with them lighted candles which, together with small offerings, were placed before the image of the Virgin at the parish mass.[5] Coming at a season when the lengthening of the days was just about perceptible, the symbolism of these lights was obvious. However, they might also be deemed to have therapeutic properties. 'Wherever it shall be lit or set up, the devil may flee away in fear and trembling with all his ministers, out of those dwellings, and never presume again to disquiet your servants'.[6] In other words the Candlemas candles were charms which could be lit to ward off evil in times of storm or pestilence. The mere preservation of such candles could be held to atone for a lifetime of sin, so it is not surprising that the parishioners of Friesthorpe in Lincolnshire were upset when the vicar removed all the candles which had been offered as soon as the mass was over.[7] The clergy were inclined to be suspicious of such popular superstitions, because it was equally the case that such sacramentals could be diverted to evil purposes. It was, for example, widely believed that if a witch got hold of a holy candle, she could drop wax from it into the footprints of anyone she wished to harm – causing their feet to fall off! So the vicar of Friesthorpe may simply have been taking sensible precautions.

In order to divert their thoughts from such ungodliness, the clergy were in the habit of encouraging their flocks to meditate on the true meaning of such ceremonies. In the case of Candlemas this meant the presentation of Christ in the temple, an event foreshadowing his future ministry. This might work for the well-instructed, particularly if they were mystically inclined, but was unlikely to be much help to the average artisan or labourer. Easter was the season for intense contemplative effort, when everyone was supposed to confess their sins and to receive communion; when the Easter sepulchre was erected and even the dullest witted could hardly escape the emotional intensity of the passion. This was the season which drove Margery Kempe and her like into a contemplative frenzy, but also stirred everyone to earnest thought about the meaning of life and death.[8] For a few days every workman laid down his tools, and would have been censured by the Church had he not done so. Easter day itself was the great feast day of the Christian year, but lesser feasts were numerous, the average church observing between forty and fifty in the course of a year. Selection might depend upon local custom or upon the whim of the incumbent, because just about every day was sacred to some saint or to some aspect of the Godhead. These feasts not only disrupted necessary work (and opportunities for profit), but were also often used as an excuse for inebriation, so there was little objection from community leaders when Henry VIII pruned the calendar heavily in 1536.[9] Fasting was almost equally ubiquitous. There were nearly seventy days in the year when adults were supposed to refrain from the eating of meat. Many of these were concentrated in the penitential seasons of Lent and Advent, but the rest were more or less evenly distributed. Ember days, for example, occupied four sets of three days each, one in each quarter of the year. Fasts might also be enjoined upon the eve of important saints' days, or as penances imposed in the confessional.[10] They seem to have been most practised, and were certainly best recorded, among the well-to-do, because abstinence from meat was scarcely penitential for the poor, who seldom saw such a luxury anyway.

Time itself also had a sacred property. It has been suggested that the first half of the year was seen as 'holy time', because the great events in the life of Christ were celebrated between January and July; Christmas (mostly), Lent, Easter and Whitsun. Ploughing and sowing, the main agricultural work, had to be fitted in between Christmas and Lent to avoid a conflict of priorities.[11] However, the corollary, that the second half of the year was seen as 'secular time', is less obvious. Michaelmas was celebrated on 29 September, All Saints on 1 November and Advent in December. Also this space had been colonized by newer observations, such as the Visitation of the Virgin (2 July), the Transfiguration (6 August) and the Holy Name of Jesus (7 August). Only the second half of August and most of September was kept clear of major events – presumably to enable the harvest to be gathered uninterrupted.[12] The layman, therefore, even if he was not particularly conscientious in his observances, would hardly have needed a calendar in the modern sense to keep track of the passing of time. Clocks were rare and watches unknown, so the sun provided the only guide to the passage of the hours, and similarly the Church provided the most complete indication of the passage of weeks and months. As Professor Duffy has observed, late medieval people were fascinated by time and the significance of its divisions; a fascination which was sometimes practical and sometimes less religious than occult.[13] There was intense concern with 'propitious days', not only for major activities like seed time and harvest, but also for minor matters such as when to gather acorns, let blood or take a laxative. Such days might be determined by approximation to a religious festival, but were just as likely to be identified by the local 'wise man' or 'wise woman', using criteria over which the Church had no control whatsoever. Not surprisingly the clergy denounced such rival activities as superstition, but equally they sought to guide them by implanting pious considerations which might have nothing to do with the decision which was required.

The Church's attitude towards astrology was equally ambivalent. That 'science' appealed mainly to the educated, who were capable of reading the almanacs and prognostications which the necromancers produced, but it had knock-on effects among the illiterate. In principle astrology was a deterministic system which was completely inimical to the idea of free will in either man or God, and provided a different division of time which had nothing to do with the Christian calendar. However, such sharp distinctions became blurred and some astrological themes, such as the ages of man and the labours of the month, became absorbed into those primers and Books of Hours which were the basic reading material of the literate.[14] The calendar for each month was illustrated, not only with the emblems of the principal saints, but also with the appropriate secular activities, such as ploughing in February. When printed primers began to appear at the end of the fifteenth century, they included what were effectively small almanacs, with a zodiacal man as a guide to blood-letting, and material on the humours which were supposed to decide issues of human health. Although formally religious guides, they became effectively all-purpose reference works, including not only such things as English rhymes listing the saints' days in each month, but also 'The Days of the week Moralized', which was more traditional folk wisdom than piety.[15] The culmination of this type of writing came in the *Kalendar of Shepheredes*, first printed in an English version by Richard Pynson in 1506 and going through numerous further editions into the reign of Elizabeth. The *Kalendar* was about two-thirds astrological almanac and one-third religious handbook, containing basic guidance to pious practice, and moralizations on the days and months in an extraordinary mixture of the sacred and the profane. Of the month of October it recorded:

> Among the other October I hyght
> Frende unto vynteners naturally.
> And in my tyme Bacchus is redy dyght,
> All maner wyne to presse and clarify,
> Of which is sacred as we se dayly
> The blyssed body of Cryst in flesshe and blode,
> Whiche is our hope/ refeccyon/ and fode[16]

Such writings should perhaps be seen as a part of that levelling process in the perception of time, which eventually reduced the significance of the great religious festivals and led to a more generalized moral and theological sensibility. However, for the early sixteenth century, they provide a readily understood indication of the way in which the religious calendar had been invaded by alien elements. Philip II, that most Catholic of monarchs, had great faith in his court astrologers and never saw anything amiss in accepting their predictions.[17] The simple visual elements of the zodiac could be understood even by the illiterate and they did not see anything inconsistent in setting such signs in a Christian context either. It is perhaps not surprising that the theologically learned were worried about the prevalence of these superstitions.

In spite of the destructive effects of alcohol abuse, which were as evident then as they are now, the Church's attitude to strong drink was always ambivalent. Church ales were a standard method of raising funds and, in days when water was seldom safe to drink, the process of brewing provided a degree of safety. Small ale (brewed without hops) was given to children and every liturgical procession was accompanied by a 'drinking', often at the home – and the expense – of a well-to-do member of the flock.[18] Bargains were concluded over similar draughts, and no reconciliation was complete without a 'pledge'. The Church no more would, or could, condemn the drinking of alcohol than it could censure the eating of cheese. Nevertheless there were problems, and the drunkard was a common pest. At best he was consuming the wages which should have supported his family, and at worst he became quarrelsome and violent in his cups. Injuries inflicted in the resulting brawls could easily be fatal. The drunken layman was bad enough, but if he had the grace to confess his fault, then he could be penanced, and if not there was always the archdeacon's court. A drunken priest was a great deal more difficult, and it was a vice to which slovenly and ill-educated curates were particularly prone. In vain did innumerable canons prohibit clergy from resorting to taverns;[19] the celibate priest was often a lonely figure, and the tavern offered the only companionship which he could find. Article 8 of Henry VIII's first royal injunctions ran

> the said deans, parsons, vicars, curates and other priests, shall in no wise, at any unlawful time, nor for any other cause than for their honest necessity, haunt or resort to any taverns or ale houses, and after their dinner and supper they shall not give themselves to drinking or riot, spending their time idly, by day or by night, at tables or card playing, or any other unlawful game[20]

Instead they were to go and read the scriptures or some improving book, bearing always in mind the need to set a virtuous and Christian example to their congregations. This counsel of perfection was repeated over and again at national and at local level, but it seems to have been only when clergy had wives to keep them in order that the problem was really addressed.

The taking of a wife might also ease another common pre-reformation problem – fornication. The Church's attitude towards sexuality in all its forms had been consistently negative from its early days, and this created dilemmas for clergy and laity alike. The only acceptable context for sexual activity was within heterosexual marriage, and since the twelfth century that had been denied to the clergy – or at least to those in major orders. Lay men and women might also find it difficult to achieve, because all sorts of conditions had to be satisfied before a contract of marriage could be entered into.[21] The inclinations of the parties themselves were not necessarily the most important. The families on both sides had to be satisfied with the allocation of property to the young people, and the prospective husband had to be in a position to support his wife and any children which she might bear. It is not surprising that responsible couples often delayed tying the knot for several years. Even those without property had economic realities to consider, of which the cost of the ceremony itself might well have been one.[22] Human nature, however, had its own imperatives, and any coming together of young people was liable to result in copulation, as a ribald Christmas carol testifies,

> As I went on Yol day in our procession
> Knew I joly Jankin by his mery ton ...
> Benedicamus Domino, Crist fro schame me shilde.
> Deo Gracias, therto – alas I go with childe![23]

If there was a betrothal, either in the future or in the present tense, such carnal knowledge might be taken as evidence of the consummation of a marriage, but very often marriage was not in the mind of either party. Women tended to be blamed for these casual encounters, partly because the bearing of an illegitimate child was irrefutable proof of misconduct and partly because of the deeply rooted misogyny of the Church. The outcome was often hard and a public penance would be the least of the girl's woes. She might well be disowned by her family and, if no man came forward to admit responsibility, she would be left to bring up the child alone, often with no employment or resources. The parish would then reluctantly intervene to protect the mother and child from destitution, but the shame involved might well condemn them both to a life on the margins of society.[24] By far the largest number of ecclesiastical cases involving women were of this nature. Usually the parish priest would endeavour to discover the identity of the man responsible, in which case he would be summoned as well. But such quests were often unsuccessful because there were no paternity tests in the sixteenth century and, if your conscience was sufficiently pliable, it was an easy offence to deny.

If, however, the guilty party was, or was suspected to be, a priest, then a different situation arose. A complaint had to be made to the archdeacon, and that required enough evidence for a *prima facie* case. The confession of the woman was not necessarily sufficient, because that might have been maliciously motivated. Consequently, although there was a great deal of colourful gossip, and endless grumbling, actual cases of clerical incontinence are relatively rare.[25] There was a popular mythology of such conduct, which was thought to come in two guises, which might be termed 'regular' and 'opportunist'. The regular offender kept a woman, ostensibly as his housekeeper, and may even have had children by her, in a kind of unrecognized marriage. Such a situation was often tolerated by the community, particularly if the priest was otherwise good at his job, and would only come to light through some change of circumstances. The opportunist was different. This was the priest who seduced men's wives or ravished their daughters under the cover of the confessional. He was the butt of a thousand jokes and the anti-hero of innumerable salacious stories, but substantiated cases are few. He was alleged to cover his crimes by using his spiritual authority to threaten excommunication on anyone who informed upon him,[26] but hardly ever was such a charge proven. The basis for all these stories was, of course, the priest's vow of celibacy, so alien to normal experience that it was hard to believe that any man could keep it. Worse still, it might encourage a man to unnatural vice, and sodomy was a capital offence under the secular laws.[27] Had any clerk been convicted under that law, he would have pleaded the benefit of his clergy, but would still have faced a lengthy term in the bishop's prison. The fact that there are so few authenticated cases of this happening may owe less to the virtues of the clergy than to the efficiency with which they could close ranks against such charges. Similar charges of 'abominable' and unmentionable vices were, of course, used against the regular orders between 1536 and 1540, and the commissioners unearthed many circumstantial stories, but very few of those were substantiated either.[28]

Visitations did produce a few scandals. In 1530 it was discovered that the abbot of St James Northampton was suspiciously familiar with the laundress of the abbey, but nothing was proved against them. As a precaution she was dismissed and he was forbidden to allow her access to the premises. At Missenden in Buckinghamshire in the same year two cases of homosexuality were uncovered, which resulted in the abbot being suspended and one of the canons imprisoned, but neither of these cases went beyond the bishop's ordinary jurisdiction.[29] Nuns were more vulnerable, partly because of contemporary perceptions of female 'weakness' and partly because many of them had been placed by their families without any real sense of vocation. At Crabhouse in Norfolk in 1524 one of the nuns had been seduced by a local gentleman, and at Littlemore in Lincolnshire the prioress was allegedly trying to conceal the fact that she had borne a child by the chaplain of the house. He had been removed from the neighbourhood, but still came visiting, and when he came they lived as man and wife. The prioress denied what she claimed was a malicious fiction, dreamed up by her undisciplined charges, at least one of whom was indeed guilty of fornication. However, Littlemore was obviously in a disordered state, and was one of the houses dissolved by Wolsey in the interests of his educational foundations.[30] Similar stories were told elsewhere, but most seem to have originated in the fertile imaginations of disgruntled young women who launched against their superiors the most obvious and most damaging charge they could think of. Objectively, the regular houses were not hotbeds of vice, natural or unnatural, but the point is that such charges were widely believed and were a part of the religious culture of the time. When the preamble to the Act for the suppression of the lesser houses spoke of 'manifest sin, vicious, carnal and abominable living', it was addressing a receptive audience.[31]

Monks and nuns did not, in any case, feature largely in the mainstream of religious consciousness, except among their own kindred. For most practical purposes they were irrelevant. Robert Aske might take them seriously, but their way of life was no longer the great Christian ideal. Piety was increasingly focused on the parish church, and it was easy to see monks as men who had opted out of real life. They were only too likely to occupy their abundant leisure by getting into mischief. Friars were different. They engaged with real problems both practical and intellectual, but they were nevertheless an intrusive element in the parish. They did not appear very often in most places, and they might be welcome; but equally they might be at odds with the incumbent, especially if he were resident.[32] This was particularly the case if, as often happened, some parishioners (particularly women) preferred to take their confessions to a relative stranger. This made the friars the butt of numerous dubious jokes, and may well have undermined the respect in which they were otherwise held. Consequently when all the religious houses were dissolved, what is rightly seen in some respects as a great disruption had little impact on the daily lives of most people. The property market was transformed, and great opportunities given to gentry and yeoman families to enhance their estates, but the only effect on ordinary families came when an unwanted aunt or cousin was returned to the bosom of her kindred, or when the friar who had visited occasionally was recycled as the parish curate. Similarly it did not matter very much that the King had replaced the Pope as the head of the Church. The educated might object to such a breach of the canon law, but they were also keenly aware that Henry himself was a divinely constituted authority, to whom obedience was owed as a religious duty.[33] To most people a few changes to the prayers of intercession were a small price to pay for getting rid of those interfering Italians who always seemed to be taking money out of the country. The most significant changes to the patterns of normal worship came when the King removed 'superfluous' saints from the calendar in 1536. If your favourite devotion was withdrawn or downgraded, you might well feel distressed, but most working men welcomed a decree which reduced disruption to their potential earnings. The major festivals of the year were not touched, and he had to make a living. If Henry's intention to dissolve the intercessory foundations had been implemented, it might have been a different story, but as it was, when the King died, no serious violence had been done to the liturgical year, or to the regular small pieties which expressed the religious feelings of the parish. The elite might be painfully aware of Henry's disruptive policies, but the parish clergy came to terms with them as best they could and tried to carry on as though nothing had happened.[34]

The change which many of them found most difficult to stomach was the imposition of the English Bible, which they saw as undermining their authority. As we have seen this innovation reached well beyond the literate, and that was a major cause of anxiety to clergy who were being urged to encourage its use. One result of this in many places was a shift of pious habit, as those of an inquisitive turn of mind set out to discover what the sacred text actually said. Furious debates developed over the meaning of particular passages. These were supposed to be referred to 'those of more learning' (meaning the parish priest) but very often this did not happen, and discussion spilled out of the church into the ale house or onto the street. This outcome, which had not apparently been anticipated, caused Henry in 1543 to attempt to restrict access to the educated, but this was hardly realistic when the Great Bible continued to be on public display in every parish church.[35] A new dimension had been added to ordinary piety which was not under direct clerical control. Even a guild run by the laity had its place within the parish church, but there was no way in which the parish priest could dictate the outcome of these debates, even if he took part in them. Many a prosperous yeoman or craftsman invested in his own copy of the scriptures, which he read at home in the company of his family, and this led to a major change in the nature of religious discourse. It was also highly controversial as conservative clergy sought to carry out damage-limitation exercises, and evangelicals found justification for their position.[36] The bases of day-by-day piety shifted all the time, often, as in this case, under pressure from above, and that seems to have happened markedly after about 1535. Pilgrimages were forbidden and the great shrines which had attracted them were torn down. When the Abbey of Bittlesden in Buckinghamshire was dissolved the abbot and monks did not merely surrender, they issued a manifesto.

> We ... do profoundly consider that the manner and trade of living, which we and other of our pretensed religion have practiced and used many days, doth most principally consist in certain dumb ceremonies and in certain constitutions of the Bishop of Rome[37]

No doubt that was a very correct thing to say in the circumstances, but they did not have to say it. Nor were they alone. The prior of the Carmelite friars of Stamford, when making his surrender on 8 October 1538, observed that 'the perfection of Christian living doth not consist in dumb ceremonies', and others expressed similar sentiments.[38] How far this shift of emphasis off rituals and onto prayer and Bible-reading really affected the daily religious practices of the average parish is hard to determine. The King's theology, which was the guiding principle, did not appear to be either stable or consistent. He clung to intercessory prayer, while rejecting purgatory; and maintained some images while rejecting others. He legislated the full traditional doctrine of the mass, while apparently speaking of converting the Eucharist into a communion service. This uncertainty was reflected during Henry's last days in endless bickerings between traditionalists and those who favoured the 'new learning'. There was also a sharp falling off of gifts and bequests to the Church as its institutional confidence ebbed. The King may have known what he wanted, but his vision did not correspond with either that of the Catholics or that of the evangelicals.

So what happened in 1547 was less a revolution than a further step in an ongoing process. The royal injunctions of the summer of that year urged the clergy to preach

> and in the same, exhort their hearers to the works of faith, mercy and charity especially prescribed and commanded in Scripture, and that works devised by man's fantasies besides Scripture, as wanderings to pilgrimages, offering of money, candles or tapers, or relics or images, or kissing or licking of the same, praying upon beads, or such like superstitions, having not only no promise of reward in Scripture for doing of them, but contrariwise great threats and maledictions of God, for that they be things tending to idolatry and superstition, which of all other offences God Almighty doth most detest and abhor[39]

This went notably further than Henry's last injunctions in discouraging traditional habits, but did not actually forbid them, and went on to encourage priests to be diligent in administering the sacraments and in hearing Lenten confessions. The homily on Justification, which was issued at the same time, indicated changes to come, but for the time being the government was trying to pace its reforms and to restrain enthusiastic evangelicals from rushing ahead. The fact that such restraint was necessary should warn us that not everyone was opposed to these changes, and that cells of Protestants were beginning to emerge, particularly in London and the south-east, whose piety was completely at odds with that of their conservative neighbours.[40] The most significant formal change of 1547 was that brought about by the Chantries Act, which dissolved all religious guilds and other intercessory foundations on the grounds that such practices were superstitious. This was no more than the implementation of a plan proposed by Henry in 1545, but it provided confirmation of the direction in which the Lord Protector was heading. A great deal of grumbling was provoked, but it was not actively resisted even in such conservative strongholds as Morebath.[41] Revolution finally came with the mandatory introduction of the English Prayer Book at Whitsun in 1549. This took the heart out of popular piety by removing the mass in favour of a communion service, and by replacing the familiar Latin liturgy with a vernacular one. This was resisted but, given the convincing evidence of the popularity of the traditional rites, neither generally nor effectively.[42] In 1552 this Prayer Book was modified to make it more Protestant, and there was no resistance at all, possibly because it was widely ignored. Nevertheless by the beginning of 1553 a complete change had come over the face of daily piety. Gone were the regular low masses which had enabled the pious to 'see their saviour'; gone were the images of the saints and the regular offerings made to them; gone were the obits, the votive candles and the small pieties in favour of the deceased. Gone, too, were the rich vestments which the clergy had been wont to wear for their celebrations, and the elaborate wall paintings which had constantly reminded the pious of their faith. In place of colourful and essentially visual and tactile images, there had emerged a religion of the word, cerebral and visually bleak, focused on the Sabbath and on the major festivals of Christmas and Easter.[43] Bible-reading and family prayers were encouraged to fill the liturgical gap, and charity to the poor was urged in place of votive offerings.

The extraordinary thing about these changes is not that they were decreed, but that they were so widely implemented. All the evidence suggests that outside of London they were deeply unpopular. The clergy resented the new demands which were being made on them, demands which they were usually ill equipped to meet. The laity resented the removal of so many familiar comforts and the fact that many clergy were now married. Yet by 1553 the vast majority of churches presented the face of authorized Protestantism.[44] The fact that these changes had been effected in the King's name, and with his increasingly active involvement, provides the only possible explanation. Edward, like his father, was Supreme Head of the Church, and the shape of the country's religion was ultimately his responsibility. Twenty years of royal direction had accustomed people to doing what they were told, and since piety was a corporate expression as well as an individual one, it was open to public scrutiny. The authorities had difficulty in persuading people to go to church to participate in the new services, but whether that means that they kept up the traditional rites in private it is difficult to say.[45] There is some evidence that conservative clergy continued to do this, at least as far as the mass was concerned. Other aspects of the old faith were demonstrative and would have been harder to conceal.

It is not, therefore, difficult to see why Mary's determined stand in defence of the mass should have made her so popular, nor why, once she had overcome the challenge of Jane Grey, there should have been a general determination to restore the old ways. However, it is not easy to define what this meant in terms of everyday piety. The Queen signalled her intentions clearly enough, but it was some months before the law was changed and longer still before the first royal and episcopal injunctions spelled out what was now required.[46] The mass was spontaneously restored in many places, and vestments and other 'gear' dug out of their hiding places, but the most obvious effect was the escalation of controversy. Small groups of Protestants and individual clergy retained their reformed regiment, sometimes publicly, until the law was changed on 20 December. It was only then that serious attempts could be made to restore Catholic discipline. About 150 beneficed clergy in the diocese of London lost their livings, and 243 in Norwich – about a quarter of all incumbents – and in Norwich about 100 unbeneficed clergy were also disciplined, the great majority for having married.[47] This responded to popular sentiment but created problems for the ecclesiastical authorities. There were simply not enough celibate priests to fill all the resultant vacancies, so most of those who had repudiated their wives were moved to new benefices, where they sometimes resumed cohabitation. One of the commonest conservative arguments against the reformers was that they encouraged sexual immortality, of which these were held to be classic examples. As Robert Parkyn in East Yorkshire wrote, expressing the general view:

> Hoo, it was ioye to here and see how these carnall preastes, which had ledde ther lyffes in fornication with ther whores and harlots, dyd lowre and looke downe when they were commandyde to leave and forsake ther concubines[48]

Bishops were instructed to 'punish and remove' anyone preaching or teaching 'naughty opinions', including all forms of heresy, but with (as yet) no indication as to what form that punishment might take. More positively, all holy days and fasting days used at the end of Henry VIII's reign were to be 'used and kept', and all 'honest ceremonies' restored.[49]

It seems clear that these instructions were generally implemented, once incumbents had worked out what were 'honest'. They were relatively cheap and easy. However, restoring the infrastructure was a different matter, which required people to begin investing in their piety again in a way which had not been seen for more than a decade. In some places wealthy donors came forward as they had been wont to do, but generally that was not the case. Churchwardens usually managed to rebuild their altars quite promptly, but struggled to replace the images which had been destroyed, and often resorted to a painted rood in place of the carved original.[50] Bishops laboured earnestly to get this work completed, but there are clear signs that the old confidence had not returned. Bequests for obits and other intercessions remained at a low level, not necessarily because people had no faith in such practices, but because they were keenly aware how vulnerable such donations could be. There was also a political dimension to such difficulties. Until the summer of 1555 all had seemed to be well, although the expected heir to the throne would be three-quarters Spanish by blood. But then came the failure of the Queen's pregnancy, and the whole landscape changed. Nobody knew what had happened, but they knew that there was no heir to the throne and that Mary's health was seriously suspect. That did not make much difference to the way they felt about God or the Church, but it did undermine the credibility of the regime.[51] What would happen if the Queen died? Would Philip seize the throne (a seriously unpopular prospect), or would Elizabeth succeed? How good a Catholic was the princess, and what would she do to religion?

In these circumstances, the momentum of the official Church held up remarkably well. Guidance and instruction continued to be issued with every appearance of confidence – God's work had to be done – but the man in the pew had his doubts. These did not affect his devotion to traditional ways, to the mass and the various processions of the liturgical year. Nor did they much affect his willingness to obey the Pope and his Legate – or the Queen. Cardinal Pole was insistent that the restoration of parish observances must take priority over such matters as the re-erection of monasteries.[52] However, they did affect his willingness to spend money in promoting has own or his kindred's spiritual well-being. A conditional bequest might be made to a dissolved friary, 'if it go up again', or even (as the Queen's health deteriorated further) to an intercession, 'if it shall be lawful'. Otherwise the designated sums were to be paid to the poor.[53] In spite of the assurance with which the Church continued to go about its business, and the manner in which it continued to persecute dissent, twenty years of turmoil and change had undermined the certainties of the old faith. The necessity of good works for salvation had been asserted, denied and then reasserted. Vows of chastity and obedience had been undermined, denied and then reaffirmed. Reading the Bible had been urged, partially withdrawn, urged again and then passed into limbo. The mass had been defined and then vilified before returning in all its ancient glory. What the piety of daily observance needed above all was stability, that sense of timeless continuity which had been so rudely disrupted since 1535. The more earnest the practitioner, the more serious the dilemma. The mass might be a comfort, but was there any merit to be gained from daily attendance? Was the layman supposed to read his English Bible, or not? Heretics might be disturbing people to have in your community, but they asked relevant questions, and did the fact that they got the answers wrong really deserve such a terrible fate?[54]

Such questions probably did not occupy the ploughman as he went about his daily tasks. He paid his tithe, went to confession and took his rights at Easter. He processed when instructed to do so and got drunk from time to time at the Church's expense, as his father and grandfather had done before him. To him Edwardian Protestantism was an aberration best forgotten, although phrases and ideas from the English Bible lingered in his mind. It was the literate who were most divided by the reformation; those whose unthinking assurance had been challenged by the availability of evangelical writings. Some repudiated all such notions; some were converted and abandoned the old certainties entirely; but most remained uncertain. They were willing enough to obey the laws currently in force, and even to believe that their betters had probably got it right, but they were not committed to any set of convictions in the full sense.[55] When Mary restored the old faith, they were happy enough, and willing to accept her decision, but when Elizabeth reversed the whole process, they were not motivated to resist, or even to object very forcefully. They were conformists, and in due course would become Anglicans. They were not indifferent to their faith, but they were thoughtful folk who believed in the Royal Supremacy. Many of them may have believed that Elizabeth had made a mistake, and would soon revert to religion 'as King Henry left it', but when it became clear that that was not going to happen, they settled into the new orthodoxy. Such an attitude would have been the despair of Cardinal Pole, and infuriated their more intellectual contemporaries, but faced with the great mysteries of the Christian faith, they took a pragmatic view.[56] They remain largely out of sight, and for that reason the reconstruction of their views is mainly circumstantial and *ex silencio*, but they formed the core of the Marian Church. It was they whom the elite leaders strove so hard to convince and to recruit into the service of Catholicism. For a while they appeared to be convinced, but when the pressures changed they reverted to a position of compromise. Their Christianity was perfectly genuine, but it was undogmatic.[57]

Some, however, could not indulge in the luxury of anonymity. Magistrates like Sir John Tyrell and Sir John Guildford had been obliged to receive indictments for heresy and to serve on commissions to investigate suspects. In many cases such participation was formal, an inescapable duty imposed by status rather than a reflection of Catholic zeal, but some, like Tyrell, appear to have gone well beyond the call of duty. The story of Sir John burning the hand of the maid Rose Allin in what appears to have been a fit of casual sadism became part of the folklore of Protestant martyrology.[58] Significantly, both Sir John and Edmund Tyrell disappear from the commission of the peace by 1562. For most purposes the justices of the peace were part of the county furniture, and only the seriously disaffected would be removed, so the Tyrells' Catholicism had caused major concern. By contrast, Sir William Cecil had remained on the commissions for Lincolnshire in 1555, in spite of having been principal secretary under the Duke of Northumberland.[59] Sir John Bourne, Mary's secretary, was less fortunate in 1562, but he was under investigation for hearing clandestine masses. Sir John Mordaunt served throughout, as did Lords Rich and Abergavenny, and Sir John Baker disappeared only because he died in August 1558. The Elizabethan bishops were anxious, and several reported that the justices in their dioceses were less than 'whole' in matters of religion, but that usually meant no more than 'conservatively inclined'. It was only after 1570, and the papal bull, that recusancy became a real disqualification from a place on the bench.[60] The continuity between the commissions of Edward and those of Mary is very marked. Many of these justices also sat as MPs, and voted through both the Protestant measures of 1549 and 1552 and their repeal in 1553 and 1555. Should they be regarded as mere time servers, or are we looking at another aspect of the Royal Supremacy? Dr Thomas Martin put Cranmer on the spot at the latter's trial in 1555 when he asked why, having professed obedience to Mary as Supreme

Head, he did not now obey her instructions?[61] The Archbishop eventually put his Protestant convictions first, but it is not surprising that most laymen, even noblemen, declined to do the same. The House of Lords had been more equivocal about the Edwardian reforms and less equivocal about repealing them than the House of Commons, but no peer was in serious trouble for nonconformity under either regime. No magistrate was prosecuted for heresy, and only the second Earl of Bedford took refuge abroad. Edward Underhill observed that there was no better place to 'shift the Easter time' – that is to avoid taking communion – than Queen Mary's court.[62] The same might be said of Elizabeth's court in the early years of her reign. In time both recusant and puritan gentlemen were to be critically important in the promotion of their respective causes, but in the turbulent middle years of the century their culture seems to have been one of obedience. They observed the required elements of the faith in public, and kept their consciences to themselves. Their example was followed by most of their social inferiors, both clerical and lay. It is not accidental that so few of Foxe's martyrs ranked even in the lowest reaches of the gentry. They had families and property to defend, and their colleagues on the bench were not anxious to pursue them. Some of the more proactive bishops may have wished to do so, but lacked the confidence to proceed against such suspects without the kind of evidence it proved impossible to obtain.

5 HERESY AND DISSENT

In the middle years of the sixteenth century, heresy was not as clearly defined as it later became, particularly at the grass-roots level. Whereas the preacher who roundly asserted that salvation came by faith and not by good works was clearly (in that respect at least) a Lutheran, and he who asserted that the bread and wine remained in the Eucharistic elements was a reformer of a more radical kind, the much vaguer mutterings among their flocks were harder to pin down. The desire to reform the Church was pervasive. Cardinal Ximenes was a reformer, so were Cajetan, Morone and Pole. Erasmus was a reformer, so too was Cardinal Caraffa, later Pope Paul IV.[1] Where the line should be drawn between the reformers' criticisms and the dissenters' heresy was largely a matter of judgement. Erasmus is a good case in point. Never condemned in his own lifetime, he considered himself to be a loyal son of the Church; yet twenty years later his works were put on the index of prohibited books.[2] Cardinal Pole, a fierce enemy of heretics in England, was himself suspected by Paul IV, and his Legateship withdrawn. Cardinal Morone was imprisoned in Rome for the same reason and Bartolomé Carranza, Pole's right-hand man while in England, later spent seventeen years in the prisons of the Inquisition.[3] Even Martin Luther considered himself to be an orthodox Augustinian, who had been condemned because of the ambiguities of the Church's teaching, and there were those in Rome in the 1530s who were inclined to agree with him. In other words, reform was nuanced. Ximenes, Pole and Morone were never condemned, while Carranza was, and Erasmus was by implication. A multitude of errors were found in the works of Luther, but his main heresy was justification by faith alone. Zwingli was guilty of far more serious deviation on the doctrine of the Eucharist, while Calvin was deemed responsible for spreading a whole raft of mistaken doctrine, from the Eucharist to predestination.[4] Moreover, there was a degree of overlap, because Benedetto de Mantova's *Trattato del beneficio di Christo*, which first caused suspicion to fall on Cardinal Pole, was largely made up of extracts from Calvin's *Christianae Religionis Institutio*. Nor was heresy exclusively defined by the Catholic Church. Radicals like Pilgram Marpeck or the Unitarian Faustus Socinus, to say nothing of the Mulhausen preacher Thomas Muntzer, were equally condemned by all established Protestant churches.

Such ideas infiltrated into England by way of books, by direct contact through trade and sometimes by the migration of those holding them. Most of the books were written in Latin, and were available only to the educated, but several old Wycliffite works were reissued in the 1530s and in 1538 Richard Taverner compiled *A Catechisme or Institution of the Christen Religion* (which was a paraphrase of Calvin) and Nicholas Wyse published *A Consolacyon for Chrysten People.*[5] The content of these books was translated into sermons by the likes of John Frith and Robert Barnes, and their ideas thus spread to a wider audience. There they impacted upon a much older and vaguer form of dissent which is generally known as 'Lollardy'. The original Lollards had been the followers of the late fourteenth-century Oxford divine John Wycliffe, and had for the most part been gentlemen and students. However the activities of some of the latter, known as the 'poor preachers', had spread these ideas around just as the reforming preachers were to do more than a century later. At that level they had been bowdlerized, misunderstood and diversified, so that hardly any two Lollards believed exactly the same things, and no *credo* or confession of faith was ever produced. The commonest manifestations were rejection of the papacy, a refusal to accept transubstantiation, and radical scepticism about the role of the saints.[6] However, there were also other more or less radical ideas in circulation: a refusal to pay tithes to 'sinful' clergy (whose sacraments were not thought to be efficacious); the rejection of purgatory and of prayers for the dead; even the uselessness of infant baptism. In other words, whatever the main culture of conformity happened to be in that place, the Lollard would deny it. The typical Lollard did not refuse to come to church, and may even have embraced its offices with every appearance of enthusiasm. He did, however, withdraw into his own circle for prayer and Bible-reading, and his most prized possession was often a battered copy of Wycliffe's Bible, a translation of which had been produced by some of the master's university followers soon after his death.[7] Outside his own family, he probably belonged to a network of 'known men', or fellow believers, who passed the secret writings among themselves, and to whose houses he would resort if forced to travel abroad on business. Lollards who shared all the principal doctrines of the movement formed a network with strong roots in certain areas; in north Kent and Essex, for example, and in parts of London, the Chilterns and the Cotswolds.[8] Men and women who had picked up some Lollard ideas, often imperfectly understood, were spread much more widely as a result of personal contacts, and in these people, who were often illiterate, the culture of dissent often shaded into the merely ribald. A man might neglect to go to church for a number of reasons, and thoughtful heresy was not necessarily among them. In 1526 Paul Lomely abjured what appears to have been a typical sacramentarian article, 'That these prestes makith us to believe that the syngynge brede they hold over there heedes is god and it is but a cake',[9] but this was an isolated case from Gravesend where there was no known Lollard network and the origin of his opinion is not clear.

By contrast the literate network of the Christian Brethren, which seems to have spread outwards from London along the trade routes, can be partially reconstructed. In 1541 Bishop Capon of Salisbury discovered that John Forsett, the vicar of St Edmunds church within the town, had been preaching the unusual doctrine that the souls of the departed sleep until the general resurrection. His congregation also complained that he was in the habit of meeting with a select band of his friends to read and discuss illicit books. These books were supplied by one Sooham, a London-based messenger who seems to have travelled the country for that purpose, and to keep these provincial cells in touch with what was going on in the capital.[10] Although Forsett commended Luther as 'a good man', and some of his books were among those discussed, neither he nor his friends were Lutherans as that is normally understood. These networks existed from the early fifteenth century to the middle of the sixteenth, and help to explain how the dissidents of Mary's reign managed to keep in touch with each other. They also help to explain why certain aspects of Henry VIII's reform programme were welcomed in some places. As early as 1423 Wyclffite scholars were denouncing prayer to the saints as idolatrous, and Lollard writings kept up this attack sporadically throughout the century and a bit which preceded the King's attack on pilgrimage shrines. Beneath the luxuriance of the early sixteenth-century cults lay this strong undertow of dissent, which divided communities and helps to explain why there was so little resistance to Henry's iconoclasm.[11] It was to these cells that the ideas of the Continental reformers made their first appeal, and the distinctions between the old and the new ideas are often difficult to perceive. William Tyndale, for example, normally thought of a straightforward Lutheran, is a case in point. His ambition to translate the scriptures into English, and to have the psalms sung at the plough, was both Erasmian and Lutheran, but it was also Lollard. Tyndale was far more emphatic against auricular confession than was Luther, and was inclined to make the efficacy of faith dependent upon repentance, which the German would never admit. His arch-enemy Sir Thomas More took some pleasure in pointing out Tyndale's indigenous roots. When describing a report that Philip Melanchthon, Luther's close ally, had been received by the King of France, More wrote to Erasmus that the English heretic 'was afraid that if by his means France should receive the Word of God, it would be confirmed in the Lutheran faith against the Wycliffites'.[12] Clearly at this stage More considered Wycliffe to be a worse heretic than Luther and, given the amorphous nature of some of the radicalism which passed for Lollardy, he may well have been right.

As with its Continental equivalent, reform in England shaded into heresy. Some conservative priests wanted to accuse John Colet after his celebrated sermon calling upon the clergy to mend their ways or lose respect. There was never the slightest chance of that happening, but the desire is indicative of a highly defensive mentality. More himself held forth against the errors of the Vulgate Bible, and denounced the regular orders in language which would certainly have got him into trouble twenty years later, if he had not become a Holy Blissful Martyr in the meantime.[13] More and Erasmus both distrusted outward ceremonies, and mocked the shrines of Walsingham and Canterbury, but both did so from within the orthodox tradition. When Thomas Bilney made the same points, but from outside that context, More hastened to their defence, and his support for popular religion was sufficiently robust.[14] Even if he had accepted the Royal Supremacy over the English Church, there might have been aspects of Henry's later proceedings which would have offended his conscience. If More was a reformer in the humanist mode, and recognizable as such, Bilney was altogether different. He has been variously described as a Lollard, an early Protestant (the term had not yet been invented) and as orthodox but eccentric, and it depends a good deal upon which aspect of his teaching is under scrutiny. His Christology was certainly radical, but he was orthodox on the mass. His thinking on the saints owed much to Wycliffe, but on justification he was closer to Luther. John Foxe, however, recognized the originality of his thought when he wrote that it

> may appear the whole sume of his preaching and doctrine to proceed chiefly against idolatry, invocation of saints, vain worship of images, false trust in man's merits, and such other gross points of religion, as seemed prejudicial and derogatory to the blood of our Saviour Jesus Christ.[15]

This was to become the mantra of those who would be known as evangelicals: the absolute priority of the sacrifice of Calvary, from which no human ceremony may detract, and which no teaching may diminish. It must be faith in that sacrifice which provides the inspiration for the Christian life. The whole Bible points to it, and beside it the ancient traditions of the Church are mere human inventions. To embrace such a vision did not require education or status, nor did it require a single interpretation of the functions of the Church. Many different schools of thought can therefore properly be labelled evangelical, and it was up to the Church to decide which were acceptable and which not. The Church did not make up its mind quickly, nor speak with a single voice, so it was some time before the vexed question of orthodoxy was answered, and Thomas Bilney was an early victim of that confusion.[16] Evangelism has been described as an 'irenic and eclectic' movement,[17] sensitive to many kinds of reform, and that is one of the reasons why it is so hard to define. By and large it embraced faith, at the expense of the penitential order which had absorbed so much of the energy of the medieval Church, and therefore rejected purgatory and all its accumulated apparatus. It held the scriptures to be more authoritative than the traditions of the Church, and it believed preaching to be central to the pastoral ministry. None of this actually excluded the believer from the Catholic regiment, at least not before the Council of Trent, but it made his orthodoxy precarious. When Henry VIII broke with the Church in 1534 for personal and political reasons, two of his chief advisers, Thomas Cromwell and Thomas Cranmer, were evangelicals in this rather loose sense.[18] That meant that, as the King's theological agenda began to emerge, the movement split into those who accepted the King's programme and those who found it inadequate. The former, who may be called the Erastians, accepted Henry's right to define the doctrines and usages of the Church, even at the cost of discomfort to their own consciences, while the latter did not, and therefore found themselves increasingly vulnerable to charges of heresy. It was, of course, no longer an offence to deny the authority of the Pope, but Thomas Cranmer was married, a fact which he was forced to conceal, and Cromwell paid the ultimate price for running ahead of the King in pursuit of evangelical goals.[19] It was Henry's conscience which was the defining factor in the orthodoxy of the last fourteen years of his reign, a fact which Cranmer recognized and accepted. Those who could not do so, like James Bainham, Anne Askew and John Lambert, paid for their scruples with their lives.[20] Although their ideas came from diverse sources, these unreconciled evangelicals tended during this period to coalesce with the old-fashioned Lollards who still existed to form a new reform movement which may by this time legitimately be called Protestant.

Genuine Lutherans were rare in England, and that is a fact which requires some explanation. In so far as English writers engaged in the theological controversies of the 1520s, it was nearly always on the orthodox side, and those whose dissent can be traced through the Church courts are usually identified as 'Lollards'.[21] Even groups such as that which assembled at the White Horse Inn in Cambridge, which was known as 'Little Germany', contained many who would not have accepted the Confession of Augsburg. Robert Barnes, who went to Wittenburg and met Luther personally, did not see eye to eye with him on all doctrinal issues. The reason for this was partly that those university teachers and students who made up this constituency preferred to be selective in their approach. Some of Luther's ideas appealed, such as his attack on indulgences and on papal authority, and some did not, like his idiosyncratic teaching on the Eucharistic presence. It was also partly because he was a condemned heretic. His books had been burned in London, and even to discuss them carried a frisson of danger. The others who may be classed as Lutherans were mainly traders and travellers who had direct contact with those parts of Germany where such ideas prevailed, or with the merchants of the Steelyard in London, the Hanseatic headquarters which harboured a number of those whose views made their residence in an unprotected environment problematic.[22] The reason why these heretical ideas did not spread lay partly in the vigilance of the authorities, but was partly (and probably more importantly) cultural. There was a vein of pragmatic scepticism which lay below the somewhat glossy appearance of late medieval religion. Even the educated found it hard to understand transubstantiation, and there were much more sensible and appealing ways of explaining some sort of divine presence. Images were obviously blocks of wood or marble carved into the semblance of the saints. What they represented was clear enough, but why should they be more? Prayers for the dead had a natural appeal, but why should they be linked to a place called purgatory, for which there was no scriptural warrant? In a culture dominated by magic and the supernatural, there was a submerged yearning for rational explanations.[23] A corporeal presence – like a human body – could surely be in only one place at a time.

These views were known at the time as Lollard, and have been so described by historians, but their connection with John Wycliffe was (and is) extremely shadowy. It is unhelpful to describe the roots of the faith of preachers like Thomas Bilney and Hugh Latimer in such terms. They were learned men, and picked out of the writings of the fathers, and out of the Bible, such passages as favoured their inclinations. Those inclinations were rooted more in natural scepticism than in the obscure and distant writings of the Oxford reformer. England did not produce a reformation theologian of the first rank, and the writers who appealed most forcibly to this sceptical streak were Ulrich Zwingli and his followers, most notably Heinrich Bullinger. This Zurich school was far more radical than Luther, denouncing not only works theology and the authority of the Pope, but the corporeal presence in the Eucharist, the cults of saints, prayers for the dead and even the use of church music.[24] In visual terms, Zwinglianism was extremely bleak; it was a religion of the word, and as far removed from the luxuriance of contemporary Catholic piety as it was possible to go. For that very reason it appealed to the iconoclastic streak in English religion, so much so that there has been earnest debate as to whether the roots of John Hooper's notoriously radical notions should be sought in Zurich or in the Lollard traditions which flourished in parts of his native Gloucestershire.[25] Zwingli's own faith was a radical extension of those humanist notions which had taken root among the educated in England in the early sixteenth century, but when the evangelical party in England split under the impact of the royal Supremacy, it did not do so cleanly along the Lutheran/Zwinglian divide. The King remained as hostile to Luther as ever, and certain aspects of the Zurich agenda were adopted, most notably over images, but the main division came over the Eucharistic presence. Henry disliked Luther's equivocation, but he absolutely loathed Bullinger's sacramentarianism. So that whereas the Erastian reformers who stayed within the establishment tended to sympathize with Luther, the reformed Protestants were excluded and remained in opposition. In so far as there was popular support for the Erastian position, as opposed to mere acquiescence to the King's will, it tended to come from the literate. The Protestants also had their educated leaders, although several of those, like John Hooper, sought refuge in exile.[26] However, their humble followers, for whom exile was scarcely an option, blended seamlessly with the old Lollards, and often seem to have been the same people. Both Lollardy and early Protestantism appealed to the same streak of iconoclastic rationalism, and consequently attempts to determine the influence of the one over the other have always been, and remain, extremely controversial.

When the politics of the succession dictated a shift in the religious establishment in 1547, the parties gradually realigned themselves. The shift to a moderate Protestant establishment under the Royal Supremacy should have reunited the Erastians with the Protestants and produced something like a reformed consensus. However, what is usually the case when two ideologically based parties come together, there are remnants on both sides which refuse to join in, with the result that there are three groups rather than two. That happened in this case. The Erastians split over the mass and related traditional ceremonies, which the Duke of Somerset, Archbishop Cranmer and reforming bishops such as Nicholas Ridley were happy to abolish, but which conservative leaders such as Stephen Gardiner, the Bishop of Winchester, Edmund Bonner of London, Cuthbert Tunstall of Durham and the Princess Mary (the heir to the throne) wished to retain.[27] Political power lay with the reformers, and they prevailed, but public sympathy was with the conservatives, and the rallying cry 'religion as King Henry left it' had a very wide appeal. The Protestants divided less obviously, and more messily, because no single issue separated them, and only the most extreme can really be described as opponents.[28] During the opening months of the reign, there was a great flood of Protestant polemic, which was broadly supportive of the intended changes, but sometimes went beyond the government's agenda, both in extent and in speed. A series of proclamations was needed, ordering punishment for assaults on clergy, silencing disputes on the Eucharist and enforcing the Lenten fast in 1548. In November 1547 a statute strove to hold the line of the government's (fairly) gradual programme against those who wanted more, and faster.[29] Most of these zealots ended by accepting what was on offer, and confined their campaigning for further reformation to lawful representations. They lost over vestments in 1551, but won over the revision of the Prayer Book in 1552.[30] However, there were those who were radically dissatisfied, and they held a rag-bag of beliefs which were classified at the time as Anabaptist, although rejection of infant baptism was not usually among their convictions. Some were Unitarians, some held a variety of Christological heresies of Continental origin, and some were just mad. They were never numerous, but they were very visible because the government made them so, denouncing them in the Forty

Two Articles which summed up the Edwardian faith, and turning the heresy laws of the old Church against Joan Bocher and George van Paris, who were the only heretics to be burned during the reign – a punishment for which there was no justification in English law.[31]

Although there was some violent resistance in the summer of 1549, and a great deal of foot-dragging in conservative areas like Devon and Lancashire, the enforcement of the Edwardian reformation was surprisingly effective, and this inevitably raises the question of how far it succeeded in bringing about a genuine shift in religious culture. Any answer must be laced with qualifications because of the patchy nature of the surviving evidence, but in some places and amidst some sections of the community there does seem to have been a change. Gentlemen and yeomen who had 'bought in' to the Henrician reformation by purchasing monastic lands had often done the same with chantry property, and had even acquired (illicitly) a quantity of the church goods which the government had confiscated in 1552. They were bound to look askance at any efforts to restore the traditional order and, although most of them made submissive noises when that came about, their zeal for the resurrected Church may be legitimately questioned.[32] The great city of London was a turmoil of conflicting practices and opinions, parishes varying with the allegiance of their incumbents and aldermen, but overall it seems to have shifted decisively in a Protestant direction. The churchwardens and clergy of St Martin's in Ironmongers Lane, for example, stripped out the crucifix and all the remaining images from their church as soon as news of the old King's death was confirmed. They replaced the crucifix with the royal arms and the images with painted texts of scripture. When summoned before the Council, they told an unconvincing tale of necessary repairs. They were reprimanded and made to replace the crucifix, but otherwise no action was taken.[33] Francois van der Delft, the imperial ambassador, who was on the spot, reported a sudden surge of advanced Protestant sentiment in the city at the same time and declared that the common people were openly hostile to Catholicism, 'of which they make all sorts of farces and pastimes.'[34] It may be that what he was witnessing was less an upsurge of Protestantism than a popular reaction to the loosening of ecclesiastical discipline. It is hard to be sure, but it is reasonable to suppose that these artisans and apprentices were motivated by something more positive than a mischievous spree. In early September 1547 the same ambassador reported that images were being taken down all over London, without any edict or authority, although he also added that the mass was being celebrated in most parishes with due decorum, which suggests that authority had been effectively reimposed.[35]

Outside of London the evidence for spontaneous Protestantism is much more sporadic, and relates mainly to towns, particularly those in cloth-working areas. At St Ives in Cambridgeshire there was a sacrilegious attack upon the mass, which may have been no more than an individual protest, but in nearby St Neots a group of parishioners removed the images from the church and resisted all commands to replace them.[36] One other phenomenon is worthy of notice in this context. In a number of parishes in East Anglia images and other church furnishings were being taken down and sold, and the money devoted to poor relief and other charitable purposes. In Saffron Walden £100 was raised in this way, which was given to the support of a free school in the town. One of the advantages of Protestant worship was that it required far less in the way of equipment, and many churches may have been tempted to realize their assets in this way.[37] At the same time that official doctrine was moving away from the idea that giving to the Church was a 'good work', and beneficial to the soul of the donor, it was moving towards the notion that giving to the poor, or to education, was a way of testifying to the grace that was in one. This change did not happen suddenly, and reflects a shift of emphasis going back many years, but it becomes much more visible (and better documented) once the official doctrine of the Church had become reformed. In this limited respect the development of lay charity expresses a change of fashion which was in tune with the Protestant reformation. The culture of charity had changed, and was to go on changing.[38]

Nevertheless the main fault line in the Edwardian Church remained that between Protestants and conservatives. Heresy, in its radical form, was irritating but quantitively insignificant. The medieval heresy laws had been repealed at the beginning of Edward's reign, along with the conservative Act of Six Articles, and would in any case not have answered to the major need. The problem was one of discipline in its widest sense – that is persuading or forcing people to do as they were told – not of heresy. With the notorious exception of John Forrest, even Henry VIII had not used the heresy laws against his Catholic opponents.[39] This might have changed had Cranmer's revised code of canon law been accepted in 1552, because most of the key Catholic doctrines were listed as heresies. 'We establish as heretics', that section of the code began,

> all those who take any decree of our common faith in a sense other than that which has been determined by sacred scripture, and who dwell in error such that they in no way allow themselves to be removed from it[40]

It went on to list twenty-one errors, embracing the mass, the authority of scripture, free will and justification, purgatory, the sacraments and the papal authority. However, there was no law in place to punish such heresies other than by ecclesiastical means, and the code was in any case rejected by the council. So conservative dissent was not treated as heresy, and became treason only in the extreme cases of rebellion, as in the south-west and in Oxfordshire in 1549. It was nonetheless very widespread and could be very vocal, as numerous consistory court records bear witness. It was not only the Devon rebels who wanted to see the Act of Six Articles restored. For example, one Margaret Harbotell was arraigned before the vicar general's court of London in July 1551, accused of remonstrating with her curate over the abolition of beads. The new order, she protested, had brought down the wrath of God,

> bycause that they wolde not suffre them to pray upon there beedes and thereupon in despite of the kinges injunctions shoke her beedes at the said Syr Nicholas [Barthram] saing contemptuously that she wold that he shulde knowe that she dydd and wold pray upon her beedes. And that men dydd dye lyke dogges bycause they cannot see there maker borne abowte by the streetes as they have seene it in tyme past.[41]

Such sentiments were widely shared, although not usually so vigorously expressed. Clergy were frequently in trouble for neglecting the royal injunctions. Robert Pytco of Aylesham, for instance was indicted for saying high mass while a sermon was actually in progress in his church, an action of which his parishioners clearly approved since they drowned out the preacher by ringing the sacring bell.[42] Such actions were not heretical, but nor were they necessarily Catholic in the proper sense. There is no mention of the Pope, or of the Universal Church, or of justification. These were the reactions of simple folk who hankered after the old ways. They did not wish to challenge the King's authority, but thought that it was being misused during his minority by those classic medieval scapegoats, evil counsellors. What they wanted was 'religion as King Henry left it'.

When Edward VI died on 6 July 1553, the Royal Supremacy was transferred to his successor, Mary, and her well-known conservative stance on religion was generally welcomed. The imperial ambassadors, who are one of our chief sources of information on this transition, expected trouble because they were convinced that the whole country was deeply sunk in heresy, but their observation was superficial, and based largely upon London.[43] There was indeed a disturbance at Paul's Cross on 13 August when the preacher Gilbert Bourne denounced as unjust the imprisonment by Edward's council of the former (and soon to be restored) Bishop of London, Edmund Bonner. But this was not a portent of worse to come. The government moved swiftly to imprison a number of Protestant preachers, not on the grounds of their faith but for the preservation of public order. On 20 August Simon Renard reported 'The popular commotions because of religion which were feared here are very much quieted since ten or twelve of the leaders have been taken prisoner and all private assemblies forbidden on pain of death'.[44]

Heresy may have been an issue in the Queen's mind, but it was not on the public agenda. What happened for the time being was that dissent was measured against the 'Queen's Proceedings', and was treated as a matter of social and ecclesiastical discipline. The Protestants had lost control of the ship of state, and that made them potentially political opponents of the regime, but it remained to be seen how this would manifest itself, and how strong they really were. When the government was challenged for the first time by the Wyatt rebellion in Kent in January 1554, it chose to represent this as a Protestant attempt to place Jane Grey on the throne.[45] Some Protestants were undoubtedly involved, but the motivation was hostility to Mary's proposed marriage to Philip of Spain, and had nothing to do with Jane Grey. Even the council's main propaganda against Wyatt admitted that he did not make an issue of religion, but insisted that such was his secret purpose.[46] There was also the involvement of Edward Courtenay, recently created Earl of Devon, which Stephen Gardiner, the Lord Chancellor, was anxious to conceal. Courtenay was a Catholic, whatever else he may have been. Gardiner had himself opposed the marriage when it was first mooted, and thereby exposed himself to charges of complicity. So it became a Protestant rebellion, in which no one could suspect him (or Courtenay) of being implicated. The Wyatt revolt is therefore no test of Protestant strength, and there is no other available. Committed reformers did their best to avoid the hated mass, either by absenting themselves from church or by other more devious means. But this was a matter for regular church discipline, and is impossible to quantify. Dissent at first was an elite matter, expressed in the arrest of reforming bishops and preachers, and their deprivation by royal commission.[47] This affected the parochial clergy mainly in so far as those who had chosen to marry were now faced with the choice between abandoning their livings or abandoning their wives, and most chose the latter alternative, sometimes at considerable cost in personal terms. The Royal Visitation of March 1554 and the disputations held at Oxford in April were the sharp end of this process, but whereas Cranmer, Ridley and Latimer were declared guilty of heresy as a result of the disputations, they were returned to prison and no further action was taken.[48]

This was not because heresy was considered to be unimportant, but because it was considered to be mainly an elite business. A majority, even of the Edwardian bishops, had accepted the new conservative dispensation – some with considerable relief – and both Mary and Gardiner seem to have believed that the reformation was only skin deep. The Protestant leaders were wicked men whose main purpose had been to plunder the Church, but ordinary people had only pretended to go along with their ideas and edicts. They could be excused by their duty of obedience to the King, and if their conversion was a little more serious, then they were simply gullible and would have to be re-educated. They might well object to their 'carnal practices' being disturbed, but committed, conscientious resistance at the parochial level was neither looked for nor prepared against.[49] Up to a point this was justified. The overwhelming majority of dissenters who were detected or denounced in the first year of the reign submitted, just as the Lollards detected in 1511 and 1528 had submitted. A few had been obstinate or evasive enough to be committed to prison, but it was only the preachers who promised to give any serious trouble. There was also a legal problem, because the early fifteenth-century statutes making heresy a capital crime had been repealed and not replaced. Consequently it remained a purely ecclesiastical offence, punishable by the bishops through their ordinary jurisdiction, but only to a certain level. The Church could fine and imprison as well as penance and excommunicate, but it could not touch either life or real property. It had been simply the general revulsion felt against the doctrines of Bocher and Van Paris which had enabled the Edwardian council to burn them, an action which was strictly illegal. It was not therefore the return of the papal jurisdiction which created the sanctions which were put in place in January 1555, but the renewal of the three Acts of Richard II, Henry IV and Henry V, which 'shall from the 20th day of January next coming [1555] be revived and in full force, strength and effect'.[50]

Cardinal Reginald Pole, whose Legatine jurisdiction was recognized by proclamation ahead of the Statute of Repeal, seems at first to have shared the Queen's convictions about the nature of the heretical challenge. On 28 January he issued a Legatine Commission for the trial of John Hooper, John Rogers, Rowland Taylor, Robert Farrer and Laurence Saunders, in the hope, and probably the expectation, that they would submit when faced with the awful alternative which was now available. This was the test which was to determine whether heresy was to be a low-key nuisance or a highly visible system of defiance. When all the original defendants went to the fire, professing their steadfast Protestant convictions, the writing was on the wall.[51] They were followed by other preachers and leaders, and the government faced a dilemma. The punishment for recalcitrant heresy was death by burning, and to have settled for anything less would have been a dereliction of duty. Stephen Gardiner, whose enthusiasm for persecution was largely informed by political priorities, probably wanted to back off, in order to contain a problem which suddenly seemed so much more difficult than had been anticipated, but Mary and Pole would have none of such equivocation. Given that nobody knew how numerous the heretics really were, or where their threshold of surrender might be, there was some logic in continuing a policy of terror.[52] We do not know to this day how close that policy may have come to success. Perhaps if Mary had not died relatively young, heresy in England would have been exterminated, leaving the thousand or so who had been driven into exile without a constituency to appeal to. However, the evidence does not suggest that. All those leaders who had stood up to be counted had indeed been tried, and the great majority of them executed. However, others remained concealed, and the influx of polemical works from abroad showed no sign of slowing down or being frustrated. Heretics went on being burned to within a few weeks of Mary's death, which suggests that the morale of those communities was holding up reasonably well.[53]

In the context of a persecution, heresy should be fairly easy to define, but in fact that is not so. The leaders were all exhaustively examined, and their doctrinal positions emerge with reasonable clarity. They were, as might be expected, orthodox Edwardian Protestants, who rejected the mass, the seven sacraments, prayers for the dead and works theology. They maintained the Prayer Book, the English Bible and the vernacular liturgy, and they defended their positions with learning and with a wealth of biblical citation. The pains which the inquisitors took with these men indicates the importance which they attached to them.[54] To obtain a single recantation, like that of Sir John Cheke, was worth a great deal of effort. However, they were seldom so rewarded, and the death sentence was often passed reluctantly and in a state of mental exhaustion, because their victims had left them no alternative. There was a certain justice in the charge that the latter sought martyrdom, but they certainly did not do so rashly.[55] They were also playing for high stakes. However, below that level, the picture is much less clear. By and large the lay elite dissembled or, in the case of women, were protected by their families. The most conspicuous of all, the Princess Elizabeth, submitted publicly and kept a careful guard upon her tongue. No one, least of all her sister, was really deceived, but she gave no occasion to take action against her. The same was true of William Cecil, who went to mass with the rest and kept his thoughts to himself. Quite a few gentlemen, and even one or two nobles, took refuge in Switzerland or the Rhineland, where they helped to support those students who would be the clergy of the next generation.[56] These exiles protected their consciences, but if it had not been for events in England they would have had nothing acceptable to return to. However, the bulk of the heretical iceberg (if such it was) remains only semi-visible below the surface.

Some 200 of those who went to the stake had no claim to elite status; they were artisans, tradesmen and servant girls, and had no motivation to sustain them beyond their religious convictions. Sometimes they too were examined carefully, usually to determine the nature of the community which they represented, and their beliefs can be ascertained from the proceedings of their trials. Sometimes, to John Foxe's embarrassment, they were radicals beyond the range of Protestant orthodoxy, a fact which he did his best to conceal, but for the most part they were simple sacramentarians, who could not see anything in the Eucharistic elements beyond the bread and wine.[57] These beliefs were sometimes supported by biblical texts, learned by heart, and were genuine enough to merit the sacrifice of their lives. However, such self sacrifice was not the normal reaction of those who got into trouble with the ecclesiastical courts. For every one who was executed there were dozens, probably scores, who submitted. The records of the ecclesiastical courts are full of these half-committed heretics. Sometimes they had simply absented themselves from church, most critically from the Easter communion; sometimes they had used scurrilous or blasphemous words to describe the sacrament of the altar, or had abused the priest in confession. That these men and women were in a way dissenters is undeniable, but what they really believed does not usually emerge. The charge is recorded, sometimes in considerable detail, and the testament of witnesses, if any, then the fact of their submission and the penance awarded.[58] However, having once been through the courts, the position of such people was precarious, because any subsequent infringement would be held as 'relapse', and result in automatic condemnation. Isolated cases of this kind occur in most dioceses, and reflect either the convictions of those who had travelled abroad or the bloody-mindedness of the individual. They were not usually taken very seriously, although the cases of George Marsh in Cheshire and the Cardiff fisherman Rawlins White should warn us that notorious ringleaders might be targeted even in otherwise conformist environments.[59] Most of the efforts of the bishops' officers were concentrated in those communities which had a tradition of heresy and where conservatives might well have been marginalized under the previous regime. A few zealous clergy, like Thomas Tye the curate of Brentford or magistrates such as Sir John Tyrell could have a field day in parts of Essex, or Nicholas Harpesfield in Kent. Sometimes the line between conformity and defiance could be a fine one. In Norwich, for example, a city which had conformed with some enthusiasm under Edward, the rapid surrender of John Barrett, the longest serving and most respected evangelical minister, seems to have taken the heart out of Protestant resistance.[60] Fifteen clergy from the diocese and cathedral were deprived for marriage in 1554, but they mostly disappear from the records thereafter. Although one or two may have fled, the assumption is that the remainder conformed. There is plenty of evidence of low-key nonconformity, and the lay magistrates were actively involved. The fate of Thomas Rose is illustrative of what could happen. A dependant of Henry Radcliffe, second Earl of Sussex, he was persuaded by Sussex into an equivocal submission, 'to the hole catholic church of Christ and the ecclesiastical laws of England', which the Earl leaned on the bishop to accept.[61] Committed to the custody of Sir William Woodhouse, Rose was allowed to 'visit friends' and thus escaped. There is no evidence that he changed his convictions. Altogether there were thirty-one burnings in the diocese of Norwich, and Foxe listed Michael Dunning, the Chancellor, as a particularly zealous persecutor, Norwich itself remained subdued. In Colchester, as in London, there were secret Protestant conventicles, and priests were abused in the streets, but nothing similar happened in Norwich, which had seemed to be a bastion of evangelicalism.

The structure of nonconformity varied very much from one community to another. Sometimes it depended upon the influence of a local nobleman or gentleman, Grimesthorpe in Lincolnshire, for instance, was evangelical because of the influence of the Duchess of Suffolk.[62] Or it might be, as at Norwich or Hadleigh in Suffolk, because of the strong personality or rhetorical skills of a particular minister. Sometimes it depended upon local trade networks, as at Burford and Witney in Oxfordshire, and sometimes upon the traditions of particularly influential families. Cranbrook and Tenterden in Kent, for example, are only a few miles apart, and shared many of the same economic circumstances, but their religious evolution was quite distinct.[63] Traditional orthodox culture remained relatively robust in Cranbrook, particularly the place of the mass in the commemoration of the dead. This was not the case in Tenterden, where gifts and bequests fell away steeply in the early sixteenth century, although the Jesus mass seems to have retained its popularity in the latter place down to 1547, and may have helped to ease the transition to the Christological focus of the reformers.[64] Cranbrook was generally far more conservative than Tenterden, and there are signs that traditional testamentary formulae were beginning to revive by the end of Mary's reign. Neither parish attracted any particular attention from Nicholas Harpesfield during his 1557 visitation, which suggests that outward conformity was being observed, but it has been noted that it was 1562 before Cranbrook took down its rood. Over a period of a hundred years or so the overall profile of family pieties is quite different between the two towns, Cranbrook giving between three and five times as much to religious causes. Admittedly it was the richer community, but the difference is still marked. Tenterden families tended to be frugal with gifts and to concentrate their bequests on their own kindred. Tenterden was more evangelically inclined, and seems to have stripped out the apparatus of Catholic worship with more enthusiasm. By 1557 there was a relatively healthy Catholic devotional life, but significant radical dissent, focused on a few families, notably the Philpots. Five of Kent's Marian martyrs came from Tenterden, while Cranbrook, which was larger and more in the public eye, provided three.[65] Both were divided communities, but the balance between the two parties was significantly different, and this was a characteristic which ran right through the reformation period.

The distinction between heresy and orthodoxy during Mary's reign was not, therefore a question of black and white. Rather it was a spectrum of many shades of grey. On the one extreme were those who welcomed not merely the return of the old ways, but the resurrection of papal authority. These Roman Catholic cannot be numbered, partly because they never got into trouble and partly because it was in the interests of everyone with a stake in the community to appear zealous in support of these changes. It might be assumed, for example, from the reaction of the members of the House of Commons to Pole's address in November 1554, that the overwhelming majority were of that opinion. However, we know from other votes, and from the behaviour of individuals, that that was not so. They were putting on a show of loyalty because the King and Queen were watching them closely.[66] Even magistrates who were apparently zealous persecutors often turned their coats with the advent of the new regime in 1559, and there was no Roman party to resist Elizabeth in the parliament of that year. Genuine Catholics in the full sense were probably a tiny minority in the community as a whole.

Then came those who welcomed the return of the mass and of the other traditional ceremonies, and rejoiced that the clergy were forced to renounce their
women. This was a wide segment, because some continued to use their English
Bibles, while others hastened to restore prayers for the dead and the images of
the saints. Most people in most places were of this way of thinking, and if there
was a prevailing religious culture, this was surely it – cautious and conservative.
Some of them had been in trouble with the Edwardian authorities, but most had
simply grumbled and conformed, as they were to do under Elizabeth. Beyond
these again came those who had accepted the reformation in good faith but had
no desire to take any risks on its behalf. Occasionally a rash word would get
them into trouble with watchful neighbours intent on a little point-scoring, but
they always submitted rapidly. The majority of those whose indiscretions fill the
archdeacons' and bishops' court records belong in this category, but they were
only a small minority. Finally we come to those with tougher consciences – the
real heretics – who drew attention to themselves by refusing to attend church
or receive the sacraments. Some of these were Edwardian Protestants, some
were radicals, and they interacted with their communities in a number of different ways. A few were unpopular with their neighbours, or were known to the
authorities, in which case they were swiftly denounced, but sometimes they were
well supported, particularly against outside interference. Divided communities
were the most likely to produce denunciations, most of all when the incumbent
was more conservative than his flock or when the local justices were attempting to curry favour with the council. Resistance was strongest in places with a
tradition of dissent, like Colchester and Tenterden, but it is clear that even at its
broadest definition, heresy was a minority problem. What makes it loom so large
in the history of the Marian Church is the seriousness with which the authorities treated it. This is understandable because no sixteenth-century government
could afford to be relaxed about ideological resistance, and Mary and Pole were
very conscious of the fact that they had to put right all that had gone amiss during twenty years of schism and heresy. With this high ideal a small number of
unreconciled consciences could not be allowed to interfere. There is also the fact
that, once their efforts had been brought to nought, the sufferings of the persecuted were recorded for posterity by the Protestant pen of John Foxe.

6 THE TRAINING OF CLERGY

On the eve of the Reformation the secular clergy formed a numerous constituency – some 12,000–15,000 altogether – and varied enormously in their standards of education and competence. Bishops were supposed to, and very often did, exercise great care in choosing those upon whom they would confer orders, but patrons were also influential and sometimes put forward candidates who were ill suited. Occasionally these were scholars who had little vocation to the ministry, but often they were clients of a more obvious kind – even serving men. Many of these men would never serve a parish cure, but would work all their lives as cantarists or domestic chaplains.[1] Episcopal oversight varied with the background and personalities of the bishops, and there was no standard test, or set of tests, designed to determine suitability. A priest needed to be basically literate; that is to be able to read and write in English, and to know enough Latin to be able to read the services with some show of comprehension. Two or three years in a grammar school would be sufficient to meet this requirement, but beyond that there was no recognized scheme of training. Many had served as altar boys, and knew what to do by virtue of imitation, and others worked out the apprenticeship of their sub-diaconate for two or three years learning the ropes in the same fashion before presenting themselves to the bishop for priestly orders. Sometimes their examination was rigorous, but often it was perfunctory enough.[2]

It may be that standards had relaxed during the 1520s. Many years later William Allen, defending his decision to establish a seminary at Douai, wrote of 'the common sort of curates ... in old time, as you may better than I remember their want then in manner even of necessary knowledge',[3] particularly their lack of theological understanding, which had left them so vulnerable to the attacks of the reformers. Nor was this mere convenience of memory. In 1531 Convocation was sufficiently worried to issue regulations appertaining to ordination, which were designed to limit the discretion of individual bishops. All candidates, even for the sub-diaconate, were henceforth to produce character references, signed by the priest of the parish in which he had lived for the last three years. These references were to be countersigned by the archdeacon, or in the case of graduates by the vice chancellor.[4] No one was to be admitted to orders at all who could not explain the meaning of the Gospel and Epistles used in the mass to the satisfaction of the examiner. There was no shortage of guides and expositions designed to help the candidate in this ordeal. As early as 1494 Wynkyn de Worde had published a small Latin treatise on the preparation required of a young cleric. This work, the *Sermo Exhortatius ... hiis qui ad sacros ordines petunt promoveri*, was by William de Meltham, a former master of Michaelhouse, Cambridge, and was aimed at those who had already acquired 'a middling knowledge', because without that it would have been of no use to them.[5] Meltham solemnly warned his aspirants that if they failed to master this degree of understanding, they would be in danger of falling into the slovenly ways favoured by so many – drinking, dicing and getting into the company of lewd women.

There was a degree of hyperbole about all this, because the authors were inspired by a high regard for the priestly calling and were ashamed of those who failed to live up to their high standards. Many years ago Peter Heath concluded that the great majority of pre-reformation English clerics were decent men, doing their best in what were often difficult circumstances. They were not, and did not pretend to be, men of learning, but they were adequately prepared to administer the sacraments, to receive confessions and to perform the spiritual tasks of their calling.[6] The criticisms which were heaped upon them, both by the reformers and by their own anxious leaders, were partly the result of high aspirations. The seriously inadequate were a small minority, but the real trouble was the lack of selective training which should have enabled these men to be weeded out before they ever got to celebrating the mass. The problem may have got worse in the early sixteenth century, but it was not a new one. In the late thirteenth century Archbishop John Pecham had been so concerned at the inadequacy of many of his clergy for the task of instructing their flocks in the rudiments of the faith that he had caused the Lambeth Council of 1281 to draw up a scheme of instruction, entitled *De informacione simplicium*. Although aimed in theory at the laity, this rapidly became the parish priests' *vade mecum*.[7] It was translated into English verse as *The Lay Folks Catechism* in 1357, and imitated or directly used all over England for more than 200 years. In 1425 John Stafford, Bishop of Bath and Wells, had another English version prepared and placed in every church in his diocese. It was reissued in its original form by Archbishop George Neville of York in 1465, and again by Cardinal Wolsey in 1518.[8]

The main emphasis of *De informacione* was upon confession and the sacrament of penance, the point at which the clergy and laity most commonly interacted. The penitent needed to know how to confess, without becoming prolix or tedious. He also needed to know when and what to confess without trivializing the exercise. The priest needed to know how to react in the best interest of the penitent, to be able to ask the right questions, and to impose penances graded according to the circumstances. In other words it was a manual of pastoral care. Nor was *De informacione* the only source of such guidance. By the late fourteenth century there was a whole literature designed to help curates to discharge their responsibilities. One of the better-known pieces was William of Pagula's *Oculus Sacerdotis*, the first section of which was a manual for confessors, instructing them (among other things) how to interrogate different lifestyles, and laying down guidelines about which sins were reserved to the bishop – or even to the Pope.[9] The various levels of excommunication which might be incurred were also described. The second section was directed in theory at the laity, but since it was highly schematized and written in Latin, it would again have been of more use to the clergy who were supposed to be conveying the information than it was to the recipients. The third part of the *Oculus* provided the priest with theological and canonical material on the sacraments and their administration. A number of other works based more or less loosely on the *Oculus* were issued in the fifteenth century, most notably John Mirk's *Instructions for Parish Priests*, and his *Festial*, or collection of homilies.[10] Mirk was more insistent than William of Pagula that his curate should have a sound grasp of the scriptures, and in that he was followed by the author of the *Manipulus Curatorum*, a practical handbook first printed in 1498, which had gone through about ten editions by 1547.[11]

With the exception of Mirk, all these derivatives were written in Latin, and aimed at the educated but unlearned clergy, but as the sixteenth century advanced vernacular devotional manuals began to appear, several of them translated from French originals. *The Ordynarye of Crystyantye* in 1502, the *Floure of the Commaundements* in 1510 and an English translation of the *Exonoratorium Curatorum* in 1534.[12] Although all these works were careful to insist upon the dignity and exclusiveness of the clerical calling, there were plenty of conservative clergy who resented them, because they were thought to undermine the dependence of congregations upon the intercessions of their priests. The modest intention of the thirteenth-century Church, to equip laymen with basic prayers and means of examining their consciences, had expanded and become more sophisticated by the early sixteenth century, as meditations on the passion and the sacraments were added to an increasingly elaborate prayer life. Although an extreme example, Margery Kempe gives a good idea of the degree to which an educated bourgeoisie could shape her own spiritual life, calling upon the services of the 'professionals' only as and when it suited her.[13] The thought was a worrying one to the priest concerned to protect his status, and it became more worrying as the educational priorities of the humanists began to permeate down to that level. It was all very well for the learned to quibble and debate theological niceties, but quite another to encourage laymen to do the same. These anxieties were raised to a new level by the appearance of the first authorized vernacular Bible in 1536. Shrouded in the decent mystery of a learned tongue, it had been the clergy's task to explain the meaning of the sacred text, which was not for irreverent minds to meddle with. Now anyone who was capable of reading at all had access, and could start asking those difficult questions for which the average unlearned priest was quite unprepared. As the clerically devised Articles of the Devon rebels were to put it in 1549, 'Item. We will have the Byble and al bokes of scrypture in Englysh to be called in again, for we be enformed that otherwise the Clergye shal not of lo[n]g tyme confound the heretykes'.[14]

There was a clash of principles involved here, because the evangelicals, including the King, believed that laymen had not only a right but a duty to familiarize themselves with the sacred text. This was a position with which otherwise conservative bishops like Stephen Gardiner tended to agree. On the other hand some humanists, such as Thomas More, demurred. In theory he was sympathetic, but the existing translation was the work of heretics such as William Tyndale and would mislead the unwary in various crucial ways.[15] It was More's line which was to be followed by Pole, whose attitude towards the Great Bible remains inscrutable. His Legatine Synod promised a new and orthodox translation, but in the meantime the use of the existing version seems to have been left to Episcopal discretion. It is, however, worth remembering that there was strong hostility to the English Bible at the grass roots, and a tendency to regard its use as an *ipso facto* indicator of heresy, an attitude which was theoretically quite unjustified.

More's attitude to the clergy, which also had a strong influence on Pole, was an interesting one. His polemical opponent, Tyndale, had savaged them, denouncing their arrogance, ignorance and dissipation. This, inevitably, More claims is gross exaggeration, but it is exaggerated, not false. Like Colet, he believes those bishops to be to blame who are more concerned to have a numerous priesthood than to have a high quality one. 'But now' he writes, 'if the bishops would once take unto priesthood better laymen and fewer (for of us be they made) all the matter were more than half amended'.[16] The trouble lay as much in the sinfulness of the critics as of the clergy themselves, but because of their pretensions, they were fair game.

> In reproach of them we be so studious, that neither good nor bad passes unreproved. If they be familiar, we call them light. If they be solitary, we call them fantastic. If they be sad, we call them solemn. If they be merry, we call them mad. If they be companionable, we call them vicious. If they be holy, we call them hypocrites ... If a lewd priest do a lewd deed, then we say 'Lo, see what an example the clergy give us', as though that priest were the clergy

If a friar was taken with a wench, 'we will jest and rail upon the whole order all the year after'.[17] More was in his turn exaggerating, but he was not inventing. Such attitudes were indeed common, and even More did not claim that they were confined to heretics. What seems to have happened, and the problem had been building for a long time, was that a clerical proletariat had developed, prompted partly by an increasing demand for 'massing priests' to serve chantries and guilds. These men were not expected to do much except to say masses for the dead. They had no pastoral responsibilities, and were frequently both underpaid and under employed. The better motivated of them taught schools or acted as parish curates, but they were under no obligation to do so. A number of them took secondary secular employment – and got into typically secular scrapes. The other reason for this oversupply of clergy was that such a career conferred a certain status, and the legal immunities of clerical privilege. It was attractive to a man with a little basic education who had no desire for the hard labour of ordinary secular work. All he needed was a patron and an indulgent bishop, who was well aware that a full complement of clergy in his diocese conferred a certain authority upon him, as a full company of soldiers gave prestige to its captain. It is hardly surprising that ordinations held up well, right to the end of Henry VIII's reign.

Then there was a complete change. Within two years the demand for massing priests and guild chaplains had disappeared entirely, leaving most of the clerical proletariat without gainful employment. Some gave up their orders and returned to secular life. Those with enough basic education became schoolmasters, often at a very humble level, but most struggled to convert themselves into parish curates. At the same time the function of the parish priest changed, with much less emphasis upon the sacraments, only two of which were recognized, and much more upon formal didacticism, particularly preaching. Sermons had always been regarded as a desirable feature of the ministry, but medieval bishops were realistic about the capabilities of their clergy, and for most people outside of London, preaching was a rare treat. Margery Kempe commented on how fast the people came running when a notable preacher visited King's Lynn.[18] John Mirk compromised, offering short and elementary Sunday homilies for use by 'simple priests', and Archbishop Cranmer did the same at a rather higher level with his book of homilies of 1547, which were specifically designed to be read by those who lacked the capacity to write their own. Meanwhile the beleaguered incumbents faced new challenges. If, like most, they were conservatively inclined, they gave formal obedience to the articles and injunctions addressed to them, and did their best to carry on as before, counselling their penitents instead of receiving their confessions, and trying to make the Prayer Book communion as much like the mass as possible.[19] This exposed them to new dangers, because in so doing they had given hostages to fortune. It only needed a small number of committed reformers in a parish to produce charges of dissimulation and backsliding, and although these usually resulted in nothing more severe than a reprimand, the mutual trust which was needed between a priest and his people was thereby undermined. In such disputes it usually happened that the majority sided with the incumbent, but by then the damage had been done. The agitators made themselves thoroughly unpopular, but the authorities (for the time being) were on their side. Charges of more ordinary turpitude also tended to be ideologically motivated. Reformers accused conservative clergy, while Protestant ministers, especially the married ones, were charged with an imaginative range of vices. Medieval parishes had often been hotbeds of contention, over tithes, over rights of patronage and over disputes arising from personal animosities, but to these were now added theological, liturgical and pastoral issues.[20] As a peacemaker, the minister was frequently hamstrung by these animosities, and there can be no doubt that in many parishes the reformation was a deeply divisive process.

However, exaggeration is unhelpful. In large areas of the north and west there was no significant Protestant presence, and disagreements arose mainly over the extent to which it was necessary to submit to authority – either that of the distant council in London or of the scarcely less distant bishop. Similarly, where a Protestant incumbent had the charge of a like-minded congregation, as happened in parts of London, Kent and Essex, conservatives could exert little leverage, and held out for the duration of the regime in resentful silence. It is not surprising that in these circumstances, candidates for ordination fell away steeply. Not only was a career in the Church less attractive in this atmosphere of strife, it was also necessary to have a genuine Protestant vocation, and they were comparatively rare. So rare, indeed, that the bishops were not able to raise the quality of their recruits in the way which they obviously wished. Protestant-ism was a religion of the word, and a knowledge of scripture was high on the list of requirements. When Bishop Hooper conducted his famous visitation of Gloucester diocese in 1551, out of 311 clergy examined, 91 were considered satisfactory, and only eight were 'utterly ignorant'.[21] However, of the remaining 212, all failed to answer one or more of the questions, and Hooper recognized that he had an uphill task. It is unlikely that Gloucester was unique. About 20 per cent of the incumbents were graduates, and only one living was actually vacant at the time. But some 60 of them were former religious, and that recruit-ment helps to explain the lack of vacancies. It is unlikely that most of these were 'Bible-learned' to the extent that the bishop now required. Very few clergy were actually deprived as a result of this visitation, and the remedial action taken was moderate, but Hooper was more careful than most in ensuring that those he ordained were up to scratch.[22] Gloucester was not a diocese where many had strong Protestant priorities, and there was no obvious link between those who failed this examination and conservative predelictions. It was later claimed that the Protestant bishops were so desperate to ordain 'gospellers' that they were willing to overlook any other inadequacy, and conferred orders upon tapsters and ostelers, but that did certainly not happen here. One of the problems of assessing the impact of the Edwardian establishment upon the clergy is that so few of them stood up to be counted. The leaders of the Oxfordshire dissidents in 1549 were priests, some of whom, having been taken in arms against the King, were summarily executed by martial law, 'hanging them from their church tow-ers'.[23] However, the most obviously religious of the risings of that year was that in Devon and Cornwall, the demands of which were written by conservative clergy, and of which the council declared 'the Commons are abused by Popish priests'. When Lord Russell was sent against the rebels in July, he was warned not to trust any of the local gentry unless they were 'fully persuaded for the matter in controversy of religion'.[24] A more typical response, however, was that of Christo-pher Trychay at Morebath. The parish was in the heart of the rebel county, and a contingent of villagers joined the insurgent army, but much as he may have sympathized with them, the priest kept a clean record, doing his best to obey the various instructions which he received, his reluctance being only apparent through the marginal notes which he wrote in the parish accounts. He was vicar from 1520 until his death in 1574.[25]

It is perhaps rather surprising that Archbishop Cranmer should have chosen to rely upon discipline and exhortation to convert his clerical workforce to the new ways. He would have been aware of the fact that most of the Protestant leaders upon whom he relied were already in orders, and he was concerned to place these committed allies in positions of responsibility. However, no training scheme was evolved – or even proposed – for the preparation of non-graduates for the ministry. Bishops required pre-ordination study, and examined candi-dates individually, but for the most part the old slipshod methods continued. It was apparently felt to be more satisfactory to ordain a promising candidate, probably as a deacon, and then for him to learn his role 'on the job' as a curate with an experienced and sympathetic vicar. Sometimes this worked well enough, as the story of Rowland Taylor and his curate demonstrates, but not every vicar was a Rowland Taylor, and the failure to evolve any systematic method for the conversion of literate Protestant laymen into ministers is remarkable.[26] It was not as if the Church was oversubscribed with zealous clergy, which perhaps helps to explain why anti-clericalism was a product of the reformation, rather than a cause of it. The new priest was supposed to be humble, not lordly, his magical 'massing powers' having been taken away; and if he was unable to live chastely, let him now take a wife as other men did. Before the godly reformation, wrote Philip Nichols of Totnes, the clergy had been proud, envious and malicious, indulging in all sorts of sexual misdemeanours. Too little had changed. The conservative clergy of Devon still tried to exercise their old tyrannical domina-tion over an exploited and often acquiescent laity.[27] Expectations of catechizing and teaching had been raised, only to be cruelly disappointed. The parish priest might be obedient to the laws of the Church and state, but that only made the disappointment harder to bear. In short, he was even less qualified for his new function than he had been for the old. Respect for the Church courts declined in proportion, Philip Gammon of Axminster denouncing excommunication as 'a merry conceit' and an 'interlude played of the priests'.[28] A godly minister could overcome such prejudices and earn the respect of his flock, but such men were too few. That minority of laymen who left their opinions on record seem to have been divided between those who were contemptuous of the clergy for failing to live up to their new expectations, and those who were equally contemptuous of them for failing to defend the 'good old ways' to which they were themselves committed. There can be little doubt that the Edwardian reformation weakened the position of the parish clergy, both institutionally and morally; and especially weakened those who were neither heroes nor trained theologians.

The graduate clergy were no more trained for a pastoral ministry than were their less educated colleagues, and a degree was no protection against moral turpitude, but the intellectual training which they had undergone did guarantee a more focused approach to the job in hand. Their numbers varied from diocese to diocese, being highest in Oxford, Ely and London, but Gloucester at 20 per cent was by no means untypical of the outlying bishoprics.[29] Cranmer turned a searching eye on the universities, commissioning visitations of both during the spring and summer of 1549. Although he was primarily concerned to issue new statutes to each, and with the regulation of their government, he was also mindful of the need to impose some control over what these aspiring ordinands were actually taught. In opening the visitation of Cambridge, Nicholas Ridley preached of the need to renounce papistry and superstition before proceeding to a detailed examination of each college. At Clare Hall the visitors expelled the master, Rowland Swinburn, and at Jesus demolished six altars in the college chapel.[30] Lest there should be any misunderstanding of the main thrust of their purpose, on Corpus Christi day, 20 June, they presided over a formal disputation on the proposition that the scriptures did not sanction transubstantiation, and that the Eucharist was purely a ceremony of thanksgiving. The former chancellor, Stephen Gardiner, who had done his best to protect the university from Protestant inroads, was by this time in prison and had been replaced by Lord Protector Somerset. Somerset had relaxed all controls on the discussion of Protestant theology, and not long before the visitation had appointed the Strasburg reformer Martin Bucer to the Regius chair of divinity.[31] Bucer was to survive the East Anglian climate for only some sixteen months, but in the course of that time he built up a devoted following, and several of those who were to die in the Marian persecution owed their conversion to his influence. Anyone graduating from Cambridge University between 1549 and 1553 was likely to be thoroughly imbued with the principles of the Swiss reformation. In June 1553 all members proceeding to the degrees of MA, BD and DD were required to assent to the Forty Two Articles.[32]

In Oxford things were rather different. In spite of having advised Henry sympathetically over his annulment issue, and accepted the Royal Supremacy without demur, it maintained a much more conservative theological tradition. Some colleges, notably Magdalen, resisted the visitation tooth and nail. Already in 1548, Somerset had required the arch-conservative Richard Smyth to stand down from the Regius chair, and had appointed the expatriate Italian Peter Martyr Vermigli in his place.[33] Martyr's theology was every bit as Protestant as Bucer's, and he lacked Bucer's irenic temperament. Placed in the hostile environment of conservative Oxford, he was soon involved in furious quarrels, and it was as much to spite him as for any other reason that in 1550 a bunch of students endeavoured to set up another disputation on transubstantiation, this time under the moderation of Dr William Chedsey, who was described as 'a great papist'.[34] However, despite these controversies (and perhaps because of them), Martyr built up a party of supporters, centred on his own college of Christ Church, where the dean, Richard Cox became a warm advocate. As a source of Protestant clergy, Oxford was less reliable than Cambridge, but at least those graduates who were of that persuasion were suitably battle-hardened for the conflicts which they would endure in their parishes. Sir John Mason, a 'trimmer' who contrived to serve on the Privy Councils of both Edward and Mary, was the chancellor. It was Cambridge which first felt the impact of Mary's success in July 1553, because it had the misfortune to be on the route which the Duke of Northumberland followed on his way to confront her. On the 15th he ordered the vice chancellor, Edwin Sandys, to preach in favour of Queen Jane, an indiscretion for which Sandys was forced to resign within a matter of days as political fortune deserted the Duke.[35] He was replaced with a safe conservative. At the same time Stephen Gardiner was reinstated as chancellor, a fact which may explain the high priority which Mary gave to the universities in her programme to re-establish the Catholic Church. In an instruction dated 20 August, she ordered Mason and Gardiner to reinstate the ancient statutes of both, and to see that they were strictly observed. Within a month the mass had been reinstated in the college chapels, and the exodus of Protestant fellows and students had begun.[36] After a brief but bitter rearguard action, Peter Martyr was allowed to return whence he had come.

As we have seen, Reginald Pole visited both institutions, and the academic curriculum was returned to its traditional mode. So effective was Pole's regiment that, in spite of its short duration, the students – and particularly the younger ones – responded enthusiastically to the allure of Catholic humanism, and would no doubt have justified his expectations as ordained clergy of the English Church. As it was, the return of Protestantism drove many of the brightest of them out, and Pole's legacy as a university reformer was to be found in Europe. Thomas Harding and Edmund Campion were among his heirs.[37] The Cardinal's concern for the state of the universities was directly linked to his desire for a preaching clergy. Sermons, he was at pains to point out, were desirable, and a necessary part of pastoral provision; but they had to be 'good' sermons. This meant not only theologically correct, but sound in their biblical exegesis. There had been far too much 'bad' preaching in recent years; not only offering unsound expositions, but often ribald and abusive of traditional doctrine. They had also been confrontational, and that was not the purpose of preaching. In London and some other major cities, sermons had become a form of popular entertainment, and star performers had attracted big crowds. What was now needed was systematic and orthodox exegisis on a regular basis, without polemical overtones, which only played into the hands of their opponents.[38] It would be better by far, he observed, if congregations would observe the ceremonies which had now been restored, and which were good exercises in discipline and obedience, rather than that they should go 'gadding' to these gladiatorial displays. He also knew his clergy well enough not to expect most of them to preach. Bishop Bonner (in imitation of Cranmer) had produced an excellent set of Catholic homilies for the use of such priests, and they should not aspire beyond their capacity. The purpose of the reform of the universities had not been so much to increase the proportion of licensed preachers as to guarantee the quality of what was on offer.

Before November 1554 the English clergy in general faced a dilemma. Because they had submitted to a heretical regime, and had conducted heretical services, they were in theory incapable of saying mass without being dispensed, and there was no authority within England which was capable of issuing such dispensations. Even Bishop Stephen Gardiner, who had gone to prison for the right to say mass (among other things), had previously served the schismatic Henry VIII, and had had no connection with Rome since 1534. A few individuals, notably Mary and Gardiner himself, seem to have sought absolution from the Cardinal Legate long before they were legally entitled to do so, but that did not amount to a full reconciliation.[39] It was cover enough for Mary to be crowned and for Gardiner to celebrate high mass on that occasion; but questions could have been asked about the legitimacy of the Queen's coronation, had anyone been disposed to ask them. A few other clergy, most notably conservative bishops, also seem to have sought Pole's good offices ahead of his restitution, but it was only in February 1555 that this anomalous situation was finally rectified. On the 15th of that month Pole issued a commission to Bonner, Bishop of London, authorizing him to reconcile to the Catholic Church anyone, priest or layman, who would require it of him.[40] He could delegate this power to any other priest or bishop who was already reconciled. Presumably thousands of men sought this dispensation, and several hundred appear to have approached Pole directly, but during the eighteen months which separated Mary's accession from the reconciliation with Rome, many thousands of clergy were celebrating mass illegally. No one seems to have minded very much.

There were plenty of worse problems to preoccupy the Cardinal Legate. One of the most obvious was the unexpected defiance of the Protestant leaders, but there were others of a more routine nature. Pluralism, for example, had been a bane of the Western Church for centuries. Stringent rules had been laid down as early as the Lateran Council of 1215. John XXII had decreed in 1317 that no priest, however distinguished, could hold more than one benefice with cure of souls, on pain of losing all his preferments.[41] However, the practice had persisted, not least because it was needed to attract talented graduates into the Church. There were simply not enough rich livings to go round, and pluralism was needed to provide a suitable level of reward. Pole was temperamentally inclined to be severe, but he also cherished graduate clergy, and so negotiated scores of dispensations during his time in office. The situation which he inherited was determined by an Act of Parliament of 1529, which decreed that any pluralist holding a benefice worth more than £8 would have the first incumbency invalidated and his dispensation annulled. The Act, however, was full of loopholes, and although Cranmer seems to have abided by it scrupulously, it went nowhere near solving the problem.[42] Pole, interestingly, seems to have accepted Cranmer's dispensations, and thereby the validity of the Act. It had been passed before the 'cut off point' of 1533, but was still an intrusion into what should have been ecclesiastical territory. There seems to have been an assumption that benefices held in plurality needed to be compatible, that is within easy reach of each other, and many of the applications for dispensations stress this aspect. However, there is no evidence that the Cardinal ever required that, and he was perfectly well aware that the pluralist would normally keep a curate in his second (and third) benefice. Richard Thornden, the Bishop of Dover, held many benefices, and did not live in any of them, but he was exceptional.[43] One of the reasons for Pole's indulgence in this respect may have been the knowledge that there was no shortage of 'massing priests' willing to do the routine work of these parishes. Having fallen off alarmingly after 1547, there was again no shortage of candidates for ordination after 1553, but although this was reassuring in respect of the status of the profession, it was also a worrying tendency. There was no guarantee that these new priests would be any better in terms of quality than their predecessors had been. Restoring the old ways meant restoring some of the old vices as well.

It was this consideration which led Pole into one of his most innovative and far-reaching experiments. The Legatine Synod which he convened in November 1556 was predominantly concerned with the state of the clergy. After starting off with two decrees of general application, one on the commemoration of the reconciliation and the other on the proper function and nature of canon law, it then got down to business with a decree on residence.[44] This was aimed principally at cathedral chapters, and laid down complex rules for the division of the prebendaries' time between the close and their parishes of title. The fourth decree was on preaching, but was aimed at bishops and other dignitaries, rather than at the general run of clergy, and was concerned to make sure that they set a good example.[45] It was, however, in the fifth and sixth decrees that the real issues began to be addressed. 'Example of life is a kind of preaching' began the fifth, 'not less effective than by the Word of God'. All clergy were to live 'soberly, chastely and piously', eschewing fashionable clothing and expensive foods. They were not to employ superfluous servants, and were to give any surplus income to the poor. Above all they were to wear clerical dress in public and to be suitably tonsured.[46] The sixth was a warning to ordinaries not to confer orders lightly, and to examine all candidates strictly. There is nothing surprising in these decrees, which reflect a proper sense of pastoral responsibility, except perhaps that they were considered to be necessary. If we take them at their face value, they indicate a considerable gulf between the aspiration and the reality, but perhaps they were doing no more than laying down benchmarks for the future.

The seventh, eighth, ninth and tenth decrees all relate to the bestowal of benefices, to advowsons and to the leasing of property, the ninth being directed against simony, but it is in the eleventh decree that these various threads are all pulled together. 'Since at this moment', it begins somewhat mendaciously,

> there is a great scarcity of ecclesiastical persons, especially of ones suitable to be put in charge of churches or clerical duties, or to serve in them; and this inconvenience can be in no way better met than by forming and preserving in cathedral churches a sort of nursery, or seminary of ministers. Therefore with the approval of this Synod, we enact and decree that all metropolitan and cathedral churches of this realm be obliged to bring up a certain number of youths in proportion to their respective incomes and means, and the size of their dioceses.[47]

The youths chosen for these academies had to be at least eleven or twelve years old, literate in English, and well disposed to the priesthood. It was expected that they would have studied for a while in a grammar school before transferring to the seminary, and would therefore have a basic knowledge of Latin. Once at the cathedral they were to be taught theology and ecclesiastical discipline, and were to be divided into two classes by age, both to be tonsured and to wear clerical dress. The older class should be in minor orders as acolytes, and when suitably advanced in age and learning should proceed to the other minor orders and 'lend their assistance to the cathedral ... in whatever office may seem fit to the bishop and chapter'.[48] The costs of this education were to be borne by the cathedral, with the younger boys receiving their keep, and the older a small stipend as befitted their greater experience and value. There could also be a reserve of boys held in the grammar school to take the place of a seminarian who dropped out for any reason, and they would also be given basic instruction to prepare them for the change. The oversight of these seminaries was to rest with the dean and chapter, who were also to be responsible for the appointments of masters to do the actual teaching.[49] Given the nature of these institutions, ordinary pedagogic competence was not sufficient. 'We therefore enact' the decree proceeds,

> that no one be appointed master in any school in any place whatsoever, or in any way exercise the office of teacher unless he has first been carefully examined and approved by the local ordinary, and charged respecting the books to be read in schools, as well for instruction in leaning as for improving the morals of youth[50]

A twelfth decree concerned the visitation of churches as being 'useful but also necessary for the removal of abuses and corruptions', but the key to understanding what Pole was about lies in this eleventh decree, which in due course was to provide the inspiration for a similar edict by the Council of Trent, and thus indirectly for seminaries all over Europe in the late sixteenth and seventeenth centuries.

The Synod was adjourned on 10 February 1557, and never reconvened because Pole's Legatine status was withdrawn, so its draft decrees have uncertain status. Both Pole and Mary died in the following November, and the scheme was never implemented. Had it been so, it might still not have solved the problem presented by untrained and poorly motivated priests, but it would at least have provided a beginning. There were rather more than thirty cathedrals and minsters in England and Wales, so if each had been equipped with a seminary there would have been well over 1,000 boys undergoing training at any one time, and these would have been released into the Church at the rate of about 300 a year.[51] They would have belonged to the 'middle class' of clergy, similar to those who had previously joined the profession directly from the grammar schools, but in addition to a reasonable education, they would also have received a theological and pastoral training which was not on offer elsewhere. The weakness of the system was that it did not seek to make the seminaries and universities the only routes into the ministry. The ordinary was supposed to examine all candidates thoroughly, but that had always been the case and too much still rested on his discretion. It would have been better if all candidates had been subject to examination by some independent body, a Legatine commission perhaps. However, such an option seems not to have been considered.

Although he was averse to confrontational preaching, Pole was very much concerned that his clergy should have the necessary equipment to combat the well-informed heretics that they were now liable to encounter. It would no doubt have been easier simply to retreat from this situation, relying upon sacraments and ceremonies to revive the traditional faith, and upon the renewed authority of the priesthood to enforce compliance. But Pole regarded such an approach as defeatist. Although at the end of the day ecclesiastical authority might have to be invoked, it was much better to use persuasion, and for that knowledge was necessary. Consequently every priest, whether educated or not, was required to familiarize himself with the scriptures, and to 'diligently study' Bonner's *Profitable and Necessarye Doctryne, with certayne Homelies*.[52] It was this positive approach to reviving the faith which lay behind the decree on seminaries. As Gilbert Burnet put it, writing more than a century later,

> There was offered to them a schedule of some terms that were to be carefully considered in the translation of the New Testament. On the 8 January [1557] that was again considered: propositions were also made, for having schools in all cathedral churches. Thus Pole found it necessary to give some instruction in the matters of religion to the nation: for an earnest desire of knowledge in these points, being once raised and encouraged, it was neither safe nor easy quite to extinguish that, which is so natural to man; and therefore instead of discouraging all knowledge, and bringing men to the state of implicit faith, without any sort of enquiry, he chose to give them such a measure of knowledge as might be governed and kept within bounds[53]

However, the Cardinal's strategy was long term. Even if the decree had been implemented at once, it would have been two or three years before the first of these newly prepared priests was posted to duty, and in the event nothing happened. Nor was the idea taken up by the Elizabethan regime which followed, although complaints about the inadequacy of the clergy went on increasing. It was not until the classical movement of the 1570s that any serious attempt was made to improve the educational standard of the non-graduate clergy.[54] From the earliest days of her reign, Mary's attitude towards clergy training had been first and foremost disciplinary. Gardiner had been much more concerned to reimpose the traditional canon law, removing heretics and married clergy, than he had been with the state of their doctrinal knowledge. His attitude seems to have been that the removal of error was sufficient, and that the sacramental nature of the restored Church made anything more sophisticated unnecessary. He may also have considered that his task was an interim one, in any case, and that it would be up to the Cardinal Legate to decide what more was needed. Although it took him some time to appraise the situation, Pole eventually came to the conclusion that a great deal more was needed – nothing less, in fact than the reconversion of England. The simple conservatism which welcomed the return of the mass and other traditional ceremonies was no more than a beginning. It lacked any degree of that positive intellectual conviction which it soon became apparent that the leading Protestants had.[55] The Church had moved on since the 1520s, and what had been an adequate clerical commitment then was no longer so. Twenty years of schism and heresy had forced the orthodox to raise their game, hence the concentration on the universities, where such challenges could best be met.

Nevertheless he had to work with the material which was to hand, and about 80 per cent of the clergy in post were non-graduates. For them the elimination of error and the imposition of discipline would have, for the time being, to suffice. Nevertheless a kind of mindless ritualism was the lowest common denominator, which may help to explain the Cardinal's lack of enthusiasm for the revival of chantries, which tended to encourage the clerical proletariat. He was entirely sympathetic to prayers for the dead, and embraced the doctrine of purgatory, but did nothing to favour those who might have aspired to a permanent commemoration.[56] In an ideal world, all priests would have been graduates, and capable of battling heresy at the highest level; but the world was not ideal, and the intellectual capacity of most of the clergy was distinctly limited. So he confined himself to the *Profitable and Necessarye Doctryne* and to the Bible. His plan for seminaries was in a way a compromise, an attempt to raise the intellectual level of the non-graduate clergy. Perhaps in due course he might have made this the only alternative route of access to the priesthood, but his time was short. What we do know is that Reginald Pole took the state of the clergy and their lack of professional training very seriously. It would not be with singing masses and going on processions that the Catholic Church would have to be defended in the future, but with the hard graft of theology and a proper devotion to the spiritual well-being of their flocks.

7 THE FACE OF PERSECUTION

Persecution is a victim's word. None of the magistrates, parochial officials and good citizens who were described as 'persecutors' in the marginalia of Foxe's great work would have acknowledged such a description of themselves. They were just doing a job in the service of the Church and of the Queen, although some of them were not above enjoying themselves in the process. 'Mr Justice Nine Holes' who was later accused of having drilled holes in the sanctuary screen in order to observe those who slept during the sermon, or failed to adore the host at mass, admitted the fact but denied the motivation. He had been concerned, he claimed 'to spy on pretty wenches'.[1] He could equally have pleaded the specific instructions which the council issued from time to time, to commit to ward all seditious persons who absented themselves from divine service. How was he supposed to know who was there, without his peep-holes? Such instructions were sent to the justices of the peace of Norfolk in May 1554, and similar letters went to other counties.[2] In a sense the persecution was very 'top-down', driven first by Gardiner and the Queen and latterly by Reginald Pole. It could hardly have been anything else, given the role of the courts, and ultimately of the Crown, in imposing penalties. Nevertheless there was also a sense in which it was community action; neighbour denounced neighbour, and even families reported their delinquent members to the authorities. Behind each story there was no doubt a different set of circumstances, and Foxe, upon whom we are reliant for most of this kind of information, often did not understand these himself.

Most of the early victims were clergy, and the nature of their beliefs was in the public domain. They were normally arrested for marriage, for preaching false doctrine or otherwise trying to discharge their usual functions. The story of Rowland Taylor, although not typical, may be taken as representative.[3] Taylor, who was backed by a strong party within his parish of Hadleigh, simply ignored the first act of repeal, abolishing the Edwardian services, and carried on as before, preaching 'most faithfully and earnestly' against the 'popish corruptions which had infected the whole country round about'. This, of course, could not carry on, and as Easter approached his opponents, who appear not to have been numerous, decided to force the issue. They imported a compliant priest, one

John Averth, described by Foxe as a 'right papist', to say mass in Hadleigh church without notifying Taylor of their intention. Clerke and Foster, the two leaders of the conspiracy, spent two days building an altar for their celebrant, only to have it demolished and to have to repeat the proceedings. Incredibly, Taylor appears to have known nothing about what was going on under his nose. When the day came, Averth, who clearly understood the attitude of most of Hadleigh, turned up with an armed escort, and Taylor, alerted by the commotion, duly appeared to forbid the celebration. In so doing, of course, he walked into a trap, 'Foster, with an irefull and furious countenance, sayd unto Doctour Taylor "Thou traitor, what doest thou here to let and disturb the Queenes proceedings … ?"'[4]

Taylor replied that it was his parish and he had every right to be there, commanding the intruders to depart in the name of God. Averth, who knew that he was canonically correct, might have given way at that point, but Clerke and Foster, using their armed escort, frogmarched the vicar out of the church and forced their mass priest to proceed. There was a riot, because such action was not at all to the taste of the people of Hadleigh, who, we are told, 'would have rent their Sacrifice in pieces', and bombarded the ceremony with rocks, hurled through the windows. Needless to say, Foster and Clerke complained to Stephen Gardiner, and within a few days Rowland Taylor was summoned to appear before the bishop. This is, of course, the story as told by Foxe, who was concerned to emphasize Taylor's popularity in the town and the 'godliness' of his stand. Modern research has suggested that there might be another way of looking at these events which would be less complimentary to the vicar, but the fact remains that he was in trouble.[5]

His friends urged him to flee, and it may be that Gardiner intended no less, giving him due warning of his interview.[6] Taylor, however, decided that it was his duty to stay and to testify to his faith, a decision which was eventually justified by events. After an exhaustive examination, in which Gardiner did his best to win his compliance, he was deprived as a married priest, and consigned to prison to await trial for heresy. He was one of those designated for the first 'show trial' of Pole's Legateship, which took place in February 1555, and thereafter, in accordance with the policy then being pursued, was sent down to Hadleigh for execution.[7] This was intended to be a terrible example to deter the like-minded, and there were no doubt some in the town who were glad enough to see him die, but to most he had been an exemplary husband and father, and a pastor who had done his duty as he perceived it. According to Foxe

> The streets of Hadley were beset on both sides the way with men and women of the town and countrey who waited to see him; whom when they beheld so led it death, with weeping eyes and lamentable voices they cryed, saying one to another, ah, good Lord, there goeth one good shepherd from us, that so faithfully hath taught us, so fatherly hath cared for us & so godly hath governed us. Oh Merciful God, what shall we poore scattered Lambes do?[8]

He was not allowed to make any public speech, but contrived to make his prayers do that work for him. He died with great courage and composure, and the whole event was something of a public relations disaster as far as the government was concerned – although it is only fair to add that the officials who were responsible would not have seen it in that light. Another heretic had been despatched in fulfilment of the law. A conservative incumbent had already been installed at Hadleigh, but he had a hard act to follow, and a hard congregation to persuade.[9]

Taylor was a learned man, and chose his course of action deliberately. He had a flock to defend, and if he could not do that by teaching, he would have to do it by example. He may well have been aware of the effect which John Barret's submission had had upon the godly congregation in Norwich, and to have been determined that no such excuse should be given to his own people.[10] He chose death rather than flight, because he considered it to be his duty. Meanwhile another drama was unfolding on the other side of the country, where duty in the formal sense was not an element. Rawlins White was an illiterate Cardiff fisherman, just about as different from Rowland Taylor as he could well be. White had become intrigued by the English Bible, and finding the task of reading beyond him, put his young son to school, so that the boy would be able to read it to him. He soon discovered that his memory was greater than his literacy, and he was able to repeat whole chapters by heart.[11] Early in the reign of Edward VI he underwent a conversion experience, and found his scriptural recitations much in demand. Cardiff was a conservative town, where the local incumbent was a conformist, and White began to find his audiences turning into converts, so that his meetings became rather like those of the 'known men' of the previous period – within the Church, but going beyond it. When Mary came to the throne, and the majority reverted to their masses and other ceremonies, White and his friends went underground.

> Rawlins [as Foxe put it], did not altogether use open instruction and admonition [as before he was wont] and therefore oftentime in some private place or another, he would call his trusty friends together, & with earnest prayer and great lamentation passed away the time[12]

Apparently the warning signs provoked by this kind of behaviour soon became apparent, and his friends urged him to escape. White, however, although he had no pastoral responsibility, elected to stay, reminding his colleagues

> that he had learned one good lesson, touching the denial and confession of Christ, advertising them that if he upon their persuasions should presume to deny his master Christ, Christ in the last day would deny and utterly condemn him[13]

Not surprisingly 'at the last he was taken by the officers of the town, as man suspected of heresie', and brought before Bishop Anthony Kitchen. Kitchen was no persecutor, and would have been glad to be rid of his prisoner. He offered him numerous opportunities to escape, but White was not in a co-operative state of mind. Both at Chepstow and at Cardiff Castle he occupied himself with prayer, and with exhortations to any who had access to him, 'admonishing them always to beware of false prophets'. After enduring this provocation for almost a year in the hope of persuading him to conformity the bishop somewhat wearily pointed out that that if he did not submit, he would be compelled to use the rigour of the law against him. Kitchen tried White by his own authority, proceeding with prayer, 'which commonly the popish persecutors are not wont to doe'. However, Rawlins, unabashed, merely told him that the false God which he worshipped would never answer his prayer, and that in any case 'I bowe not to this Idoll, meaning the Host that the priest held over his head' during the mass which preceded the trial.[14] After this demonstration he was duly condemned, and (when someone had remembered to obtain the necessary writ) led out to execution. What then transpired is ostensibly an eyewitness account by one Mr Dane, and narrates the struggle of White's conscience between his duty to God (as he saw it) and his duty to his wife and family, who were present to witness his death. This was something of a trope for the godly death of any married man, but there is no reason to doubt that it actually happened. Slightly less convincing is the story that a man who had always walked with a stoop should suddenly appear at the stake upright and dignified. A similar story is told of Hugh Latimer, and seems to have been taken as evidence of divine favour. According to Dane, Rawlins's friends rallied round him at the end, taking him by the hand, much to the chagrin of the 'popish priest' who had been brought in to preach the usual edifying sermon. Apparently the sheriff made no attempt to stop this procedure, but from the absence of any report to the contrary, it does not do to assume a sympathetic crowd. Most of them had probably turned up with same kind of indifferent curiosity that attracted them to the public hanging of felons.[15] Rawlins White had made his point, but it would be hard to say whether anyone benefited very much from it. Like other acts of self sacrifice, it was a gesture of personal integrity, made in terms which his contemporaries would have understood.

George Marsh is interesting from a different point of view, not because of his doctrine or the circumstances of his death, but for the manner of his arrest. Marsh was a Lancashire man and a Cambridge graduate, who had taken orders under Edward VI and returned to a curacy in his native Bolton, where he built up a circle of like-minded friends. Unusually, Bolton was a divided town, with a significant Protestant minority, to which Marsh went on ministering after Mary's accession. Then, on 12 March 1554, while visiting his mother's house, he was warned that several of Mr Barton's servants were seeking for him.[16] Barton was an officer of the Earl of Derby, and his intention was to bring Marsh before the Earl 'to be examined in matters of Religion'. Derby was a well-known religious conservative, but he appears to have been acting in this connection without any specific commission, simply using the weight of his traditional authority in the area. Marsh's friends, of course, advised flight, but after a rather perfunctory struggle with his conscience, he took leave of his family and gave himself up. Barton placed him under bonds to appear before the Earl at Lathom. So he said goodbye to his mother, and the next day rode over to Lathom. The Earl was in session with his council, most of whom were laymen, and immediately challenged him with sowing 'evill sede and dissention among the people', a charge which he denied. Accused of being an evil priest, he also denied being any such thing, because 'by the lawes nowe used in this Realme (as farre an I do know) I am none'.[17] This was strictly accurate because his orders had been conferred under the 1550 ordinal, which was not recognized in Marian England.[18] He was also frank with his interrogators. He had ministered to his congregation as long as the laws allowed, and if the present laws changed, he would do so again. He was commanded to write his answers, and committed to prison for two days. When he was summoned again on Palm Sunday, he found that the Earl's council had been augmented by one or two of the bishop's chaplains.

With these clergy he then had a long and predictable debate about the mass, punctuated with pleas to return to the truth of the Catholic Church. At the end of this time he was committed to Lancaster Castle, to appear before the next sessions. It was only at this late stage that the Bishop of Chester, George Cotes, became involved. Visiting Lancaster about some other business, he was apprised of Marsh's presence in the prison, and at once decided that he was a heretic. Whisking him off to Chester, he brought him before his consistory court, sitting in the cathedral, where in due course he was condemned.[19] Presumably Marsh would have ended up before the bishop in any case, but the initiative was taken against him by the Earl of Derby, not by any private informant and not, as far as we can see, as a result of any unlawful activity upon which he was actively engaged. The Earl was concerned to demonstrate his loyalty and zeal, and probably to live down his reluctant conformity to the Edwardian Church, so he acted on the basis of information which was already in his possession. An even better example of the same motivation is provided by Lord Rich of Leighs in Essex, who, as Foxe notes in bitter aside, had passed for an ardent gospeller under the Protestant government.[20] Having effectively turned his coat in the summer of 1553, he had a lot to prove, and was on the lookout for cases to help his cause. Such a one was provided by Thomas Wattes, a linen draper of Billericay. Wattes had been a leading member of the Protestant movement in the town, and had attracted personal as well as religious animosity. Seeing which way the wind was setting after Mary's accession, he sold off the contents of his shop and, having made provision for his wife and children, gave the balance to the poor, 'for he looked always to be taken by God's adversaries and his'.[21] Who these enemies were is not apparent, but they must have included some of the constables or other officers of the town, because on 26 April 1555 he was arrested and brought before Lord Rich and the other commissioners of oyer and terminer at Chelmsford.[22] This time the involvement of the justices was brief. Having examined him and decided that he was a heretic – and one moreover who had the temerity to remind Rich of his previous allegiance – the very next day they sent him, with an appropriate covering letter, to Bishop Bonner. The charge of refusing to go to church was adequately proved, and the rest was down to the Consistory court. Wattes was given comparatively short shrift, and on 10 June went to stake at Chelmsford, blaming Lord Rich for his death, rather than the bishop who had condemned him.

On the whole, there seems to have been little animosity against Protestants as such, although personal quarrels sometimes resulted in denunciations. Usually some specific incentive was required. Thomas Whittle, an Essex minister, was, we are told, denounced by one Edward Alblaster 'in the hope of reward or promotion', although whether this was a hope or an expectation is not clear.[23] Alblaster may have been the sort of parish promoter whom Edward Underhill noticed at work in the capital. 'This Banbery ... was the spy for Stepney parish; as John Avales, Beard and such others were for London',[24] although whether these were self appointed or had any official status is not clear. Given the perceived need to clear out nests of heretics, and the apparent lack of enthusiasm for such tasks among the people at large, it is quite likely that they were akin to the old summoners and pardoners, and worked on a commission basis. How widespread this practice may have been is not apparent. Because he is concerned to argue the godliness and determination of his victims, Foxe is not much concerned with false accusations, nor with the large number of those who submitted. The typical face of Marian Protestantism was not the martyr, or the exile, but the humble convert who had 'tasted the gospel' in Edward's reign, and had liked what he saw. Sometimes, as with the congregations at Norwich, they had submitted at once to 'the Queen's proceedings'. Sometimes they used a simple device, like moving house, to avoid drawing attention to themselves, as Edward Underhill did in London.[25] Sometimes they waited until the churchwardens or other officers came around, and then, having had their day in court and testified (after a fashion), submitted and performed the penance assigned.

Private issues can sometimes be read between the lines. Alice Benden was denounced by her husband, in what was surely more than an act of pious devotion. Richard Woodman was handed over by his brother, apparently with the connivance of their father, who hoped to lay hands on Richard's goods. In this they would appear to have displayed an ignorance of the law, because when Woodman was executed (as he eventually was) all his property was forfeit to the Crown.[26] However the most conspicuous (and rare) case of a prosecution being driven by private malice comes in the trial of three Guernsey women, Catherine Cawches and her two daughters Guillemine Gilbert and Perotine Massey. Arrested originally upon a false charge of receiving stolen goods, when they were acquitted the constable, Nicholas Cary, who was no doubt feeling rather foolish, had them rearrested on a charge of not going to church. This being an ecclesiastical issue, they were then handed over to the dean of the island, Jacques Amy.[27] Amy seems to have decided that these were undesirables, perhaps because Perotine was married to the fugitive Protestant pastor David Jores, a marriage which Amy would not have recognized. The women were undoubtedly Protestants, but when confronted with the court, they submitted unconditionally to the King's and Queen's Acts, and to the church as it was presently constituted. Nevertheless witnesses were called against them, who testified that they had been absent from church, and had used various insulting epithets to describe the mass. On this basis, they were condemned and burned.[28] Quite apart from the impropriety of executing heretics who had submitted, and not relapsed, Perotine was heavily pregnant at the time, and should at least have been reprieved until after the birth had taken place. The result was one of the most graphic and horrible scenes of the whole persecution, when, in the agony of the fire, the woman actually gave birth, and the presiding official ordered the newly born infant to be consigned to the flames also.

Much of the evidence of the Guernsey case was provided by Thomas Effart, who served as a jurat from 1558, and would have had access to all the trial papers. He may also have been an eyewitness of the events themselves, and although his sympathies were with the victims, there is no reason to doubt the substantial accuracy of his account.[29] The case is also unusual in that it was investigated by an Elizabethan commission, which came substantially to the same conclusion. The exact reason for the animus which was displayed against these women remains unclear, but it was an exceptional case, and the fact that Thomas Harding went out of his way to blacken their reputation – even accusing Perotine of murder – is an indication that the Church had an uneasy conscience about these victims, which certainly did not apply to the majority of those executed.[30]

The Guernsey case is also unusual in that it involved the testimony of witnesses. Indeed the only evidence against them came from that source, because the women were not examined as to the state of their beliefs. The normal procedure was for the accused to be interrogated. If these (sometimes colourful) exchanges were with the secular magistrates it was to establish a *prima facie* case for heresy proceedings, in the same way as a similar examination in quarter sessions would be designed to create a case which could be submitted to the assizes. Once a case had been referred to the bishop's consistory, or to the legatine commissioners, the whole process began again, sometimes at intolerable length and on numerous occasions. In the case of a learned cleric, or a gentleman (of whom there were a few), these sessions might well be interspersed with private consultations, either with the bishop himself or with some learned man designated by him.[31] The efforts made to secure recantations were often considerable, and no doubt succeeded on many occasions. Foxe was only concerned with those which failed. It may also be that witnesses were more frequently called in cases where the accused denied the charges, and which resulted in submissions, because Foxe was concerned to show his martyrs testifying to the truth that was in them, and conviction by the testimony of witnesses does not conform to that model. Minor laity were handled much more briefly. A set of articles would be issued to them, covering the main points of the faith, such as transubstantiation, to which they would be invited to subscribe. When they refused, various threats and inducements would be offered, which would vary with the person and circumstances. If these were unavailing, sentence would be pronounced and the condemned person handed over to the secular authorities.[32] The whole process might take only a matter of days. On the other hand, they might be returned to prison and left for several months. This was done, less in the hope of a recantation than because of delays in obtaining the necessary writ, or sheer administrative indifference. It may also have been in the mind of the officials that a spell in prison would do their work for them. According to John Foxe, five such victims were 'famished to death' in Canterbury Castle in 1556, because they had either fallen out with their families, or had no family to appeal to.[33] It was the responsibility of each prisoner to provide for his own food and clothing, and in the absence, or unwillingness, of a family to shoulder the responsibility, it fell upon the 'godly brethren', and it may have been in this case that the congregation was too intimidated to act. There were many, particularly gentlewomen, who were prepared to brave ecclesiastical displeasure to perform this necessary service, even for the very humble, but in this case there was no one to act. As Foxe observed, it is hard to say whether a swift and agonizing death in the flames is to be preferred to the slow death of starvation. Both were to him unacceptable faces of persecution.

On the whole, and with certain notorious exceptions, conforming parishioners were much less likely to denounce their suspect neighbours than were incumbents and parish officials. It usually required some calculated act of defiance to draw attention to the delinquents, and it is surprising to notice how often deliberate words or gestures resulted in arrests.[34] It frequently seems as though the Protestants were challenging the authorities to take action against them – and perhaps in a sense they were. But how did those same conformists react when their Protestant neighbours were led out to be burned? Foxe's accounts are suspect in this connection, because he was trying to make a point, and reading between the lines a more ambiguous picture emerges. In some cases the victims' sympathizers crowded around the stake, praying audibly for God to strengthen them in their ordeal. They took him (or her) by the hand, and even pledged them in draughts of ale.[35] Either the presiding sheriff was unable to check this behaviour, or refrained from doing so in order to avoid a 'commotion', or riot, that most dreaded of all sixteenth-century signs of discontent. His authority was upheld by a contingent of 'billmen', or soldiers, but these would have been drawn from the local levies, and even if they had tried to do their duty, would have been too few to pit against an angry crowd. The crowds, however, were never that threatening, and no one was ever rescued from a burning by that means. At the same time, although less commonly, there were hostile demonstrations, cries of 'heretic' from the spectators, and even on one occasion a log of wood thrown at the victim.[36] The presiding sheriffs also varied. Some were doing their duty with evident distaste, and were prepared to allow the victims as many comforts as they conveniently could, most notably opportunities to address the crowd, and to pray with their supporters. Some were 'cruel', and either out of zeal or apprehension insisted upon silence, even curtailing the use of gunpowder with which some sympathizers hoped to shorten the sufferings of those about to die. On various occasions 'spies' were planted in the crowd, often but not always priests, who made it their business to note the names of any who were conspicuous among the supporters, and to 'trouble' them thereafter. Cecily Ormes was taken by this means for pledging Elizabeth Cooper at her burning by one 'Master Corbet of Sprowston', and was subsequently tried and executed for the same offence.[37]

When Joyce Lewes was burned in Lichfield in September 1557, she had been at some pains to organize such a gesture of support. The night before her death, she had

> desired certain of her friends to come to her, with whom, when they came, she consulted how she might behave herself, that her death might be more glorious to the name of God, comfortable to His people, and also most discomfortable to the enemies of God.[38]

What then happened is somewhat confused, because although the demonstration duly took place, there was also a counter-demonstration which may (or may not) have been organized by the authorities, and a 'plant' detected the names of nine Lichfield women and two men who had 'pledged' with her. There were more than that involved, but they came from Coventry, and the informant did not know their names. This was certainly not a spontaneous gesture of support, but rather a calculated activity by the evangelical community of Lichfield, but all those arraigned for their part in it subsequently recanted. Some demonstrations appear to have been genuinely spontaneous, as when John Laurence was burned at Colchester in March 1555, and was surrounded by children crying 'Lord strengthen thy servant' or when Alexander Grouche and Alice Driver went to the stake at Ipswich in November 1558, and the support was so strong that the sheriff decided to refrain from trying to arrest all those who were involved in the community psalm-singing, which was the method of support chosen on that occasion.[39] Such gestures were by no means risk-free, and Foxe's chronicling of them should be taken seriously, but when he makes no mention of them, it is reasonable to suppose that they did not happen.

The authorities were well aware that they had a battle on their hands, and that in a sense every burning was a defeat for them. They tried executing heretics in their places of origin or, in the case of clergy, the place where they had last ministered, but this usually meant taking them where Protestantism was strong and the crowds likely to be hostile. Even taking John Hooper to conservative Gloucester did not really work, because his courage won the respect even of those who had opposed him as bishop.[40] Latterly this didactic aspect of the reign of terror was abandoned in cases which were considered to be potentially troublesome, and it was seriously urged that heretics should be executed very early in the morning, before the crowds were likely to be about. This would, its advocate noted, reduce the need for an armed escort, as well as preserving the sheriff's dignity.[41] In a sense, every burning became a kind of gladiatorial encounter, and one of the chief weapons in the hands of the authorities was the sermon which was invariably preached on such occasions. This was usually delivered by a local incumbent of well-known Catholic sympathies, and sometimes provoked altercations, either with the victim or with a section of the crowd, unless or until the sheriff silenced the dissenters. One of the most famous of these sermons was that preached by Richard Smyth at the burning of Ridley and Latimer in Oxford on 16 October 1555. Smyth was the Regius professor of divinity, and a somewhat battered war-horse who had been forced to recant his 'popery' before going into exile under Edward. He preached on the inevitable text 'If I yield my body to the fire to be burned and have not charity I gain nothing' and pointed out that by refusing conformity and the Queen's pardon, the delinquents were effectively committing suicide. This was something of a trope among the persecutors, but neither the victims (who gestured furious dissent) nor the crowd seems on this occasion to have been convinced.[42] Smyth was mercifully brief, and the reformers were not strong in Oxford, but such as they were, they were palpably unpersuaded by this performance.

When Henry Cole was given the even more sensitive task of preaching at Cranmer's burning in the following March, he made a mess of it. The Archbishop had ostensibly recanted, and therefore by the canon law should not have been executed at all. This awkward fact the preacher was compelled to gloss over, welcoming his submission as ensuring the safety of his soul. He then went on to make the extraordinary statement that the deaths of Cranmer, Ridley and Latimer were a just compensation for the executions of Fisher and More, suggesting that the motivation of the Church was contaminated by the issue of revenge.[43] Whether this performance played any part in Cranmer's famous repudiation of his submission, or in his heroic performance at the stake, we do not know, but it was generally acknowledged to be one of the regime's worst public relations disasters, and Henry Cole's sermon played its part.[44] Usually, the preacher was just part of the furniture, like the priest or minister who regularly attended secular executions. It is unlikely that he persuaded many by his arguments, but he did provide a part of the necessary ritual, which was designed to satisfy the onlookers that the requirements of justice had been satisfied. Every burning was a piece of political theatre, and attractive to those who felt that they had a point to make. It was for this reason that there was usually a section of the crowd prepared to demonstrate in support of one of their own. At Smithfield, where the victims were not usually local, the motivation was slightly different. There the troublemakers were usually the city apprentices, who in addition to being generally Protestant in their sympathies, also welcomed the opportunity to make a bit of mischief. The Privy Council acknowledged this in January 1556, when it instructed the city authorities to ensure a strong guard at every execution, and 'to see that such as shall misuse themselves either by comforting, aiding or praising the offenders ... (are deterred, and that) ... no householder suffer any of his apprentices or other servants to be abroad' at the time of any such burning.[45] The Protestants were gaining far too much public exposure by these antics. After another disturbance at Smithfield in June 1558, it was Bonner himself who suggested that future executions should be conducted in the country, irrespective of the offenders' place of origin.[46]

Foxe is our main source of information about these reactions, which is why the stories need to be treated with caution, but he is not the only one. The Spanish ambassadors were consistently cynical about the regime's efficiency and, although prepared to concede the worthiness of the Queen's motives, regularly attacked her tactics.[47] Renard was convinced that Protestantism was strong among the people, and was confidently expecting an uprising when the Prayer Book services were brought to an end in December 1553. He was astonished when nothing happened, but did not revise his opinion, agreeing wholeheartedly with Gardiner that the Wyatt rebellion was religiously motivated – that was just what he would have expected. His successor (as Philip's special representative), the Count of Feria, was equally unimpressed. Feria's pessimistic assessment of Cardinal Pole is now generally dismissed as a piece of special pleading,[48] but he also believed that the hostile reactions of some parts of the crowd at burnings for heresy were symptomatic of a deep-seated malaise. His pithy (and on the whole accurate) assessment of Elizabeth's religious position in the days immediately before her accession included the observations that all her ladies were heretics, and that there was not a heretic or traitor in the land who would not rally to her cause.[49] However, the Spaniards were interested parties with their own agenda. More impressive in this context is the testimony of Giovanni Michieli, the Vene-

tian envoy, who had no particular axe to grind. Referring to the executions of
John Cardmaker and John Warne on 30 May 1555, he wrote

> two days ago, to the displeasure as usual of the population here, two Londoners were
> burned alive, one of them having been public lecturer in scripture, a person sixty years
> of age, who was held in great esteem. In a few days the like will be done to four or five
> more; and thus from time to time to many others who are in prison for this cause, and
> will not recant, although such sudden severity is odious to many people.[50]

This is an important despatch from the front line of the battle, if only for its mat-
ter-of-factness. The people of London are displeased at the burning 'as usual'. It is
not apparent whether the demonstrations of sympathy which accompanied this
particular execution were orchestrated or not, or whether they were particularly
vociferous, but to an outside observer like Michieli they were normal. To say that
the authorities were alarmed would probably be an exaggeration, but the situation in London needed careful managing. This was reflected also in the popular
writings of that indefatigable publicist, Miles Huggarde. Huggarde had a bitter wit, which he exercised at the expense of Protestants in general, but he was
particularly outraged by the imagery which these 'false stinking martyrs' were
creating for themselves. He could perfectly well have ignored them altogether,
but the tone of his invective suggests anxiety. They were madmen, he claims,
desperately hurling themselves into the flames.[51] However, mad or not, they constituted a calculated and deliberate challenge which the authorities could not
afford to neglect. Nevertheless, Huggarde's humour sometimes has an appealing
edge. In describing the death of John Rogers in February 1555 (a death which
was believed by many to be the inspiration of what followed) he wrote

> when Rogers their pseudomartyr (protomartyr I would say) was burned in Smith-
> field, were there not divers merchant men and others which seeing certain pigeons
> flying over the fire that haunted to a house adjoining, being amazed with the smoke
> forsook their nests and flew over the fire, were not ashamed boldly to affirm that the
> same was the Holy Ghost in the likeness of a dove

As far as Huggarde was concerned, all Protestants were either fools or knaves,
and this contempt was returned with interest against 'the hosier that dwells in
Pudding Lane', and who was not supposed to have the knowledge to address
such issues.[52] Nevertheless his books sold well, and his deflationary attacks
were probably more effective in puncturing the mystique of martyrdom which
these dissidents were building up than direct attacks such as that launched in
The Treatise on the Masse. The treatise was concerned to argue that, far from
being martyrs, those executed were simply criminals 'by iuste lawes cast and condemned to burne for their obstinate heresie'. The author went on at great length
to denounce the gullibility of those taken in by their pious frauds.[53] Again his

vehemence suggests the anxiety of one who knows that he is in a fight which he may well lose. His thumping rhetoric was also popular, and the *Treatise* went through several editions, but beyond demonstrating that the government was fighting its corner with vigour, it is impossible to say how many people were influenced, and to what extent.

One of the strangest features of the Church's otherwise earnest campaign to combat the mythology of martyrdom which was building up around the executed Protestants was its failure to contain their outreach through letters. Nearly all those who were sufficiently literate wrote screeds to their friends, supporters and followers, without any apparent intervention from their jailers.[54] Occasionally we read of pen and ink being denied, or smuggled into the prison by visitors. Sometimes 'privy searches' were made which resulted in the confiscation of papers and writing materials, but by and large the flow of this correspondence continued uninterrupted. Many of the recipients were individuals, who no doubt kept silent about them, at least until quieter times, but on other occasions whole congregations were addressed, or the inhabitants of a particular town.[55] Whether these missives were ever received as intended, or what impact they may have had, is unknown, but they create the impression of a tightly knit community being held together by letters.

Often the victims wrote accounts of their own examinations and trials, which were sometimes found after their deaths, in John Bradford's case by his wife, clearing his effects from his prison cell.[56] Sometimes these 'stories' were smuggled out of the country to waiting collectors, such as Edwin Sandys or John Foxe. The main impact of these narratives came later, when Foxe incorporated them into his *Actes and Monuments*, either in 1563 or, more usually, in 1570, but the fact that they were written in the first place is astonishing. The system of imprisonment operated by the Church seems to have varied from place to place and from time to time. Some prisoners were allowed to come and go virtually as they pleased, while others were kept in squalid dungeons, occasionally in chains, and where many of them died. Bonner's coal hole had a particularly sinister reputation. Some jailers were 'cruel' and some were lenient. This may have had more to do with the prisoner's resources than with any ideological sympathy.[57] It was quite normal for a prisoner with money (or with money behind him), to get favourable treatment, but that did not always work. Alderman Irish, with whom Ridley was lodged during his imprisonment in Oxford, was allegedly hostile to his prisoner because he was dominated by his wife. He may have been immune to bribery, but that did not prevent Ridley both sending and receiving many letters.[58] Sometimes such letters were allegedly written in conditions of extreme difficulty, without light, and in one case in the prisoner's own blood for lack of ink. The Protestants clearly set great store by them, and the recipients cherished them, but the government's attempts to stop them were at best inefficient and at worst hopelessly negligent.

There is no doubt that Pole and the council realized that they had a battle on their hands over the way in which the persecution was perceived. Numerous tracts were written which included a defence of severity among their other aims.[59] Some of these were theological, aiming to out-argue, or to shout down, Protestant objections to transubstantiation, the worship of the saints and prayers for the dead. Some argued that the law must be enforced and that the so-called martyrs were simply offenders against the relevant statutes; others again resorted to bitter mockery. It used to be believed that the government's case more or less went by default, and that the result was a country which became increasingly sickened by the butchery, blamed on either 'the papists' or the Spaniards. In other words the persecution was counter-productive in terms of the Church's declared policy of Catholic reconversion. Recent research has not only cast doubt on that interpretation, but has presented the alternative scenario of a Church winning its battle for hearts and minds against an increasingly beleaguered and diminishing minority, and frustrated merely by the deaths of its two protagonists in November 1558.[60] The truth is probably somewhere between the two. In London, Colchester and Canterbury, where there was significant Protestantism, the demonstrations were probably spontaneous as well as organized. Elsewhere they are more likely to have been the work of small committed groups. On the whole, the English did not take heresy very seriously as a crime, unlike treason or murder, particularly when the offenders were 'unlearned'. In that they differed very significantly from the Spaniards, for whom an *auto da fe* was a cleansing of offences against the national consciousness.[61] Demonstrations against the offenders were rare, and the prevailing atmosphere seems to have been one of rather puzzled curiosity. It is probably safest to conclude that the government's earnestness in pursuing a policy of persecution was accepted by most people as a part of its job. They did not particularly approve of it, but then it was none of their business. Protestants as such were not particularly popular. They tended to be self righteous and were always going on about the scriptures, but on the other hand they were decent people and good neighbours. It was hard to see why they had deserved such a terrible end. In so far as there was positive hostility to the persecution, it was aimed mostly at the Spaniards, who were blamed for everything which the people did not like, from the decline of the Netherlands cloth trade to the loss of Calais.[62]

When Pole and Mary both died, the momentum of the Catholic reformation carried it forward for several months, but the burnings stopped at once. It was not only the citizens of London who were unhappy with the way the persecution had developed. There were doubters at the highest level, particularly among the lay magistrates and the bishops. Justice should be done, and should be seen to be done, but the burning of six, or even ten, humble men and women at a session for doctrinal offences which they barely comprehended did not necessarily confirm the Catholic Church as the loving mother and spiritual guardian which it claimed to be.[63] In presenting so implacable a face of persecution to the country, the Church was not, in fact, furthering its own mission. In addition, it had probably given to its Protestant opponents a credibility which they might otherwise have struggled to find. It was one thing to swim with the Edwardian tide, but quite another to stand by those convictions when faced with such a formidable combination of state and ecclesiastical power.

8 THE IMAGERY OF JOHN FOXE

As a work of cultural propaganda, the *Actes and Monuments* was an unprecedented success. In spite of its enormous bulk (over 2,000 pages in the 1583 edition), and consequent expensiveness, its influence permeated down to the lowest social levels and helped to create that popular anti-Catholicism which was such a feature of the England of the 1580s. Its first edition, in 1563, was supported among others by Sir William Cecil, but it was never officially promoted, and indeed its second edition of 1570 was by implication highly critical of the Queen for failing to press on with the reform programme.[1] What it did, most effectively, was to present the Catholic Church as a conspiracy of clerical pride and cruelty, anti-Christian and inspired by the devil.

> We find in all ages from the beginning (gentle reader) that Satan hath not ceased at all times to molest the church of Christ, with one affliction or another to the trial of their faith, but yet never so apparent at any time to all the world as when the Lord hath permitted him power over the bodies of his saints to the shedding of their blood, and perverting of religion, for then sleepeth he not, I warrant you, from murdering of the same unless they will fall down with Ahab and Jesabell, to worship him and so kill and poison their own souls eternally. As in these, the miserable latter days of Queen Mary hard by our doors, yea even in our houses sometimes, and also afar off we have felt heard and seen the practice of the same[2]

Queen Mary herself was represented as a victim of this clerical conspiracy, the protagonists of which were Stephen Gardiner and Edmund Bonner. She was guilty mainly by association for having married a Spaniard, who not only reintroduced the Pope, but brought in the ungodly ways of his own nation, so that Catholicism became not only cruel and unnatural, but also foreign. Foxe was not the first to argue along these lines. John Bale, who was in a sense his mentor, John Ponet, Christopher Goodman and John Knox had all written works of similar import, while his contemporaries Thomas Brice and John Aylmer were doing the same.[3] However, none had the sheer impact of John Foxe, who, thanks to his contacts in the Protestant communities of the Home Counties, had unprecedented quantities of information at his disposal. Indeed, he was not so much the author of the *Actes and Monuments* as its editor. Although some passages bear the unmistakable imprint of his thinking, large parts, particularly in the later editions, consist of collections of letters or what purport to be verbatim transcripts of the martyrs' own accounts of their sufferings. Some of these had been smuggled out of the country within months of the events; others were collected by Foxe or one of his agents soon after his return. Other letters and 'eyewitness' accounts were handed over only when the first edition had already caused a controversial storm, and aroused interest in his project.[4] On a number of occasions, Foxe sent amenuenses to take transcripts from the relevant bishops' registers – some of which are no longer extant – and occasionally seems to have ripped out the pages. Where the documents which he printed can be checked, either against the original or against his own transcripts, they were on the whole rendered accurately. This was notably the case with the Guernsey women, where the whole proceedings of the court and the Elizabethan commission of enquiry survive.[5] When Henry Bull published his edition of the *Letters of the Martyrs* in 1564 he altered the gender of the authors in a few cases, because it was not 'edifying' for a clergyman to be receiving spiritual counsel from a woman, and Foxe followed him in the 1570 edition, but generally such editorial interference was rare.

Sometimes the name of Foxe's source is given, as with Thomas Effart in the Guernsey case, but more usually not. Often they seem to have been the widows or children of the victims, who were anxious to secure his, or her, place in the martyrology which was now clearly emerging. In the case of Isobel Malt, who was (allegedly) asked to give up her son for adoption after the Queen's false pregnancy, he notes 'this much, I say, I was told by the woman herself', and he cites the existence of Timothy Malt (aged fifteen in 1570) as further proof.[6] Occasionally he allowed biblical or patristic precedents to carry him away, and one of his most telling passages comes into that category. Hugh Latimer's exhortation to Nicholas Ridley as they both went to the stake in Oxford, 'Be of good comfort, master Ridley, and play the man. We shall this day light such a candle, by God's grace, in England, as I trust shall never be put out.'[7]

The original account of this burning, derived probably from George Shipside, and published in 1563, contains no such words, but someone, possibly Foxe himself, realized the appropriateness of Eusebius's account of the execution of Polycarp in the second century, and adapted it accordingly.[8] In that narrative a voice from heaven urges him to 'play the man', but we do not know the immediate source of the words attributed to Latimer, which do not occur in any of Foxe's remaining notes and drafts. John Hooper was also compared to Polycarp, but at least in that case the source of the comparison is clear. He is unlikely to have invented Latimer's words, that not being his way. He researched his subject assiduously, both before 1563 and between editions, and neither Nicholas Harpesfield nor Robert Parsons, both of whom savaged his interpretation, accused him of inventing executions.[9] Harpesfield criticized him for a number of errors of individual identification, which were duly corrected in the second edition; but Parsons, whose work was published only after Foxe's death, confined himself to a general attack upon the whole concept of Protestant martyrdom. It was, he insisted, the cause which made the martyr, not the death, and in any case Foxe's 'martyrs' were simply criminals who had broken the laws under which the state was then governed.[10]

John Foxe was one of the relatively few protagonists on either side of the ideological debate who believed that the death penalty was inappropriate for heresy, and this gave a white-hot quality to his indignation, which burns through a number of his accounts of individual executions. For example, his narrative of the burning of Prest's wife at Exeter in the last days of the persecution runs

> Then was she delivered to the sheriff, and innumerable people beholding her, she was led by the officers to the place of execution, without the walls of Exeter called Sothernhey, where again these superstitious priests assailed her: and she prayed them to have no more talk with her, but cried still God be merciful to me, a sinner ... And so whilst they were tying her to the stake, thus still she cried and would give no answer to them, but with much patience took her cruel death, and was with the fire and flames consumed[11]

It was a part of his basic argument that the True Church did not behave in such a way, and that the Catholics' cruelty, shown not only in respect of the actual burnings, but in the foul conditions in which the victims were often held in prison, branded them as a False Church and disciples of the Antichrist. This created problems for him, because it was not an attitude shared by either Henry VIII or Thomas Cranmer. He was particularly embarrassed by the role of Archbishop Cranmer in the proceedings against John Lambert, who was burned in 1538 for holding precisely those views on the Eucharist which Cranmer later embraced himself.[12] He was reduced to explaining that the Archbishop had only gradually come to that full enlightenment which he was to display after 1548, and in which, by a merciful turn of providence, he was to die. The King himself had been an enigma – now godly (as when he abolished the papal authority), now ungodly (as when he passed the Act of Six Articles). There was no room for Henry's idiosyncratic religion in Fox's scheme of things, so he was reduced to representing the King as gullible and easily led. While he was listening to the good advice of Thomas Cromwell, all was well, but when he was deceived by the corrupt counsel of Stephen Gardiner, things went seriously wrong.[13] If the acid test was the burning of heretics, then Henry's Church remained unregenerate to the time of his death, in spite of his reforming initiatives. This was difficult enough, but mild by comparison with the burning of Joan Bocher and George van Paris, which had occurred in the otherwise impeccably godly reign of Edward VI. Both of these held Christological heresies which would later have been called Melchiorite, which were unacceptable alike to the Catholic and the Protestant Churches, but they should not have been burned by a True Church.

The villains of Foxe's stories were always the traditional clergy, like Thomas Tye in Essex, who presented a number of dissidents, or those who sought to stir up the crowds against the victims at executions. There was invariably a sermon preached on such occasions, and frequently bad-tempered exchanges resulted between the preacher and the victim(s) which Foxe inevitably represents in the latter's favour.[14] His descriptions of crowd reactions on these occasions need to be treated with caution as evidence of the general religious culture. For example of the burning of Ridley and Latimer in Oxford he writes

> For I think there was none that had not clean exiled all humanity and mercy, which would not have lamented to behold the fury of the fire to rage upon their bodies. Signs there were of sorrow on every side. Some took it grievously to see their deaths whose lives they held full dear. Some pitied their persons that thought their souls had no need thereof[15]

Nevertheless we know that George Shipside was doing his best to stir up such reactions amongst a crowd which seems to have been largely indifferent. Similarly, at the burning of John Rogers, 'all the people wonderfully rejoice[ed] at his constancy, with great praises and thanks to God for the same',[16] whereas, as we have seen, Miles Huggarde represented the crowd reaction quite differently.

Sympathetic demonstrations by a section of the crowd seem to have been quite normal, but these were nearly always staged by the victim's fellow believers, which is why the sheriffs often tried to have them apprehended. It should not necessarily be assumed that the spectators in general were hostile to the authorities, although, as we have seen impartial observers sometimes assumed that they were.[17] Foxe was writing after the event, and was seeking to defend the idea of a godly community which had always existed among the unregenerate, and was therefore concerned not only to celebrate the martyrs as the heroes of that community, but also to argue that they were well supported. It is very largely from Foxe's evidence that the idea of a counter-productive persecution has been derived. The thesis that the population at large was becoming increasingly sickened by the butchery is at best unproven.[18] The social status of the victims certainly declined, because the clerical leadership had largely been eliminated, but there is no reason to suppose that executions carried out in 1557 or 1558 were worse received than those of 1555. The government's popularity declined, but that was rather due to the Spanish connection and to the war with France than to the persecution. For those who wanted to see it, there was plentiful evidence that God was not pleased with the English in general and with the Queen in particular. Mary's false pregnancy, the harvest failures of 1555 and 1556, the influenza epidemic and the loss of Calais could be made to add up to a formidable indictment. In 1563 Foxe wrote

> we shall never find any reign of any Prince of this land, or any other, which did ever show in it (for the proportion of time) so many great arguments of God's wrath and displeasure, as were to be seen in the reign of this Queen Mary; whether we behold the shortness of her time, or the unfortunate event of all her purposes[19]

It was all very well for Miles Huggarde to argue that all this was due to the ingratitude and rebelliousness of the English people, rather than to the Queen's actions, but such an explanation tells its own story, and the role of the 'false stinking martyrs'[20] in creating such an impression offers some indirect support for Foxe's interpretation.

He was not in England during the persecution, and therefore his reconstruction of events is all at second hand, and his representation of the godly remnant based on first principles. The first and most important of these is the idea that the truth of the scriptures is simple and readily understood by any right-minded person.[21] Since the Bible had been sincerely presented by the preachers of King Edward's reign, there was no excuse even for the illiterate not to understand it. It therefore followed that the return of the mass and its attendant ceremonies was less the result of spontaneous reaction than of the subtle and deceitful promptings of the popish clergy. The idea that the Bible needs a 'lively expositor' in the person of the priest, and that the Church consequently had a monopoly of interpretation, was a basic tenet of the Catholic position.[22] It also appealed to the common sense of most of those who had been exposed to the Edwardian battery. The simple were often confused by apparent contradictions within the text itself, and did not necessarily find the explanations so confidently offered by the Protestant ministers convincing. The better educated were only too keenly aware that the Bible is a multilayered text and that doctrinal guidance is in fact necessary. This was, after all, the purpose of the biblical glosses and commentaries which were offered in such profusion by the reformed Churches. There was consequently a certain schizophrenia within the Protestant position. If challenged directly (as Ridley was at his trial), they denied the need for the Church as interpreter, but they offered plenty of explanations themselves, and ultimately took refuge in the idea that the Holy Spirit was needed for a proper understanding.[23] The real reason why the role of the Church was denied was less confidence in the working of the Holy Spirit than the need to refute the Catholic arguments about tradition. In spite of Protestant claims to the contrary, the Church never neglected the Bible, or pretended that it was not a fundamental text, but it also argued that its own historical practices and traditions were of equal validity.[24] This the reformers vehemently denied, labelling them as human inventions, and asserting that faith could only be based on the Bible – *sola scriptura*. It was ultimately a battle over authority, in which those who were temperamentally inclined to rebelliousness were likely to accept the reformed position, while those of a more biddable disposition remained conservatives. This was particularly the case when the 'Queen's proceedings' pointed in the same direction. When it comes to defining the Marian Church, therefore the 'clerical conspiracy' is merely a figment of Foxe's imagination, and when it comes to identifying the godly remnant, the working of the Holy Spirit is as good an explanation as any.

It also meant, however, that he could not afford to admit any disagreements within the persecuted Church. Those who were inspired by the Holy Ghost to resist an ungodly tyranny could not by definition fall out among themselves. Consequently, while he was happy to emphasize any disagreements which arose on the Catholic side, the Protestant differences were airbrushed away. This was especially true of Kent, where, in the words of Patrick Collinson, 'The heretics were not yet a field of wheat but the cockles growing here and there amongst the corn'.[25] The cockles were, however, fairly thick in parts of this particular field, and there were Protestant communities before 1547 in Maidstone, Herne, Cranbrook, Tenterden and a number of other towns and villages. A total of 61 were burned, over 40 of them in Canterbury, which thus became, after Smithfield, the commonest site for executions.[26] These were at the cutting edge of the faith. In 1556 ten parishioners from Herne were prosecuted for insulting words against the sacrament of the altar, but all seem to have conformed when brought into court. They were much more typical of the average dissenter than were the martyrs, and their experience argues a significant minority in many parts of the county. It is, in fact, difficult to define exactly what is meant by the term 'Protestant', even as late as the reign of Edward VI. In one sense it simply means one who conformed to the new legislation, but that became unsatisfactory as soon as the Edwardian establishment had disappeared. From the point of view of the Marian authorities all nonconformists were heretics, and the nature or degree of their nonconformity did not greatly matter.[27] However, Foxe's position was to argue for the continuity of the True Church through the ages, and therefore it was of crucial importance, not only that Protestants should agree among themselves, but that their doctrine should be consistent with that of the early Church.[28]

Cranmer had been greatly concerned with the existence of what he called 'Anabaptists' in Kent, which was used as a blanket term for any radical. True Anabaptists, that is those who rejected infant baptism and believed in a 'gathered church' of believers, probably did exist, but the radicals who surfaced during Edward's reign were rather different. The militant Joan Bocher, for example, denied the humanity of Christ, arguing that the incarnation was simply a rite of passage and that Jesus took no flesh of the Virgin Mary. She claimed that there were a thousand of her sect in London, and although this was probably an exaggeration, she was a leader of some note.[29] Her doctrine originated on the Continent with the Dutch heretic Melchior Hoffman, but how it had been transmitted to her remains unknown. Joan had a strong desire for martyrdom, and succeeded in provoking the Protestant authorities into burning her, to the Archbishop's acute embarrassment. Foxe, as we have seen, was scandalized that a godly Church should have blood and ashes on its hands, and skated thinly over the whole episode. Joan was the most troublesome, but she was not the only radical to disturb the godly peace of Kent. There was also the Freewiller Henry Hart and his following, who were a milder nuisance in that they argued against the orthodox Protestant doctrine of predestination. This was not a thumping heresy, and it is not clear that the Freewillers were actually a sect in the proper sense at all, but Hart argued vehemently that predestination was a demoralizing doctrine propagated by academic pedants and actually published a book to that effect in 1548, entitled *A Godly newe short Treatise Instructyng every Parson, howe they shulde Trade theyr Lyves*.[30] They were numerous and geographically widespread in Kent, but whether they were separatists is less clear. Foxe had no time for them, but he did not ignore them, and reported a debate which took place in the King's Bench Prison in 1555 between Hart and the orthodox predestinarian John Bradford when both were incarcerated for heresy. This debate appears to have been facilitated by the authorities in order to demonstrate Protestant divisions, but Foxe does not acknowledge this, handing a decisive victory to Bradford.[31]

Nicholas Harpesfield and justices like Sir John Baker did not make any subtle distinctions as they went out to eradicate heresy in Kent, and Foxe was careful not to let such divisions appear as he told their stories. He was to a large extent dependent upon what he was told, but it was in the interest of the Elizabethan faithful to connive at any misrepresentations which may have been necessary. A good example of this is the vivid and circumstantial account of the burning of Christopher Wade of Dartford in the summer of 1555, which includes the victim singing psalms as he went to his fate, and fruiterers selling horse loads of cherries to the spectators.[32] However, the full version of the story only reached Foxe in time to be included in the 1583 edition from Richard Fletcher, the vicar of Rye in Sussex, although the latter had been an eyewitness of the event. This final version included an exhortation by Wade at the stake that the spectators should flee Babylon and 'embrace the doctrine of the gospel preached in King Edward his daies'.[33] The reason for this sudden accretion of memory lay in the fact that in the 1570s Richard Fletcher senior, who was the vicar of Cranbrook, was involved in a dispute with the radical puritan John Strowd, and the Fletchers were anxious to establish their Protestant credentials.[34] Not only had they supported Wade at the stake, they had recorded his impeccably orthodox exhortation. Wade appears from his antecedents to have been something of a radical himself, but his story was appropriated in the service of Elizabethan orthodoxy, and we have no means now of knowing what he actually said. Correct responses to the days of persecution were a necessary aspect of the formation of the Elizabethan Church, and this always needs to be remembered in evaluating Foxe's narratives. When John Bland and John Frankesh, the only two clergy to be burned in Kent, were executed together on 12 July 1555, their impeccably orthodox utterances were duly recorded, but what was not made clear was that the two laymen who were burned with them, Nicholas Sheterden and Humphrey Middleton, were Free-willers, with whom Bland had been in fierce controversy.[35] Their sentiments, if they uttered any, were subsumed under those of their orthodox colleagues.

A slightly better-authenticated deception was practised in the case of those whom Collinson calls 'the Maidstone Seven', executed together on 18 June 1557. Foxe duly records their deaths, but the circumstantial story sent to him by Roger Hall, the brother of another victim, Alice Benden, was not used. This is remark-able because it contains some vivid and unexceptionable remarks made at the stake by one of the women, Joan Bradbridge.[36] However, Foxe merely says of the schedule of heresies for which the seven were condemned, 'It differeth not much from the usuall manner expressed before, page 1585, neither did their aunsweres in effect much differ from the others who suffered'.[37] This is suspicious, and the doubts are confirmed by another story of the defence which John Day, a local priest who had preached on that occasion and had subsequently conformed to the Elizabethan settlement, advanced to justify his action. 'But this I know', he declared, 'that some of them did deny the humanity of Christ and the equalitie of the Trinitie, and no man dowbteth but such ar heretykes'.[38]

Foxe may have had other evidence corroborating this statement, but for what-ever reason he skirted lightly around this group of martyrs, desiring to exploit their deaths without being specific about exactly why they had died. Hall's letter was mainly concerned with his case against Day, whom he represents as wilting under a challenge to the veracity of this statement, but for Foxe the mere suspi-cion was enough. This was doubly the case because he had in his possession other evidence which specifically charged several of the later martyrs in Kent with radical heresies. These charges were contained in several pages which appear to have been torn out of Harpesfield's register, a document not otherwise surviving. Moreover, since the pagination is not continuous, it has been speculated that even more incriminating evidence was deliberately destroyed in the course of Foxe's search.[39] The cross reference to page 1585 is also revealing in this context, because that is to the articles charged against John Bland of Adisham, an impec-cably orthodox martyr. However these were only seven in number, whereas we are told that the charges against the group numbered twenty, so it is reasonable to suppose that the other thirteen dealt with more unacceptable matter.

Foxe is not easy to pin down in his evasions, most of the evidence being cir-cumstantial, but from what we know about others who were interrogated, and who submitted, it seems that radical ideas were widespread. John Symmes of

Brenchley and Rober Kyne of East Peckham both recanted anti-Trinitarian views which would not have commended them to the martyrologist. John Fishcocke of Headcorn appears (from further evidence not used by Foxe) to have been a fairly radical Freewiller.[40] He was burned on 19 June 1557 on the same godly pyre as Alice Benden, beneath the cloak of whose orthodoxy he was allowed to pass. It would be a great exaggeration to suggest that Foxe falsified the record wholesale in order to make his martyrs appear to be godly Edwardians, but he did tweak the evidence in some cases, particularly in regard to Essex and Kent, where the radicals were relatively strong, and the picture which he presented of the unanimity of the Church under the cross was largely propaganda aimed at his Elizabethan readership.

Another aspect of his account of the persecution which is particularly interesting is the role played by women. The Catholic Church was guilty of institutionalized misogyny, but that was not really the point. Miles Huggarde made merciless fun of the 'fleering flirts' of London, who went gadding to radical sermons, and who would instantly betray their husbands if they did the same, 'so that they might have other'.[41] Social anarchy would inevitably follow the leadership of these headstrong dames, and that was an anarchy which even the most responsible leaders of the Church were eager to associate with their enemies. To John Foxe, on the other hand, the female martyrs were 'sisters on Christ', who were specially strengthened by the Holy Spirit to bear tribulations and pains to which nature would normally have succumbed. Although women were naturally weak, and inferior to men in both intellect and spirituality, those who embraced the gospel were transformed by the experience.[42] This applied not only to those who were burned, but to those like Mrs Cotton, who supported John Careless through his long imprisonment, and to the women who provided clean linen and other comforts to prisoners like Thomas Cranmer and Nicholas Ridley, who either had no wives or whose wives were far away. To John Foxe, as to John Careless, the transforming effect of the gospel upon its female devotees was one of the hallmarks of the True Church.[43] It was, of course, axiomatic that the True Church depended upon God, whereas the counterfeit Church depended upon human power and institutions. This was well expressed in the confrontations between these 'silly women' and their interrogators, where even the illiterate were empowered to debate points of scriptural interpretation and to overcome the ignorant priests who questioned them. This did not, however, make the martyrologist some kind of a feminist. Foxe shared the general perception of female inferiority and represented the consciences of these tough controversialists as having been made male by miraculous intervention. 'Blessed be the Lord omnipotent, who supernaturallie hath indued from above such weak creatures with such manly stomach and fortitude, so contantantlie to withstande the uttermost extreamitie of these pitilesse persecutors.'[44] It is this transformation which emancipates the women concerned from the silence and submissiveness which were otherwise recognized as the feminine ideal. Altogether about 55 women were burned during the persecution, rather more than 20 per cent of the total, and each story was moulded to fit with this notion of godly freedom.

This also made it necessary, however, to defend his heroines against Catholic charges of mere female wilfulness and disorder, particularly in view of the flamboyant display of Joan Bocher at the stake, where she had shouted down the preacher and repeatedly made the sign of the gallows at him.[45] Such overt defiance was not appropriate to a godly martyr, but it was not always easy to draw the line, and the 'pledging' which accompanied the executions of Alice Benden or Joyce Lewes gave some ammunition to his critics. Nor were the Elizabethans always happy with these notions of female autonomy. Richard Hooker, while acknowledging the power of female piety, nevertheless blamed female volubility and 'wild affection' for the spread of puritan ideas later in the century.[46] It was, in fact, a rather similar situation to that of the Marian period, except that these puritan women were not threatened with death, and were given no opportunity to testify. There was among Foxe's readers an uneasy feeling of the world turned upside down about the stories of these martyrs, where women turned 'doctors' and instructed the clergy in the performance of their duties. The story of Elizabeth Young is an example of the kind of unease which was caused. Elizabeth was arrested in 1558 for the not very feminine activity of importing heretical books from Emden and selling them in London. When asked why she refused to go to mass, she responded that her conscience would not suffer it, a response which her examiner sought to reduce to mere fastidiousness. When she replied 'it is but an easy conscience that a man can make', she was trespassing into the realm of theological debate which was supposed to be forbidden to women, and created an ambiguous situation where her virtue could be impugned by associating her with the traditional loquacity of the whore.[47] At her second examination Dr Martin, then her interrogator, took full advantage of this ambiguity, accusing her openly of being a 'rebell whore' as well as a heretic. In reporting these exchanges, Foxe was seeking to represent Martin as an unscrupulous and pitiless persecutor, but he was sailing close to the wind. Similar language was reportedly used by Sir John Tyrell in attempting to extract the tears of feminine weakness from Rose Allin, but that was provoked by her silence rather than her speech, and was consequently better able to engage the sympathy of the reader.[48] In the case of Elizabeth Young, her examiners kept on hammering away at the gender issue. When she refused to swear an oath, she was accused of being a man in women's clothing, and when she persisted in disputation, she was accused of being a priest's leman. 'What priest hast thou lien withal, that thou hast so much scripture? Thou art some priests woman, I thinke, for thou wilt take upon thee to reason and teach, the best doctor in all the land, thou.'[49] Foxe's point is that

Elizabeth's ability to dispute arises directly from the infusion of the Holy Spirit, but the opposing view, that it must be derived from some man or other – not her husband because she was unmarried – must have commanded the tacit allegiance of most Elizabethan conservatives.

At the same time, the whole Protestant imagery of the Church was female, derived from its presentation as the bride of Christ. The True Church was the Woman clothed with the Sun, immaculate and faithful, while the False Church was characterized as the Whore of Babylon, bloodstained and decked out with fripperies.[50] This had nothing to do with the behaviour of real women, as distinct from men, but then the special conditions induced by the persecution did not have much to do with their ongoing role in the Church either. If anything the demotion of the Virgin Mary in Protestant hagiography deprived women of their most conspicuous role model, but since that role was one of obedience and submission, it may have been no great loss. Once the persecution was over, pious women retreated from the public to the private sphere, but they did not forget their earlier prominence – as witnessed by their role in the later puritan agitation. The idea that the female conscience was autonomous and answerable only to God, which was to have a vital role to play in the future history of the Church, can be traced back to the *Actes and Monuments* and to Foxe coming (somewhat uneasily) to terms with the heroic deaths of over fifty women.[51]

John Foxe wrote a number of other books, and published numerous sermons, but the *Actes and Monuments* was his *magnum opus*. It was originally a compromise, because his first intention had been to write in Latin for a European audience, and the two (fairly modest) early editions were in that language.[52] However, the accession of Elizabeth and her decision to settle for an Edwardian Protestant Church altered the political landscape. There was now a task to be performed at home, because Foxe knew as well as anyone that the government was locked in a battle for the hearts and minds of Englishmen. There was more than a touch of triumphalism about the introduction, to the first English edition, hailing the Queen as the New Constantine, but that was incidental to the main purpose of the work. He was concerned, first and foremost, to discredit the Catholic Church.[53] The celebration of the lives of the Protestant martyrs was a means to that end rather than an end in itself. He printed the whole text of the Lady Mass in order to demonstrate its 'absurdities', and went out of his way to emphasize the malice and cruelty of some of the persecutors. This 1563 edition, which owed its appearance to the printer, John Day, as much as to the author, was aimed at the educated, not only (or even chiefly) at the clergy but at that literate laity which played such a key part in the making of public opinion – whose opinions were those of the 'public' for most practical purposes.[54]

What it aimed to do was to trace the development of the True Church in England from the days of its reawakening by John Wycliffe in the late fourteenth century to its triumph under Elizabeth. This was done largely through the lives and confessions of those who had died in its defence, which necessitated the careful selection of evidence. Fifteenth-century Lollards are thus reinvented as early Protestants, their testimony, taken basically from the bishops' registers, being moulded with this end in view. Sir John Oldcastle, executed for rebellion, becomes a hero and martyr because of his Lollard associations, and the later Wycliffites (who had never heard of justification by faith) merge seamlessly with the early Lutherans.[55] John Wycliffe thus becomes the 'morning star' of the reformation,[56] which is given English roots, and John Hus, executed by the Council of Constance, becomes an Englishman by association. Although he had no desire to deny the Continental roots of his own faith, John Foxe knew his fellow countrymen well enough to realize that adding a nationalist touch to his narrative would give it credibility, especially since Mary's Spanish marriage had been so unpopular.

The storm which was stirred up by this first edition must in a way have been gratifying to its author. Given its bulk and cost it could have fallen from the press with a dull thud. As it was, influential supporters and the sensational nature of much of the story guaranteed that it was taken up and read. Many of the events were so recent that the protagonists were still alive, to be gratified or outraged according to how they were represented. Mr Justice Drayner was not the only one to seek to set the record straight; ex-Bishop Edmund Bonner was (justifiably) annoyed to be described as a pitiless bloodsucker, and was also put out by the suggestions that he took a perverse delight in flogging small boys.[57] In 1566 Nicholas Harpesfield, from his not very rigorous confinement in the Tower, wrote a detailed refutation both of the *Actes and Monuments* and of Jewel's *Apologie*, which he published abroad under the pseudonym of Alan Cope. However, since the *Dialogi Sex* was written in Latin, its influence did not extend far into Foxe's core constituency. Nevertheless he took it seriously as criticism, and made some detailed corrections in response.[58] What the 1563 edition also did was to establish John Foxe as the martyrologist of the English reformation, and the man to whom all corrective and supplementary material should be sent. From his position within the Duke of Norfolk's household, he developed a team of assistants, paid for in all probability by Sir William Cecil, and began to work towards a second edition.

By the time that this appeared in 1570, a number of things had changed, which made it a timely intervention in the ongoing debate. In that same year the Pope issued his bull *Regnans in Excelsis*, deposing Elizabeth and absolving her subjects from their allegiance. The worldly pretensions of Rome were thus emphasized and the boundaries of English religious allegiance redrawn, to make Foxe's insistence on the Englishness of the reformation more relevant than ever.[59] The Queen, on the other hand, had shown a marked reluctance to use her authority to finish the restructuring of the English Church, and in the eyes of zealous Protestants had left the reformation half completed. The second edition was respectfully dedicated to Elizabeth, but the encomium on her as the New Constantine was withdrawn. Thanks to Pius V, the main battle had been won. Elizabeth had not succumbed to popish blandishments, nor had she married a Catholic prince, but the result was far from satisfactory. Where was the godly zeal of the martyrs? Or even the ambition of 1563? Both seemed to have subsided into a complacent conformity, and to have been overtaken by worldly preoccupations.[60] Consequently the battle of 1570 was different in many ways from that of seven years earlier. The godly, and particularly the Queen, needed to be reanimated, so even heavier guns were wheeled out. Some dubious stories were removed and replaced with others which might be more edifying. A great deal of supplementary material was also included, not only narratives but also documents, as though to bury all doubters under the weight of the evidence. The whole work was recast as a history of the Church, and taken back to imperial Rome.[61] In spite of this, the emphasis remained upon England, and particularly upon the origins of English Christianity. The Roman position on this was that the faith had been introduced by St Augustine in the sixth century, and consequently owed its origins to the Holy See. The ingratitude involved in its subsequent apostasy was therefore doubly to be deplored. Not so, argued the reformers. Christianity had been present in Britain centuries before Augustine, having been introduced either by King Lucius in the second century, or even by Joseph of Arimethea within a generation of the crucifixion.[62] All that Augustine had done was to distort and pervert what was already well established. Foxe was taking a chance with his scholarship here, and modern work has dismissed both Joseph and Lucius as figments of the imagination. However, British Christianity was a reality, and although the monks of Bangor may not have been massacred as the historian believed, they did exist and were the focus of a lively regional devotion.[63] Within a year convocation had instructed all bishops to have copies of the *Actes and Monuments* placed in parish churches, alongside the Bible. This may have been very imperfectly implemented, but it greatly increased the exposure of the illiterate to 'readings' in which (not surprisingly) the favourite topics were the more sensational of the Marian burnings.

There were two further editions during Foxe's lifetime; one in 1576 and one in 1583, neither of which saw major revisions on the scale of the 1570 edition. The 1576 edition was a 'cheap print' version in one volume, designed in part to meet the demand for an abridgement, which Foxe would not allow. By contrast, 1583 was a 'de luxe' edition, in which some of the original excisions were restored. Editorially it is a somewhat weary piece of work, concentrating on holding the ground that had been gained, but no longer convinced that either the puritans or the Catholics constituted an immediate threat.[64] Given the worldliness of the English, much remained to be done, but Foxe now felt at the end of his life that he had done what he could, and the *Actes and Monuments* would march on into the future. Within a couple of years of Foxe's death, Timothy Bright had published the desired abridgement, but that did not prevent the production of further full editions in 1596, 1610 and 1632, each with a slightly different agenda.[65] In spite of numerous Catholic attempts to undermine it, Foxe's narrative and interpretation of the Marian persecution had entered the folklore of England. It was accurate in the narrow sense, of getting the dates and circumstances of executions right, and quoting documents correctly, but it was also misleading in the sense that it did not tell the whole truth, even when the facts were available. So it created an impression of theological unanimity amongst the martyrs which research has demonstrated to be specious, and of spontaneous support for their cause which we know to have been largely bogus. So Foxe's providentialism led him to present an evangelical community which was both larger and more coherent than was in fact the case. More importantly, he did not make any serious attempt to describe or analyse the prevailing religious culture of the period. He conceded that most people were much given to their 'old mumpsimus', but attributed this to the influence of wicked priests, who had been deprived of their status by the Edwardian reforms, and were now out to gain revenge.[66] They were able to do this by taking advantage of the popular taste for superstition, but Foxe was very careful not to blame the persecution on the people at large, bearing in mind that that was the constituency which he was aiming to convert. Formally, the executions were the responsibility of the government which had revived the heresy laws, and of the royal council which was pressing for their implementation, but Foxe made little of this. He was prepared to blame individual magistrates for their 'cruelty' in specific cases, and attributed the 'rotten stinking death' of Alexander, the keeper of Newgate, to his severity to those entrusted to his charge, but he was not prepared to concede that these represented a general culture of hostility to dissenters.[67] Most of the evidence which we have upon the other side is contained in the writings of those (primarily clergy) who were concerned to discredit the 'martyrs', and is consequently no more reliable than Foxe. A somewhat fairer picture is probably presented by the case of Elizabeth Folkes, an Essex woman burned in 1555. William Chedsey, the archdeacon, had done his best to get Folkes released on the grounds that she was just an ignorant girl. John Boswell, a member of Bonner's staff, had earlier written to the bishop apropos of a similar case

> Yt may please your good lordship to be advertised that I do se by experience that the sworne inquest for heresies do most comenly induct the simple, ignorant and wretched heretikes, & so do let the acrhheretikes go, which is one greate cause that moveth the rude multitude to murmur when they see the simple wretches (not knowing what heresy is) to burne. I wysh (if it may be) that this common disease might be

cured amongst the iurates of Essex. But I feare mee it will not bee so long as some of them be (as they are) infected with the like disease.[68]

The commissioners, in other words, were purging their own consciences by prosecuting the humble. This was not at all the picture of evangelical solidarity which Foxe was anxious to promote. The loyalties of the local elites were tangled up with their desire to be good citizens and to obey the laws, which might cut right across their religious sympathies. The humble were expendable, and burning them might distract attention from their more substantial neighbours. This may sound unduly cynical, but it draws attention to the extreme importance of obedience to authority in shaping the culture of the educated. In so far as there was a culture of dissent, it was bound up with the 'natural rebelliousness' of the lower orders, and when the clerical leaders of Protestantism were removed, this bedrock was exposed. With the Elizabethan settlement, the culture of obedience changed direction, which may account for the fact that there were many conformists but few zealous Protestants in the years after 1559. So it was Foxe's main concern to make the heirs of the martyrs worthy of the inheritance which had been so painfully acquired.

POSTSCRIPT: THE EARLY ELIZABETHAN CHURCH

On 17 November 1558, between five and six in the morning, and in the sixth year of her reign, Queen Mary died. The news came as no very great surprise, either to the court or to the citizens of London, because her health, never very robust, had been in visible decline for over a month. Elizabeth cannot have been very surprised either because although, according to the traditional story, she was walking in the park at Hatfield when the news reached her, she had in fact been preparing for this moment for some time.[1] Her supporters had been quietly mobilized in case Mary should change her mind at the last minute, and she had been tormenting Philip's special envoy, the Count of Feria, with speculations about her intentions. Between eleven and twelve o'clock that same morning Elizabeth was proclaimed in Cheapside as Queen of England, France and Ireland, and Defender of the Faith by 'dyvers haroldes of armes', supported by the assembled nobility of England. The same day the bells of all the city churches rang out, and that night parties and bonfires were set in the streets 'for the newe quen Elizabeth, quen Mare syster'.[2] Feria had been rightly apprehensive about the Queen's attitude to religion, but for the time being nothing was said. On 19 November Te Deum Laudamus was sung in every church in London, and the following day William Bill, her chaplain, preached at Paul's Cross and made (according to Henry Machyn) a 'godly sermon', from which we may conclude that it was uncontroversial.[3] There had been a great deal of anxiety abroad about what would, or might, happen when Queen Mary died. Elizabeth was illegitimate, and relations between the two women were notoriously bad. Would King Philip attempt to ignore his marriage treaty and secure the succession for himself, or would some other pretender emerge? When the new Queen was unchallenged, the country breathed a collective sigh of relief.

Elizabeth's warm reception in London seems to have been echoed up and down the country. At Much Wenlock in Shropshire on 25 November (St Catherine's day) the people were gathered in the parish church for mass, when the service was interrupted by the arrival of the sheriff with the news. At the offertory, the vicar came down into the body of the church and invited the congregation to pray 'for the prosperous estate of our most noble Queen Elizabeth', whereupon the choir sang the Te Deum, as it was set out in the processional for a royal accession, before the vicar went back to his place and completed the mass. Two days later, he put on his best cope and, accompanied by the leading men of the town, processed to the church again to proclaim the new Queen. The choir then sang the litanies and collects for a Catholic ruler, and the service was followed by a bonfire at the church gate, and a dole of bread, cheese and beer to the poor.[4] The rejoicing seems to have been just as genuine and spontaneous as it was in London. Meanwhile, in the Archbishop of Canterbury's prison, those heretics awaiting execution learned that they had been reprieved. Cardinal Pole had died only hours after Mary, and it remained to be seen what the new Queen would do about the state of her Church.[5] Far away in Rome, Pope Paul IV rejoiced that the heretical Cardinal and his Habsburg-dominated mistress were gone, and looked for an easing of diplomatic relations; while in Strasburg and Frankfurt English Protestant exiles began to pack their bags in anticipation of a swift passage home. Meanwhile, all over the country, Elizabeth was welcomed with impeccable Catholic ceremonial.

It did not take very long for these uncertainties to be resolved at a political level. In spite of a determined rearguard action, the remaining bishops were outvoted in the House of Lords and the Acts of Supremacy and Uniformity became law.[6] From the summer of 1559 the Church again became Protestant, and the Edwardian liturgy was restored. In July the Queen issued a fresh set of injunctions for the suppression of superstition, and 'to plant true religion'. At first sight this looks like a rerun of the Edwardian Articles, and in a sense it was, but there was a subtle difference. The parishes had been this way before and, although they might not like it, they knew what was expected of them. In Exeter diocese, Bishop James Turberville had refused the oath of supremacy, and at the time of the visitation was awaiting deprivation, so it was conducted to all intents and purposes *sede vacante*.[7] The visitors, who included the returned Marian exile John Jewel, started by embargoing any further masses or other popish services, and summoned the churchwardens of every parish to prepare an inventory of their church's goods. This was not quite as sinister as it looked, because although they were supposed to destroy their vestments and mass books, nobody followed up to make sure that they did so, and in most places these items were placed in the hands of sympathetic parishioners in case (or until) they were wanted again. Morebath, typically, spent money on re-equipping itself for reformed services; 4s. 4d. for a new Book of Common Prayer; 2s. 1d. for a copy of the English Litany and Psalter; 20s. for a Bible and a copy of the *Paraphrases*.[8] It dutifully took down its altar and restored its communion table, and in every outward way conformed with promptness and apparent willingness. This was the reaction throughout the south-west, and prompted Jewel to the surprised observation 'We found everywhere the people sufficiently well disposed towards religion ... even in those quarters where we expected most difficulty ... if inveterate obstinacy was found anywhere, it was altogether among the priests'.[9] However, this 'inveterate obstinacy' did not usually extend as far as risking deprivation. Most, like Christopher Trychay of Morebath, conformed, and he confined himself to reminding his flock each year where their 'massing gear' had been bestowed. Some took the not very serious risk of celebrating the occasional clandestine mass, but it is unlikely that Trychay indulged himself in this way, not least because he was (to an extent) under the watchful eye of his Protestant patron, Stephen Tristram.

This relatively prompt conformity to the new Protestant establishment, which was not confined to the south-west of England, presents some problems, because it was not occasioned by any great enthusiasm for Protestantism itself, nor by revulsion against what had gone before. All the evidence suggests that the culture of Catholic piety was flourishing, right up to the autumn of 1559, and that it continued to command the allegiance of many people after the changes had been made.[10] It is possible, indeed probable, that Mary's government was unpopular, but that did not indicate anti-Catholicism. Similarly, Elizabeth was welcomed, but that was because of who she was, and does not indicate any inclination towards her faith. Part of the answer probably lies in a lingering enthusiasm for the Royal Supremacy. Distance was lending enchantment to the view. King Henry had known how to stand up these foreigners, and when he fought wars, it had been in his own interests, not theirs. However, that alone is not a sufficient explanation. More important was the Queen's relatively tolerant attitude. Her visitors made fierce noises about superstition, the removal of images and the destruction of altars, but the actual enforcement was slow and restrained.[11] There was none of the abrasive haste which had characterized the Edwardian regime. Most sees were vacant for several months following the death or deprivation of the Marian incumbent, and a soft answer by the churchwardens usually turned aside what wrath there was.[12] A great gulf separated the clerical elite from their parochial colleagues who provided the spiritual leadership in every locality. With one exception, Mary's remaining bishops all refused the oath of supremacy and were deprived, and when the Convocations met alongside parliament at the beginning of 1559 both reaffirmed Catholic doctrine and the papal obedience. Parliament ignored them, but many of the deans, archdeacons and other senior clergy who made up the Lower Houses were similarly deprived for the same reason.[13] The refusal of co-operation at that level may well have finally convinced the Queen of the need for a fully Protestant settlement, because there was no prospect of finding an obedient but conservative bench of bishops within the existing establishment. Little as the Queen might relish it, there was no alternative to placing a number of the returning exiles. However the zeal of a Grindal or a Pilkington might well need to be curbed by a little cold water from Elizabeth, and consciences of parishes like Much Wenlock were eased in consequence.

The conformity of most of the rank and file clergy was highly significant. For every Thomas Harding or William Allen, whose consciences could not abide the new regime, there were a hundred Christopher Trychays. Trychay was a conservative. His age alone would indicate that, because he was nearly seventy in 1559, but his comments on the Edwardian changes (to which he nevertheless conformed) were abrasive and the warm welcome which he gave to the Marian restoration confirms the same impression.[14] Nevertheless, his obedience to the Elizabethan Church was not altogether constrained. Although he went on using the parochial saint Sidwell's name for baptismal purposes down to 1570, he gave up reminding his parishioners where the chasuble and mass book were deposited after 1562, and dutifully took down the rood loft in the same year, well ahead of any penalty for neglect. This may partly be explained by the frequency of visitations, because there were three in 1559 and another three in 1561, but it was also partly due to the sense of Christian community which existed in each parish.[15] The pressure from the diocesan courts was continuous, but it was also mild, and a 12*d*. fine to the bishop's official for some tardiness in compliance was neither here nor there. The gentleness of this pressure was due partly to the personality of Bishop William Alley of Exeter, who had been installed in July 1560 and was to serve for the remainder of the decade. Alley was diligent, but genial. He toured his see industriously, and knew all his clergy personally, as a result of which he was uniquely well informed about what was going on. Although strenuously anti-Catholic, he seems to have appreciated the difference between committed popery and mere conservatism. He could not afford to tolerate the latter in any formal sense, but preferred to use the tactics of constant chivvying to bring about conformity rather than the occasional imposition of draconian penalties. His use of excommunication was typical of this strategy.[16] Although dismissed as a 'money matter' by many of the well to do – particularly those of a reformed persuasion – it did pose a real threat to the cohesion of rural parishes, making it impossible for the person so sentenced to hold a parish office, for example. This was at least a serious nuisance, and usually led the offending parties to seek immediate release. Since their infringements had been caused more by conservative habits of thought than by deep-seated Catholic convictions, such submission was less painful than it might appear.

There was also the possibility of genuine conversion, or at least the creation of a 'comfort zone' within the practice of conformity. This can be seen in the case of Christopher Trychay of Morebath, who was unusual only in that he was a keen preacher. Since there were but 28 preachers among the 255 benefice holders in the diocese, this subjected him to exceptional scrutiny, and there is no suggestion that his sermons were anything but acceptable to the authorities.[17] None of his texts survive, and we can assume that his content was ethical rather than doctrinal, but he cannot have avoided doctrine altogether, and what he preached must have been recognizably Protestant. This was perhaps less surprising than it might appear, because the Queen kept the evangelical enthusiasm of her bishops on a tight rein and did not allow the more extreme attitudes which had characterized the latter part of her brother's reign to reappear. Although the communion service remained unequivocally reformed, little touches like the use of vestments and the kneeling position for reception made its bleakness easier to bear, and there was, after all, some merit in communicating the people in both kinds.[18] Moreover, many of the rhythms of the old Church year, banned under Edward and restored under Mary, were allowed to continue. Women were churched, rogation processions visited the familiar boundaries and church ales raised funds for parochial purposes. Practices which had been changing slowly over the years were not interrupted by the new regime. The desire to remember the dead was not diminished, but intercessory gifts and bequests had, as we have seen, been declining for years and, although partly restored under Mary, had not resumed anything like their previous vigour. Now they were forbidden again, but this created nothing like the shock of ten years earlier. Benefactors had grown accustomed to making their donations to the poor, or to the local school, and inviting their prayers, but no longer with the assumption that this would benefit the deceased.[19] 'Month minds' could still be kept, and the better off began to endow commemorative sermons, which might be repeated over a number of years. In spite of the absence of the mass, and of images from the churches, there was a comfortable familiarity about all this. Most important of all, perhaps, there was no attempt to confiscate what had been so painfully restored. The vestments and mass books might be sold off, but at least the parishes kept the proceeds, or most of them. The Queen's commissioners insisted on their cut from the sale of rejected silverware, but this seems to have been exceptional.[20] Those moneys which had been bequeathed to the Church during the Catholic years for purposes which were now unacceptable could usually be diverted to other uses.

There was also the professional responsibility of the clergy, particularly those who had been in post for a number of years. They had baptized, married, counselled and buried the members of their community. Very often they had resolved their quarrels and reconciled their feuds. It required a particular kind of conscience to walk away from all that in the cause of theological principle. The more educated senior clergy often lacked these kinds of direct ties. If they held a living alongside their other offices, the chances were that it would be served by a curate, and it would be he to whom the community related.[21] Such a man would be more doctrinally learned than his parochial colleagues, and that no doubt gave him a sharper perception of such issues, but the real difference was caused by his lack of roots. As a dean, archdeacon or fellow of an Oxford college he would have spent his time in official business or in study, not in dealing with the spiritual crises of the humble. Christopher Trychay is again an extreme example. He had been at Morebath for forty years, guiding and living alongside his parishioners. He had survived two radical regime changes already and it was not likely that he would succumb to a third. He seems also to have found in his later years an empathy with that Protestantism which at first he had so much resented. Perhaps he was merely responding positively to an authority which tolerated his conservative mindset in return for an assiduous outward conformity.[22] Bishop Alley, like his mistress, was not concerned to make windows into men's souls, and he was repaid with a more whole-hearted conformity than he might have expected. By 1570 the reformation was, as Eamon Duffy has put it, 'part of the furniture' at Morebath. In 1564 a new seat was placed by the quire door for Sir Christopher to sit in at service time, and in 1568 a new set of tables of the commandments was commissioned to occupy the space where the high altar had once stood.[23] None of this was constrained, and indeed the vicar's co-operation was rewarded in 1560 by the grant of a second living at nearby Molland, where a similar regime was followed. Not many clergy were deprived in the south-west, but natural wastage was hard to make good because the number of candidates for ordination had taken another disastrous tumble with the return of the reformed faith, and Bishop Alley was no doubt suitably grateful for the vicar of Morebath's complaisance.

Although we know more about Christopher Trychay than we do about most incumbents because of the records which he kept, his attitude was typical rather than exceptional. Even Robert Parkyn, who had been so fierce against married clergy at the beginning of Mary's reign, continued to serve the cure of Adwick-le-Street under the new regime, perhaps encouraged by the Queen's own aversion to married priests (if he had known about it), but more probably out of the same sense of responsibility.[24] Similarly William Shepherd, a former monk of Leeds Priory in Kent, who had been appointed to the tiny Essex benefice of Heydon in 1541. Heydon was about the same size as Morebath, but in a much more theologically disturbed environment. Shepherd set off, as might have been expected, with a full set of conservative convictions, including a belief in purgatory and a devotion to the cult of the Holy Name, but having gritted his teeth through the Edwardian revolution, and no doubt rejoiced at the return of Mary, after 1559 he began to show signs of accepting what might be described as 'mainstream' Protestantism. He campaigned locally against fairs and Sabbath day games on the grounds that they kept 'the younger sort' from hearing the gospel. Like Trychay he preached, energetically and acceptably, and came to describe the Prayer Book as 'the decent rites of the Church of Christ'.[25] There is no sign of reluctance about his acceptance of the Elizabethan settlement, and he went on to serve his little cure until his death in 1586. The mindset of such men is not hard to understand. The gospel was the gospel, whether it was read in English or Latin, and there was actually much to be said for a communion of the people which happened more often than once a year. They were occasions for reconciliation, and whether you called the counselling which accompanied such settlements 'confession' or not did not really matter. The nature of the Eucharistic presence was a mystery anyway, and not worth disrupting the peace of the community over. So they recycled their vestments as altar cloths and their chalices as communion cups, preached or read the homilies and ministered to their people as before.[26] Although there were notorious exceptions, which have probably attracted more than their fair share of attention, the prevailing culture of the early Elizabethan Church was one of conformity, and in that it probably did not differ very much from its Marian predecessor.

By 1570 churches generally were recognizably Protestant places of worship, with the communion table in the body of the church, a reading desk and a pulpit in place, and the plain walls adorned with the tables of the law and the memorials of departed worthies. The government had played its part in this transformation, not only through the constant proddings of Episcopal visitations but also by prescribing intercessions from time to time. There were prayers of support for the French Huguenots, prayers for captives in Barbary or Turkey, prayers against the plague and, most significant perhaps, prayers against the northern rebels in 1569.[27] The latter posed no serious threat to the stability of the regime, but they did serve as a warning against the subversive possibilities of popery. Whereas in 1536 there had been considerable sympathy for 'the northern men' in central and southern England and the government had had difficulty in raising forces against them, no such sympathy was felt for the northern earls. Even on their home ground in the north-east, they rapidly ran out of credibility, and had retreated and disbanded before the royal army ever arrived.[28] Nevertheless, the rising did serve as a stimulus to the growing anti-Catholicism of both the council and the people. Whereas twenty-four years earlier, Morebath had burned its Prayer Book and sent a contingent off to join the south-western rebellion, in 1573 Christopher Trychay recorded 'Item they [the church] resseyvd a communion bok and a sawter of the gefth of William Hurley and of Eylone hys wyffe prisse of xs by sydis the caryage from London – deo gracias'.[29] Hurley had died in 1558, but the gift was no less welcome for being delayed. It would be an exaggeration to describe Trychay, even in the year of his death, as anti-Catholic, and he still clung to many of his old habits of thought. But he had been genuinely converted to the new faith, and he took his congregation with him.

One of the claims made for the Elizabethan settlement is that it marked the change from a clergy-dominated Church to one controlled by the laity, and consequently a cultural shift in the direction of secularization.[30] In a sense that is true. At the political level authority was vested in the Crown and exercised through an ecclesiastical commission. The bishops were left under no illusions that they were anything more than the Queen's servants. The Archbishop of Canterbury was not even a member of the Privy Council. In principle this marked a big change from a Church obedient to the Pope and run by a Cardinal Legate but, in view of Mary's proactive role in ecclesiastical affairs, the change may not have been so great after all. Catholic bishops had spent quite a lot of time sitting on royal commissions, and not all these were concerned with religious discipline. At a parochial level the old Church was undoubtedly sacerdotal in its rites and practices. There was no pretence of lay participation in the mass, and every soul was dependent upon the priest for confession and absolution. This was perhaps more so in Mary's reign than earlier because of the failure of those bastions of lay power, the fraternities, to revive on any significant scale. Nevertheless, it was upon the gifts and bequests of laymen and women that the Church operated and the auxiliary clergy were paid.[31] The churchwardens were the key supporters of the priest and the culture leaders of the laity within the parish. With the reformation, as we have seen, the priest lost most of his liturgical power, but he gained authority of a different kind. The minister's job was to teach and to console. Like the priest he might well be a mediator in quarrels and a counsellor to the afflicted, but his main work was no longer sacramental but pedagogic. He was supposed to be the expert who interpreted the Holy Scriptures, not in the name of the Church, but in the name of the Holy Spirit. This gave him an authority akin to that of the old priest, and meant that nearly all the divergent movements of the Elizabethan Church were clergy-led. This was particularly true of the puritans because although lay support, particularly from the gentry and nobility, was critical to their political power, their leaders were all clergy, like Thomas Cartwright and William Perkins.[32] In theory the layman now had the right to read the scriptures for himself, and to draw what conclusions he thought fit, but in practice very few did so. The eccentric interpretations which circulated in the 1570s and 1580s were nearly all derived from the writings or sermons of dissident ministers.

Similarly the movement towards secular priorities in giving was more apparent than real, and only partly connected with the Elizabethan establishment. Obviously gifts for intercessory prayer finally disappeared, along with bequests designed to support lights or images, but these had been in decline for several years. It is a matter of opinion whether the increasingly generous donations for the education of children and the support of the poor were less motivated by the faith of the donors than the more obviously sacramental gifts of the past. They were less likely to be under the control of the minister or churchwardens and to that extent were secularized, but they were no less a product of the Christian desire to do good works.[33] Similarly the age of church building was over. No longer were generous benefactors going to build a new chapel, or replace the south porch, but repairs were, with some exceptions, kept up to date. Leaking roofs were patched and windows replaced. The high water mark of dilapidation had come under Edward VI, when interest in maintaining the buildings seems genuinely to have declined. As late as 1557, Archdeacon Harpesfield's visitation of Canterbury diocese had revealed many churches still to be in a sorry state of disrepair.[34] Thereafter the situation steadily improved as the industrious visitations of the Elizabethan bishops makes clear.

Generosity might also take the form of endowed sermons, or even the appointment of fully funded lecturers to support (or challenge) the incumbent. These were usually placed in corporate towns and were controlled either by the council of the town or by specially appointed trustees.[35] These lecturers might well have a divisive effect upon the community, but cannot be adduced as symptoms of religious indifference. Inevitably, the Church courts show cases, not merely of indifference, but even of hostility to the Church which cannot be ascribed to either puritanism or recusancy, but that had always been the case. The woman in Mary's reign who had claimed that her daughter could piss as good holy water as that which the priest made was not necessarily a heretic, but was expressing contempt for the whole sacramental set up of the Church.[36]

What did change with Elizabeth's accession was the preoccupation with heresy. This did not mean that either the Queen or her first-generation bishops were indifferent to its solvent effects. Their visitation returns show them struggling hard to impose some degree of uniformity, but they were not interested in the doctrinal beliefs of the dissidents.[37] They no longer administered the careful inquisitions into the exact nature of the Eucharistic presence which had characterized so many Marian heresy trials, and which had awakened the principled resistance – or sheer obstinacy – of many defendants. It was one thing to be fined 12*d.* for non-attendance at church, and quite another to put your life on the line. In due course this changed, but the issue remained one of obedience rather than belief. The rebellion of the earls and the papal bull which followed it made clear the subversive potential of Catholicism – not a belief in transubstantiation but a willingness to accept the Pope's deposing power. It was in a sense a fiction for William Cecil to pretend, when he wrote *The Execution of Justice in England* in 1583, that no one was put to death for their religion, but only for treason.[38] As William Allen pointed out, if you made papal obedience a capital offence, you were effectively penalizing people for their beliefs.[39] However, in another sense it was a real distinction, because no one in power was much interested in the sacramental faith of the accused, but only in their allegiance to the Queen. It was not for their pastoral care that the death penalty was decreed for priests, but rather for the assumption that their first political duty was to Rome.[40] It was for this reason that there arose the phenomenon of 'church popery', or outward conformity, against which the Catholic clergy set their faces so adamantly. Over time church popery inevitably drifted into conformity and its practitioners were largely ignored in the anti-Catholic legislation of the 1580s.[41]

So what happened to the culture of Mary Tudor's Church? At an elite level the answer is clear. Cardinal Pole's legatees were those who fled, either from their appointments or from the universities, to avoid the reimposition of heresy. Thomas Harding, Thomas Stapleton, William Allen, Thomas Goldwell, and a little later Edmund Campion and Robert Parsons, all got themselves out of England.[42] The heirs of those Marian divines who had so strenuously promoted their faith, like Thomas Watson, were the recusants who faced fines, imprisonment and even death for their devotion to the Holy See. However, whether clergy or laity, these formed only a small part of the population. Far more numerous were those who clung onto the old ways as far as they could, but were not prepared to make great sacrifices for them. These were the clergy who celebrated Holy Communion in the morning and mass in the evening, unless or until they were found out; or the gentleman who went to church with his eldest son, but who avoided taking communion as far as possible, and whose wife and daughters remained aloof; whose tenants and servants went through the motions of conformity, but who celebrated the old rituals in private.[43] However there were also others, and these may have been the most numerous of all, who conformed more or less willingly, not because they were convinced about justification by faith or transubstantiation, but because they took their community seriously and followed the lead which was given them. They were, for the most part, the same people who had lived through Mary's reign, when they had done much the same thing. They saw themselves as Christians, but were uncertain as to quite what that meant, having been told one thing under Edward VI, and the exact opposite under Queen Mary – often by the same people.[44] Their culture was Christian rather than specifically Catholic or Protestant, and their fondness for traditional forms did not have deep doctrinal roots. A procession was a good excuse for a communal get together – never mind the liturgical pretext. Heresy was deplorable, as much because it disrupted the unity of the village as because it destroyed the souls of those infected with it. However if the alleged heretic was an honest and good neighbour, why should he (or she) be prosecuted?

It is deceptively easy to take elite attitudes as being representative. Edmund Bonner, William Barlow, Thomas Watson and other authoritative writers did their best to inculcate sound doctrine into the laity. Sermons hammered away at the same themes, but Cardinal Pole was probably right when he argued that ceremonies observed for obedience's sake were better for conformity than any amount of Bible-reading.[45] Pole was not averse to Bible-reading, but like Henry VIII was distressed to learn that it was wrangled over in every ale house. The English Bible, even more than the sermon, could easily get out of control, and it was control, particularly clerical control, which preoccupied him most. Like every Catholic leader, he saw the alleged 'liberty' of Protestantism as its greatest vice, and it was the sheer obstinacy of the heretic as much as his doctrinal deviance which called forth the severity of punishment.[46] These attitudes were imperfectly reflected at grass-roots level, but obedience was a word which everyone understood. Consequently 'the Queen's proceedings' attracted an immediate response, and Stephen Gardiner would have had almost everyone behind him when he told James Hales to pay more attention to the Queen than to the law. We simply do not know what the popular response to the restoration of the papacy might have been, and the ostentatious enthusiasm of parliament is no guide in that respect. However, the King was unpopular and the restoration was (rightly) seen as being his work. So this new level of obedience would have been tempered by hostility over foreign interference. This played into the hands of those who were dissenters anyway, but had no noticeable impact on the general level of conformity. It should also be remembered that these dissenters, although relatively few, constituted a counterculture. These were the people to whom the religion of the word had appealed, and who had been convinced by the Edwardian message. They were a minority, but may have been more numerous than has generally been supposed. They were more common in the towns than in the countryside, but were to be found from Newcastle-upon-Tyne to Exeter. They were not heroes, and although they may have grumbled and 'looked down' when ordered to go to mass, the most that they did by way of resistance was to try and avoid attendance.[47] Had the Catholic Church been content to accept this grudging acquiescence, and imposed small fines for absence, there would have been no great persecution. It was the inquisitorial insistence on the fine points of doctrinal orthodoxy which caused the trouble. This was understandable in the case of elite clergy who were seeking 'soul conformity', and who deluded themselves into believing that every Protestant conscience concealed a subversive anxious to overthrow the Queen's government. There was a failure on the part of the elite to understand or to connect with the culture of popular religion; that culture which kept all but the most zealous of reformers within the bounds of their communities, and led to an outward acceptance of the regime change of 1553. This was simply not good enough for Queen Mary and her loyal servants, who were desperately concerned with the salvation of the souls entrusted to their charge. The Church had to be satisfied that conformity was from the heart, and thereby stimulated that opposition which it then had to take draconian measures to overcome. If Elizabeth's Church had been allowed to go the same way to work (and there were some who wanted that) there could well have been far more than 300 Catholic martyrs in the first ten years of her reign.[48]

As it was, the heresy laws were repealed again in 1559, and with them went the legal framework of the persecution. Elizabeth believed herself to be responsible for the souls of her subjects, no less than for their bodies, but she interpreted her role in a different way. It would not be true to say that she was not interested in what they believed, but her indifference to godly preaching tells its own story. She knew the common man well enough to understand that his faith waited upon his obedience rather than the other way round. There was no point in starting with sophisticated points of doctrine, and she discouraged zealous bishops from probing beneath the surface. Elizabeth understood, as Mary had not, the compromises which circumstances make necessary. She was a Protestant, the faith in which she had been reared, but was sufficiently pragmatic to recognize the exposed nature of her position in 1553.[49] She was also aware, as Mary had not been, of the grey areas between the Catholic and reformed churches, and of the wide range of doctrine which they had in common. She liked church music, having her family's talent in that direction, preferred her clergy simply robed, and was notoriously keen on the cross and candles on the communion table in the Chapel Royal. These were not calculated gestures, but expressions of her own faith, which was markedly less austere than that of her Zwinglian brother.[50] Her attitude is only a puzzle to those whose mindset is conditioned by the absolutes laid down by the intellectuals upon both sides, who abused each other in print over refined points of doctrine and deliberately emphasized the differences between them in order to score debating points. The Queen was not interested in debating points; what she was interested in was using the Church as a form of social and political cement, and in that she was eventually highly successful. Whether she was more successful than her shorter-lived sister and whether the recusants after 1570 were more disruptive that the Protestants before 1558 remains debateable. What is clear is that John Foxe's martyrology was more popular and effective than those of Richard Verstegen or Robert Parsons.[51] This was partly because Foxe was writing in the heat of the battle, while both Verstegen and Parsons were retrospective, but it is also partly because the Marian persecution was specifically doctrinal, whereas that of the recusants was overtly political, particularly after 1585. Gardiner and Pole never succeeded in branding the reformers as enemies of the state in the way which the Catholics were branded during the Anglo-Spanish War. Nor is there any evidence that they were so perceived by their conforming neighbours. The culture of the Marian Church was at its roots much more tolerant and pragmatic than its elite leaders would have liked. The strength of its commitment to the papacy and to the old canon law was ruthlessly exposed by the events of 1558–9 when the lay elite defected almost to a man, and the commons followed their lead. Those who have observed that this had nothing to do with Protestantism are almost certainly right. What it did have to do with was authority. By 1559 the English people were much more comfortable with a Church led and defined within the realm, particularly if it was 'user friendly' in terms of its rituals and practice. This had applied in 1553, and was to apply again in 1559. The Church had an enormous social function, which it could discharge almost irrespective of its doctrinal foundations, and it was the consensus generated by that function which determined the religious culture both of Mary's Church and that of Elizabeth which followed. To concentrate too much on the polemic posturings of divines on either side of the division is to give that division an emphasis which it does not really deserve.

NOTES

Introduction

1. J. Burckhardt, *The Age of Constantine the Great*, trans. M. Hadas (London: Routledge & Kegan Paul, 1949); N. Davies, *Europe: A History* (London: Pimlico, 1997), pp. 208–9.
2. P. Jaffe (ed.), *Regesta pontificum romanorum annum 1198*, 2nd edn, ed. S. Loewenfeld et al., 2 vols (Leipzig: Veit, 1885–8).
3. C. Oman, *The Dark Ages, ad 476–918*, 6th edn (London: Rivington, 1919); F. Lot, *The End of the Ancient World* (London: Routledge, 1966).
4. *Bede's Ecclesiastical History of the English People*, ed. B. Colgrave and R. A. B. Mynors, corrected edn (Oxford: Oxford University Press, 1991), pp. 73–6; H. Mayr-Harting, *The Coming of Christianity to Anglo-Saxon England* (London: Batsford, 1972), pp. 117–28.
5. N. Orme, *English Schools in the Middle Ages* (London: Methuen, 1973); P. Binski, *Medieval Death: Ritual and Representation* (New Haven, CT: Yale University Press, 1996); K. L. Wood Legh, *Perpetual Chantries in Britain* (Oxford: Oxford University Press, 1965).
6. E. Duffy, *The Stripping of the Altars* (New Haven, CT: Yale University Press, 1992), 'How the Plowman Learned his Paternoster', pp. 53–88.
7. Ibid, 'Encountering the Holy', pp. 89–130.
8. For instance Arians, who did not believe in the humanity of Christ, Nestorians, who did not believe in his divinity, Donatists and many others. A. McGrath, *Christian Theology: An Introduction* (Oxford: Blackwell, 1994), pp. 5–25.
9. E. Cameron, *The Reformation of the Heretics: The Waldenses of the Alps, 1480–1580* (Oxford: Oxford University Press, 1984), pp. 65–94.
10. E. LeRoy Ladurie, *Montaillou: Cathars and Catholics in a French Village, 1294–1324*, trans. B. Bray (Harmondsworth: Penguin, 1980); J. Sumption, *The Albigensian Crusade* (London: Faber, 1999); Z. Oldenbourg, *Massacre at Montsegur: History of the Albigensian Crusade* (1961; London: Phoenix, 2000).
11. A. Hudson, *The Premature Reformation: Wycliffite Texts and Lollard History* (Oxford: Oxford University Press, 1988); R. Rex, *The Lollards* (Basingstoke: Macmillan, 2002); R. Lutton, *Lollardy and Orthodox Religion in Pre-Reformation England* (London: Royal Historical Society, 2006).
12. 16 Richard II, c. 5, in *Statutes of the Realm*, ed. A Luders, T. E. Tomlins, J. Raithby et al., 11 vols (London, 1810–28), vol. 2, pp. 84–6.
13. K. Dockray, *Henry V* (Stroud: Tempus, 2004), pp. 13–15.
14. Duffy, *The Stripping of the Altars*, 'Now and at the Hour of our Death', pp. 299–377.

15. Ibid, pp. 354–7.
16. Dom D. Knowles, *The Religious Orders in England*, 3 vols (Cambridge: Cambridge University Press, 1955), vol. 2, pp. 8–13; B. F. Harvey, *Living and Dying in England, 1100–1540: The Monastic Experience* (Oxford: Oxford University Press, 1993), pp. 112–45.
17. R. Rex, 'The Friars in the English Reformation', in P. Marshall and A. Ryrie (eds), *The Beginnings of English Protestantism* (Cambridge: Cambridge University Press, 2002), pp. 38–59.
18. Duffy, *The Stripping of the Altars*, 'Encountering the Holy', pp. 91–130.
19. D. Loades, 'The Sanctuary', in C. S. Knighton and R. Mortimer (eds), *Westminster Abbey Reformed, 1540–1640* (Aldershot: Ashgate, 2003), pp. 75–93.
20. M. Aston, *Lollards and Reformers: Images and Literacy in Late Medieval Religion* (London: Hambledon, 1984). For the Burford Lollards, see J. Foxe, *The Actes and Monuments of the English Martyrs* (1583 edn), p. 841. The 1583 edition is cited throughout unless otherwise stated.
21. G. W. H. Lampe (ed.), *The Cambridge History of the Bible, Vol. 2: The West, from the Fathers to the Reformation* (Cambridge: Cambridge University Press, 1969), pp. 492–505.
22. H. Jedin, *A History of the Council of Trent*, trans. E. Graf, 2 vols (London: T. Nelson, 1949), vol. 2, pp. 58–92.
23. A. G. Dickens, *The English Reformation* (London: Batsford, 1964), p. 94.
24. D. Loades, *The Six Wives of Henry VIII* (Stroud: Amberley, 2009), pp. 44–5.
25. Leviticus 20:21 forbids a man from taking his brother's wife and condemns the couple to childlessness. Henry and Catherine were not childless, they had a daughter, but a Hebraist named Robbert Wakefield convinced Henry that the original Hebrew said 'they should be without sons', which fitted his case.
26. 26 Henry VIII, c. 1, in *Statutes of the Realm*, vol. 3, p. 492.
27. D. Loades, *Henry VIII: Court, Church and Conflict* (London: National Archives, 2009), pp. 89–90.
28. 26 Henry VIII, c. 1; G. R. Elton, *The Tudor Constitution* (Cambridge: Cambridge University Press, 1982), p. 341.
29. For the most recent full discussion of the Pilgrimage of Grace, see R. W. Hoyle, *The Pilgrimage of Grace and the Politics of the 1530s* (Oxford: Oxford University Press, 2001).
30. G. R. Elton, *Policy and Police* (Cambridge: Cambridge University Press, 1972), pp. 217–64. For the creation and maintenance of the royal image, see G. Walker, *Persuasive Fictions; Faction, Faith and Political Culture in the Reign of Henry VIII* (Aldershot: Scolar, 1996).
31. D. Daniell, *The Bible in English: Its History and Influence* (New Haven, CT: Yale University Press, 2003), pp. 198–204.
32. A. Jenkins and P. Preston, *Biblical Scholarship and the Church: A Sixteenth-Century Crisis of Authority* (Aldershot: Ashgate, 2007).
33. J. J. Scarisbrick, *Henry VIII* (London: Eyre & Spottiswoode, 1968), pp. 406–17.
34. J. Youings, *The Dissolution of the Monasteries* (London: Penguin, 1971); W. C. Richardson, *A History of the Court of Augmentations, 1536–1554* (Baton Rouge, LA: University of Louisiana Press, 1961); Dom D. Knowles, *Bare Ruined Choirs: The Dissolution of the English Monasteries* (Cambridge: Cambridge University Press, 1976).
35. Dickens, *The English Reformation*, p. 148.

36. D. Loades, *John Dudley, Duke of Northumberland* (Oxford: Oxford University Press, 1996), pp. 82–5.

37. 'Furthermore, because the place where the souls remain, the name thereof, the state and condition which they be in, be to us uncertain, therefore these, with all other such things, must also be left to Almighty God'. *The King's Book*, ed. T. A. Lacey (London: SPCK, 1932), p. 164.

38. G. Redworth, *In Defence of the Church Catholic: The Life of Stephen Gardiner* (Oxford: Blackwell, 1990), pp. 235–57.

39. W. K. Jordan, *Edward VI: The Young King* (London: Allen & Unwin, 1968), pp. 52–9; Loades, *John Dudley*, pp. 83–4.

40. For a full discussion of Henry's relationship with Cranmer, see D. MacCulloch, *Thomas Cranmer* (New Haven, CT: Yale University Press, 1996).

41. D. MacCulloch, *Tudor Church Militant: Edward VI and the Protestant Reformation* (London: Allen Lane, 1999); Jordan, *Edward VI: The Young King*, pp. 125–66; M. L. Bush, *The Government Policy of Protector Somerset* (Manchester: Manchester University Press, 1975), pp. 100–26.

42. S. Brigden, *London and the Reformation* (Oxford: Clarendon Press, 1989), pp. 433–46.

43. 1 Edward VI, c. 14; 2 & 3 Edward VI, c. 1, in *Statutes of the Realm*, vol. 4, pp. 24–33, 37–9.

44. J. J. Scarisbrick, *The Reformation and the English People* (Oxford: Blackwell, 1984), pp. 19–39.

45. Ibid., pp. 109–35; J. Simon, *Education and Society in Tudor England* (Cambridge: Cambridge University Press, 1979), pp. 223–44.

46. F. Rose-Troup, *The Western Rebellion of 1549* (London: Smith Elder, 1913), appendix K; R. Whiting, *The Blind Devotion of the People: Popular Religion and the English Reformation* (Cambridge: Cambridge University Press, 1989).

47. E. Duffy, *The Voices of Morebath* (New Haven, CT: Yale University Press, 2001), pp. 123–4.

48. 'The Autobiographical Narrative of Thomas Hancock', British Library, Harley MS 425, f. 124, in J. G. Nichols (ed.), *Narratives of the Days of the Reformation* (London: Camden Society, 1859), pp. 74–84.

49. Loades, *John Dudley*, pp. 191–5.

50. The Forty Two Articles, which were appended to the Second Act of Uniformity of 1552, 5 & 6 Edward VI, c. 1.

51. *Acts of the Privy Council*, ed. J. R. Dasent, 32 vols (London: HMSO, 1890–1907), vol. 3, p. 467. Order of 29 January 1552.

52. D. Loades, *Mary Tudor: A Life* (Oxford: Blackwell, 1989), pp. 143–5.

53. J. A. Muller, *Stephen Gardiner and the Tudor Reaction* (1926; London: Octagon, 1970), pp. 161–73.

54. Rose-Troup, *The Western Rebellion*, appendix K.

55. J. Loach, *Edward VI* (New Haven, CT: Yale University Press, 1999); W. K. Jordan, *Edward VI: The Threshold of Power* (London: Allen & Unwin, 1970), pp. 510–15.

56. In liberties such as the palatinates of Durham and Chester, pleas of the Crown belonged to the bishop and the earl respectively. All these franchises were resumed to the Crown by statute in 1536 (27 Henry VII, c. 24).

57. R. Houlbrooke, *Church Courts and the People during the English Reformation* (Oxford: Oxford University Press, 1979), pp. 7–20.

58. Petty treason was the crime of killing or resisting another person who had a proper claim to the accused's allegiance – a lord, master or father. Misprision was the crime of concealing another person's high treason. It was high treason to kill, injure or resist in arms the king or a member of his close family.

59. J. C. Holt, *Magna Carta and Medieval Government* (London: Hambledon, 1985); R. Turner, *King John* (London: Longmans, 1994); J. C. Davies, *The Baronial Opposition to Edward II* (Cambridge: Cambridge University Press, 1918); M. Bennett, *Richard II and the Revolution of 1399* (Stroud: Sutton, 1999).

60. 'He [the King] being also institute and furnished by the goodness and sufferance of Almighty God with plenary, whole and entire power ...', The Act of Appeals (1533), 24 Henry VIII, c. 12.

61. Elton, *The Tudor Constitution*, pp. 239–47.

62. Loades, *Henry VIII*, pp. 229–37.

63. Scarisbrick, *Henry VIII*, pp. 333–4. Charles V hoped that Henry would take a Portuguese princess as his fourth wife.

64. 'Item, that every parson ... of any parish church within this realm, shall ... provide a book of the whole bible, both in Latin and also in English, and lay the same in the choir for every man that will to look and read thereon'. The first Royal Injunctions of Henry VIII (1536), in *Visitation Articles and Injunctions of the Period of the Reformation*, ed. W. H. Frere and W. M. Kennedy, Alcuin Club Collections, 14–16, 3 vols (London: Longmans, Green, 1910), vol. 2, p. 9.

65. *Foxe's Book of Martyrs: Select Narratives*, ed. J. N. King (Oxford: Oxford University Press, 2009), pp. 22–34.

66. P. Marshall, *Beliefs and the Dead in Reformation England* (Oxford: Oxford University Press, 2002), pp. 47–123.

67. J. N. King, *English Reformation Literature: The Tudor Origins of the Protestant Tradition* (Princeton, NJ: Princeton University Press, 1982); I. Green, *Print and Protestantism in Early Modern England* (Oxford: Oxford University Press, 2000).

68. Brigden, *London and the Reformation*; D. Loades, *Tudor Government* (Oxford: Blackwell, 1997), pp. 143–55.

69. 1 Edward VI, c. 1, in *Statutes of the Realm*, vol. 4, p. 2; *Tudor Royal Proclamations*, ed. P. L. Hughes and J. F. Larkin, 3 vols (New Haven, CT: Yale University Press, 1964–9), vol. 1, pp. 410–12.

70. J. Cornwall, *The Revolt of the Peasantry, 1549* (London: Routledge, 1977); Rose-Troup, *The Western Rebellion*, pp. 122–37.

71. G. G. Gibbs, 'Marking the Days; Henry Machyn's Manuscript and the Mid-Tudor Era', in E. Duffy and D. Loades (eds), *The Church of Mary Tudor* (Aldershot: Ashgate, 2006), pp. 281–308.

72. Royal Injunctions of Edward VI, in *Visitation Articles*, vol. 2, p. 115.

73. Jordan, *Edward VI: The Threshold of Power*, pp. 456–93.

74. Marshall, *Beliefs and the Dead*, pp. 188–231; R. Houlbrooke, *Death, Religion and the Family in England, 1480–1750* (Oxford: Oxford University Press, 1998).

75. MacCulloch, *Tudor Church Militant*, pp. 105–55.

76. Ridley's Articles for the Diocese of London, in *Visitation Articles*, vol. 2, pp. 230–40.

77. Loades, *Mary Tudor*, pp. 145–8.

78. This was intended to take the form of letters patent, but it never passed the Great Seal. Loades, *John Dudley*, pp. 239–41. For the part played by Jane in the crisis, see E. Ives, *Lady Jane Grey: A Tudor Mystery* (Oxford: Wiley/Blackwells, 2009).

79. Loades, *John Dudley*, pp. 239–41.
80. *Tudor Royal Proclamations*, vol. 2, p. 3.
81. J. D. Alsop, 'A Regime at Sea: The Navy and the Succession Crisis of 1553', *Albion*, 24 (1992), pp. 577–90.
82. Loades, *Mary Tudor*, p. 181.
83. Ambassadors to the Emperor, 14 July 1553, in *Calendar of State Papers, Spanish*, ed. R. Tyler et al., 13 vols in 20 (London: Longman, Green, Longman & Roberts, 1862–1964), vol. 11, p. 89. The ambassadors' instructions were to do business with whoever came out on top in the succession crisis.
84. National Archives, KB8/21, mm. 23, 24 [Baga de Secretis], *Fourth Report of the Deputy Keeper of the Public Records* (London: HMSO, 1843), Appendix II, pp. 232–4. Indictment found against John, Duke of Northumberland (and others), 18 August 1553, 'Conspiring to deprive the Queen of her Crown and Dignity, [he] did with arms artillery etc. on the 14th and 15th July 1 Mary, at Ware, levy war against the Queen ....'.
85. *Tudor Royal Proclamations*, vol. 2, pp. 5–8.
86. Cardinal Pole advised Mary to ignore both her father's and her brother's statutes as being *ultra vires*, but Mary did not choose to take this logical advice.
87. The rights of a married woman were negligible in law.

1 The Structure of Coercion

1. J. Blair, 'From Minster to Parish', in J. Blair (ed.), *Minsters and Parish Churches: The Local Church in Transition, 950–1200* (Oxford: Oxford Committee for Archaeology, 1988), pp. 1–19.
2. On the archdeacon and his jurisdiction, see Houlbrooke, *Church Courts*, pp. 30–4.
3. B. Kumin, *The Shaping of a Community: The Rise and Reformation of the English Parish, c. 1400–1560* (Aldershot, Ashgate, 1996), pp. 227–8.
4. B. L. Woodcock, *Medieval Ecclesiastical Courts in the Diocese of Canterbury* (Oxford: Oxford University Press, 1952), pp. 89–92; Houlbrooke, *Church Courts*, p. 9.
5. G. D. Squibb, *Doctors Commons: A History of the College of Advocates and Doctors of Law* (Oxford: Clarendon Press, 1977), pp. 5–7.
6. For the story of Richard Hunne, see Foxe, *Actes and Monuments*, pp. 806–10.
7. J. Bossy (ed.), *Disputes and Settlements: Law and Human Relations in the West* (Cambridge: Cambridge University Press, 1983).
8. See, for example, the case of Rawlins White, convented before the Bishop of Llandaff. Foxe, *Actes and Monuments*, p. 1556.
9. Houlbrooke, *Church Courts*, pp. 30–5.
10. In some cases Foxe complained that executions were carried out in haste, without waiting for the arrival of the writ. See the case of Richard Woodman and others, burned at Lewes in August 1557. *Actes and Monuments*, p. 2003.
11. P. Gwyn, *The Kings Cardinal: The Rise and Fall of Thomas Wolsey* (London: Barrie & Jenkins, 1990), pp. 269–70.
12. Carne to Philip and Mary, 2 July 1557, National Archives, SP69/11/641.
13. 2 Henry IV, c. 15; 2 Henry V, c. 7, in *Statutes of the Realm*, vol. 2, pp. 125–8, 181–4.
14. J. A. F. Thompson, *The Later Lollards, 1414–1520* (Oxford: Oxford University Press, 1965); Lutton, *Lollardy and Orthodox Religion*.
15. *Visitation Articles*, vol. 2, pp. 1–11.

16. Elton, *The Tudor Constitution*, p. 223; S. E. Lehmberg, 'Supremacy and Vicegerency: A Re-Examination', *English Historical Review*, 81 (1966), pp. 225–35, on p. 225.

17. Foxe, *Actes and Monuments*, pp. 1120–1.

18. 31 Henry VIII, c. 14, 'An Act Abolishing Diversity of Opinions', in *Statutes of the Realm*, vol. 3, pp. 739–43.

19. Foxe, *Actes and Monuments*, pp. 1135–77, 1203–5.

20. Redworth, *In Defence of the Church Catholic*, pp. 285–9; Loades, *Mary Tudor*, pp. 142–50; MacCulloch, *Tudor Church Militant*, pp. 36–9.

21. To affirm the same in writing or printing, or by overt act or deed. 1 Edward VI, c. 12, in *Statutes of the Realm*, vol. 4, pp. 18–22.

22. These burnings must have been carried out under the old canon law, because there was no statute in being authorizing such a penalty. MacCulloch, *Tudor Church Militant*, p. 141.

23. 5 & 6 Edward VI, c. 1, in *Statutes of the Realm*, vol. 4, pp. 37–9.

24. Foxe, *Actes and Monuments*, pp. 152–3.

25. *Tudor Royal Proclamations*, vol. 2, no. 390.

26. *Calendar of the Patent Rolls, Philip and Mary*, 4 vols (London: HMSO, 1936–9), vol. 1, p. 77.

27. 1 October 1553, in *Tudor Royal Proclamations*, vol. 2, no. 393.5.

28. *Visitation Articles*, vol. 2, pp. 322–9.

29. Ibid., vol. 2, p. 325.

30. 28 Henry VIII, c. 10, 'An Act Extinguishing the authority of the Bishop of Rome' (vii), in *Statutes of the Realm*, vol. 3, pp. 663–6.

31. D.G. Newcombe, *John Hooper: Tudor Bishop and Martyr* (Oxford: Davenant, 2009), p. 224.

32. A. G. Dickens, *Robert Holgate*, St Anthony's Hall Publications, 8 (London: St Anthony's Press, 1955); Newcombe, *John Hooper*, p. 230.

33. *Calendar of the Patent Rolls, Philip and Mary*, vol. 2, p. 261.

34. 14 April 1554, ibid., p. 302.

35. D. Loades, *The Reign of Mary Tudor* (London: Longmans, 1991), pp. 119–20.

36. Redworth, *In Defence of the Church Catholic*, pp. 323–4.

37. 1 & 2 Philip and Mary, c. 8, in *Statutes of the Realm*, vol. 4, pp. 246–54.

38. For example Thomas Hawkes, denounced by servants of the Earl of Oxford: Foxe, *Actes and Monuments*, pp. 1585–91.

39. For example by John Proctor, whose *Historie of Wiatts Rebellion* (London, 1554) [*RSTC* 20407] was a work of government propaganda. The work is reprinted in Pollard, *Tudor Tracts*, pp. 199–259.

40. Rich, whose evidence had been responsible for the conviction of Thomas More in 1535, had appeared to be a keen evangelical during Edward's reign. *ODNB*.

41. Foxe, *Actes and Monuments*, pp. 1562–5.

42. Ibid., pp. 1497–2050.

43. Ibid., p. 1483; D. Loades, *The Oxford Martyrs* (London: Batsford, 1970), p. 149.

44. Loades, *The Oxford Martyrs*, p. 149.

45. 'Processus contra Cranmerum', in *The Works of Thomas Cranmer*, ed. J. E. Cox, 2 vols (London: Parker Society, 1844–6), vol. 2, p. 541.

46. Mary's attitude towards the Royal Supremacy before January 1555 is obscure. She gave up using the title, but certainly used the power. For practical purposes she seems to have treated it rather as she argued it should have been treated while Edward was a child.

47. 1 Mary, st. 2, c. 3, in *Statutes of the Realm*, vol. 4, p. 203.
48. For example, 1 Mary, st. 3, c. 10, 'For re-edifying the parish churches of Ongar and Greensted in Essex', which had been united by statute under Edward VI, in *Statutes of the Realm*, vol. 4, p. 234.
49. Loades, *the Oxford Martyrs*, p. 165.
50. *Calendar of the Patent Rolls, Philip and Mary*, vol. 3, p. 24.
51. Ibid.
52. On Pole's exercise of his Legatine authority, see T. F. Mayer, *Reginald Pole: Prince and Prophet* (Cambridge: Cambridge University Press, 2000), pp. 252–301.
53. *Calendar of the Patent Rolls, Philip and Mary*, vol. 3, p. 281.
54. It is not at all clear what law the commissioners would have been using, because the Act of Six Articles had not been restored and no other statute gave them a basis upon which to act. This would seem to be another hangover from the Royal Supremacy, when the King had administered to canon law.
55. T. F. Mayer, 'The Success of Cardinal Pole's Final Legation', in Duffy and Loades (eds) *The Church of Mary Tudor*, pp. 149–75.
56. *Calendar of the Patent Rolls, Philip and Mary*, vol. 4, p. 14.
57. *Acts of the Privy Council*, vol. 4, p. 411. The remark was made in the context of the flog- gings of Thomas Hinshaw and John Mills. Foxe, *Actes and Monuments*, pp. 2043–4. See also the royal letter of 24 May 1555 in ibid., p. 1582.
58. Foxe, *Actes and Monuments*, pp. 1796–829.
59. Foxe makes frequent references to 'adversaries' as being responsible for the arrest of vic- tims of the persecution, and it is not clear who these people were. A magistrate or an incumbent who was responsible was normally named, and marginalia sometimes iden- tify the 'persecutors' by name, but many of these seem to have held no official position.
60. John Chambers and David Pole, bishops of Peterborough, hardly feature in the records of the persecution, nor does Maurice Griffith of Rochester. The most reluctant of all was Cuthbert Tunstall of Durham – but he was hardly in the front line. By contrast John Hopton of Norwich was exceptionally zealous.
61. Foxe, *Actes and Monuments*, pp. 1573–7.

2 Elite Religion

1. M. Huggarde, *The Displaying of the Protestantes* (London, 1556) [*RSTC* 13557–8], p. 12. Huggarde was an educated artisan – a hosier – rather than an elite writer.
2. Mayer, *Reginald Pole*, pp. 157–8.
3. Jedin, *A History of the Council of Trent*, vol. 2, pp. 92–3.
4. Duffy, *The Voices of Morebath*, p. 162.
5. Mayer, *Reginald Pole*. Lampe (ed.), *The Cambridge History of the Bible, Vol. 2*, pp. 492–505, examines the positive attitude of Erasmus towards vernacular scripture, which Pole largely followed.
6. E. Duffy, 'Cardinal Pole Preaching: St. Andrew's Day 1557', in Duffy and Loades (eds), *The Church of Mary Tudor*, pp. 176–200.
7. Pole's oration to the citizens of London in support of ceremonies, in J. Strype, *Ecclesiasti- cal Memorials* (London, 1721), vol. 3, ii, pp. 482–510. This discipline had been largely restored since Mary's accession.
8. W. Wizeman, *The Theology and Spirituality of Mary Tudor's Church* (Aldershot: Ash- gate, 2006), pp. 14–20.

9. For an examination of the state of the Church at this time, and the nature of these controversies, see Jedin, *A History of the Council of Trent*.
10. 1 Mary, st. 2, c. 2, in *Statutes of the Realm*, vol. 4, p. 202.
11. Wizeman, *The Theology and Spirituality*, p. 38. Smyth stood down from his chair in 1555, on appointment as Vice Chancellor. His replacement was Juan de Villagarcia.
12. D. Hoak, 'The Coronations of Edward VI, Mary I and Elizabeth I', in Knighton and Mortimer (eds), *Westminster Abbey Reformed*, pp. 114–52; D. Loades, *Intrigue and Treason, the Tudor Court 1547–1558* (London: Pearson, 2004), pp. 137–40.
13. Loades, *Mary Tudor*, pp. 117–18; S. James, *Katheryn Parr: The Making of a Queen* (Stroud: Sutton, 1999).
14. Preface to St John's Gospel, in N. Udall, *The First Tome or Volume of the Paraphrases of Erasmus upon the New Testament* (London, 1548) [*RSTC* 2854].
15. According to Renard's report, in *Calendar of State Papers, Spanish*, vol. 11, p. 134; D. Loades, 'The Personal Religion of Mary I', in Duffy and Loades (eds), *The Church of Mary Tudor*, pp. 1–29, on pp. 18–19.
16. A mood reported in a number of the ambassadors' despatches. See also 'The Vita Mariae Angliae Reginae of Robert Wingfield of Brantham', ed. D. MacCulloch, *Camden Miscellany*, 28 (1984), pp. 181–301, on pp. 252–5.
17. As one contemporary verse put it, 'Ay que Ingalterra ya no es para mi!' F. Diaz-Plaja (ed.), *La Historia de Espana en sus Documentos* (Madrid: Instituto de Estudios Políticos, 1958), p. 149.
18. Loades, *Mary Tudor*, p. 229; *Tres Cartas de la sucedido en el viaje de su Alteza in Ingalterra* (Madrid: La Sociedad de Bibliofilos Espanoles, 1877), primera carta, p. 91.
19. J. I. Tellechea Idigoras, 'Fray Bartolomé Carranza: A Spanish Dominican in the England of Mary Tudor', trans. R. Truman, in J. Edwards and R. Truman (eds), *Reforming Catholicism in the England of Mary Tudor: The Achievement of Fray Bartolomé Carranza* (Aldershot: Ashgate, 2005), pp. 21–33.
20. J. Edwards, 'Corpus Christi at Kingston upon Thames: Bartolomé Carranza and the Eucharist in Marian England', in Edwards and Truman (eds), *Reforming Catholicism*, pp. 139–53.
21. Ibid., p. 142; J. I. Tellechea Idigoras, *Fray Bartoloma Carranza y el Cardenal Pole* (Pamplona: Diputación Foral de Navarra, Institución Príncipe de Viana, Consejo Superior de Investigaciones Científicas, 1977), p. 67.
22. D. Baldwin, *The Chapel Royal, Ancient and Modern* (London: Duckworth, 1990), pp. 89–91.
23. Loades, *Mary Tudor*.
24. 29 May 1554, in *Calendar of the Patent Rolls, Philip and Mary*, vol. 1, p. 203. In her will she also left £500 to each university 'for the relief of poor scholars', Loades, *Mary Tudor*, p. 372.
25. Mayer, *Reginald Pole*, pp. 190–1; *ODNB*; E. Duffy, *Fires of Faith: Catholic England under Mary Tudor* (New Haven, CT: Yale University Press, 2009), pp. 29–52.
26. Duffy, *Fires of Faith*, p. 42; *The Letters of Stephen Gardiner*, ed. J. A. Muller (Cambridge: Cambridge University Press, 1933), pp. 496–501.
27. J. Edwards, 'Spanish Influence in Marian England', in Duffy and Loades (eds), *The Church of Mary Tudor*, pp. 201–26, on p. 203. An English or Latin translation was planned, but never took place.
28. Mayer, 'The Success of Cardinal Pole's Final Legation', p. 149.

29. Notably her own secret dispensation ahead of her coronation. Report by Henry Penning (messenger of Cardinal Pole), in *Calendar of State Papers, Venetian*, ed. R. Brown et al., 38 vols (London: Longman, Green, Longman & Roberts, 1864–1947), vol. 5, p. 429. See also C. H. Garrett, 'The Legatine Register of Cardinal Pole, 1554–7', *Journal of Modern History*, 13 (1941), pp. 189–94.

30. *The Correspondence of Reginald Pole. 3. A Calendar 1555–8: Restoring the English Church*, ed. T. F. Mayer (Aldershot: Ashgate, 2004), pp. 75 ff.

31. C. Cross, 'The English Universities, 1553–1558', in Duffy and Loades (eds), *The Church of Mary Tudor*, pp. 57–76, on p. 62.

32. Ibid., *passim*.

33. Ibid, p. 70; A. Wood, *History and Antiquities of the University of Oxford*, 2 vols (Oxford, 1792–6), vol. 2, pp. 130–4.

34. J. Lamb (ed.), *A Collection of Letters, Statutes and other Documents, from the MS Library of Corp. Christ. Coll.* (London: J. W. Parker, 1838), pp. 184–236; J. B. Mullinger, *The University of Cambridge*, 3 vols (Cambridge: Cambridge University Press, 1873–1911), vol. 2, p. 157.

35. A. Hegarty, 'Carranza and the English Universities', in Edwards and Truman (eds), *Reforming Catholicism*, pp. 153–72.

36. Cross, 'The English Universities', p. 71.

37. Ibid.

38. Foxe, *Actes and Monuments*, pp. 1951–64.

39. Duffy, *Fires of Faith*, pp. 188–207.

40. *Epistolarum Reginaldi Poli, SRE Cardinalis et aliorum ad ipsum*, ed. A. M. Quirini, 5 vols (Brescia: Rizzardi, 1744–57), vol. 5, p. 74.

41. D. Cressy, *Literacy and the Social Order: Reading and Writing in Tudor and Stuart England* (Cambridge: Cambridge University Press, 1980); H. Kearney, *Scholars and Gentlemen: Universities and Society in Pre-Industrial Britain, 1500–1700* (London: Faber, 1970).

42. There was much emphasis among the elite writers upon 'those ... who deceive the simple' (British Library, Harley MS 444, f. 27), acknowledging the fact that many had been so influenced. John Foxe records the stories of many of these humble and illiterate heretics.

43. Wizeman, *The Theology and Spirituality*, pp. 251–5.

44. Ibid., pp. 264, 259; Duffy, *Fires of Faith*, p. 232.

45. L. Stopes, *An Ave Maria in Commendation of our Most Vertuous Quene* (London, 1553) [*RSTC* 23292]; T. Watson, *Holsome and Catholyke Doctryne concerning the Seven Sacraments* (London, 1558) [*RSTC* 25112].

46. T. More, *A Dialoge of Comfort against Tribulacion, made by Syr Thomas More Knyght* (London, 1553) [*RSTC* 18082]; T. More, *The Workes of Sir Thomas More Knyght, sometime Lorde Chauncellour of England* (London, 1557) [*RSTC* 18076].

47. It was normal practice to circulate texts of sermons among colleagues and friends, which was how some of them came to be published. S. Wabuda, *Preaching during the English Reformation* (Cambridge: Cambridge University Press, 2002).

48. J. Gwynneth, *A Brief Declaration of the Notable Victory geven of God* (London, 1554) [*RSTC* 12556.7]; Proctor, *The Historie of Wiatts Rebellion*.

49. J. Christopherson, *An Exhortation to all Menne to Take Hede and Beware of Rebellion* (London, 1554) [*RSTC* 5207].

50. J. Fisher, *A Sermon very Notable Fruicteful, and Godlie* (London, 1554) [*RSTC* 10896]; J. Standish, *The Triall of the Supremacie* (London, 1556) [*RSTC* 23211].

51. *A Plaine and Godlye Treatise concernyng the Masse* (London, 1555) [*RSTC* 17629, 17629.5]; *An Exclamation upon the Erronious and Fantasticall Sprite of Heresy* (London, [1553?]) [*RSTC* 10615].

52. Mayer, 'The Success of Cardinal Pole's Final Legation'.

53. E. Bonner, *A Profytable and Necessarye Doctryne, with certayne Homelies* (London: 1555) [*RSTC* 3283].

54. Ibid., p. 14v.

55. Wizeman, *The Theology and Spirituality*, p. 130; L. Pollard, *Fyve Homilies* (London: 1556) [*RSTC* 20091], sigs G4r–H1r.

56. Wizeman, *The Theology and Spirituality*, pp. 137–40.

57. Duffy, *Fires of Faith*, pp. 48–9; Loades, *The Reign of Mary Tudor*, pp. 106–7; *Visitation Articles*, vol. 2, pp. 322–9.

58. Bonner, *A Profytable and Necessarye Doctryne*, preface.

59. Watson, *Holsome and Catholyke Doctryne*, p. 58.

60. Ibid., p. 94. See Wizeman, 'The Sermons of Thomas Watson', in Duffy and Loades (eds), *The Church of Mary Tudor*, pp. 258–80.

61. Duffy, *The Stripping of the Altars*, pp. 534–7.

62. E. Bonner, *An Honest Godlye Instruction: And Information for the Tranynge, and Bringinge up of Children* (London, 1556) [*RSTC* 3281].

63. *Visitation Articles*, vol. 2, pp. 360–1.

64. Ibid., vol. 2, pp. 360–72.

65. Bonner's Articles, in ibid., vol. 2, p. 339.

66. James Brooks's Injunctions for Gloucester Diocese, in ibid., vol. 2, pp. 401–2.

67. Ibid., vol. 2, p. 404. For the celebration of St Andrew's day, see Duffy, 'Cardinal Pole Preaching'.

68. Goldwell's Injunctions for St Asaph Diocese, in *Visitation Articles*, vol. 2, pp. 409–11.

69. *Two Sermons Preached by the Boy Bishop, one at St. Pauls, temp. Henry VII, the other at Gloucester, temp. Mary*, ed. J. G. Nichols, Camden Miscellany, 7 (London: Camden Society, 1875).

70. *Tudor Royal Proclamations*, vol. 2, p. 302.

71. *The Diary of Henry Machyn*, ed. J. G. Nichols, Camden Society, 42 (London: Camden Society, 1848), p. 75.

72. *Two Sermons Preached by the Boy Bishop*, p. 14.

73. Ibid., p. 21.

74. Foxe, *Actes and Monuments*, pp. 2145–6.

3 Popular Religion

1. F. J. Furnivall (ed.), *Political, Religious and Love Poems from the Archbishop of Canterbury's Lambeth MS no. 306* (London: Early English Text Society, 1866), p. 227.

2. Duffy, *The Stripping of the Altars*, pp. 301–3.

3. There was a great deal of calculation about the power of intercession. An indulgence, for example was for a given number of years remission, which varied according to the price.

4. Most Lollards were regular, even assiduous, attenders at their parish churches, because although they were sceptical about the physical presence of Christ in the elements, they continued to believe that the sacrament was a channel of grace. Rex, *The Lollards*.

5. D. Loades, 'Anticlericalism in the Church of England before 1558: An "Eating Canker"?', in N. Aston and M. Cragoe (eds), *Anticlericalism* (Stroud: Sutton, 2000), pp. 18–41.

6. P. Aries, *The Hour of Our Death*, trans. H. Weaver (London: Allen Lane, 1981), pp. 107–10; Duffy, *The Stripping of the Altars*, plates 117–19; *Ars Moriendi* (London: Wynkyn de Worde, 1506) [*RSTC* 788].

7. W. Tyndale, *The Practice of Prelates* (Antwerp, 1530) and numerous other reformers' works.

8. Duffy, *The Stripping of the Altars*, pp. 155–206, citing Cambridge University Library, Add. MS 2792; H. Farmer, *The Oxford Dictionary of the Saints* (Oxford: Oxford University Press, 1978).

9. Duffy, *The Stripping of the Altars*, p. 157.

10. Ibid., pp. 159–60, citing All Saints Churchwardens' Accounts (b), p. 226.

11. Farmer, *The Oxford Dictionary of the Saints*.

12. Duffy, *The Stripping of the Altars*, pp. 155–6; *Mirk's Festial: A Collection of Homilies by Johannes Mirkus*, ed. T. Erbe (London: Early English Text Society, 1905), pp. 241–2.

13. Henry VIII's last pilgrimage was to Walsingham in 1511, to give thanks for the birth of his short-lived son. Catherine of Aragon was a frequent visitor to Caversham. R. Finucane, *Miracles and Pilgrims: Popular Beliefs in Medieval England* (London: Dent, 1977); J. Adair, *The Pilgrims Way: Shrines and Saints in Britain and Ireland* (London: Thames & Hudson, 1978). The King gave up on pilgrimages after his disappointment, and Mary never followed her mother's example.

14. Joan Bocher was not alone in regarding Mary as a mere channel for the Holy Spirit. A. Hope, 'Martyrs of the Marsh: Elizabeth Barton, Joan Bocher and Trajectories of Martyrdom in Reformation Kent', in R. Lutton and E. Salter (eds), *Pieties in Transition: Religious Practices and Experiences, c. 1400–1640* (Aldershot: Ashgate, 2007), pp. 41–58.

15. See for example, the will of John Major, a London scrivener, written in the 1540s, which specifically instructed that prayers should not be offered for his soul. S. Sweetinburgh, 'The Poor, Hospitals and Charity in Sixteenth-Century Canterbury', in Lutton and Salter (eds), *Pieties in Transition*, pp. 59–73, on p. 60, citing Guildhall Library, MS 9172/1b, f. 153.

16. This commission of reforming cardinals produced its famous, and embarrassing, report, the *Consilium ... de emendanda ecclesia*, in 1537, which was heavily critical of the friars and of certain aspects of curial administration. The report is reprinted in B. J. Kidd, *Documents Illustrative of the Continental Reformation* (Oxford: Oxford University Press, 1911), pp. 307–18.

17. 'The First Royal Injunctions of Henry VIII', para. 4, in *Visitation Articles*, vol. 2, p. 5.

18. Ibid., n. 3, citing the Ten Articles.

19. 'Second Injunctions', item 7, in ibid, vol. 2, p. 38.

20. Gardiner to Protector Somerset, 6 June 1547, in *The Letters of Stephen Gardiner*, pp. 286–95.

21. *Visitation Articles*, vol. 2, p. 327.

22. In the thirteenth century theologians had endeavoured to explain this transformation by using the Aristotelian concepts of substance and accidents; the substance being the inner reality and the accidents the apparent specifics, such as taste, sight and smell. This distinction continued to be used into the Reformation period.

23. C. Horstmann (ed.), *The Minor Poems of the Vernon Manuscript*, 2 vols (London: Early English Text Society, 1892–1901), vol. 1, p. 177.

24. *The Book of Margery Kempe*, ed. S. B Meech and H. E. Allen (London: Early English Text Society, 1940). Some of her neighbours found her ostentatious piety profoundly irritating, p. 11.

25. Duffy, *The Stripping of the Altars*, pp. 100–3.

26. '[M]oche peple ... go nyghe and about the aulter and stond so nyghe the aulter that they trouble oftimes the preest'. Guy de Roye, *Thus Endeth the Doctrinal of Sapyence*, ed. W. Caxton (London, 1489) [*RSTC* 21431], f. 63v.

27. Duffy, *The Stripping of the Altars*, pp. 109–15.

28. N. Davis (ed.), *Non-Cycle Plays and Fragments* (London: Early English Text Society, 1970).

29. *The English Works of John Fisher*, ed. J. E. B. Mayor (London: Early English Text Society, 1876), p. 109.

30. Duffy, *The Stripping of the Altars*, plate 49, taken from a Sarum primer of 1497.

31. 31 Henry VIII, c. 14. Henry's will is calendared in *Letters and Papers, Foreign and Domestic, of the Reign of Henry VIII*, ed. J. Gairdner et al., 23 vols in 35 (London: Longman, Green, Longman, Roberts & Green, 1862–1932), vol. 21, ii, no. 634, from an original in the National Archives. It was printed in full by T. Rymer in *Foedera, Conventiones, Litterae, etc.*, 20 vols (London: A. & J. Churchill, 1704–35), vol. 15, p. 110.

32. *The Works of Thomas Cranmer*, vol. 2, p. 442.

33. This case is argued in full in K. Thomas, *Religion and the Decline of Magic* (London: Weidenfeld & Nicholson, 1971).

34. *The Manual of Prayers, or the Primer in Englysh and Laten ... set forth by John [Hilsey] ... Bysshope of Rochester* (Antwerp, 1539) [*RSTC* 16009.5], pp. 1–9, 25–43.

35. For the office of churchwarden and other minor offices, see F. Makower, *The Constitutional History of the Church of England* (London: Swan Sonnenschein, 1895), pp. 345–8.

36. Loades, *Tudor Government*, pp. 138–66; A. D. Dyer, *Decline and Growth in English Towns, 1400–1640* (London: Macmillan, 1992).

37. Scarisbrick, *The Reformation and the English People*, 'The Importance of Lay Fraternities', pp. 19–39.

38. British Library, Egerton MS 2886, f. 294; *Victoria History of the County of Shropshire*, 7 vols (London: Constable, 1908–98), vol. 2, pp. 134–7.

39. Scarisbrick, *The Reformation and the English People*, p. 25.

40. C. J. Kitching (ed.), *The London and Middlesex Chantry Certificates, 1548*, London Record Society Publications, 16 (London: London Record Society, 1980), pp. 16, 52.

41. Scarisbrick, *The Reformation and the English People*, p. 28.

42. H. F. Westlake, *The Parish Gilds of Mediaeval England* (London: SPCK, 1919), p. 54.

43. Kitching (ed.), *The London and Middlesex Chantry Certificates*, pp. xxiii–xxviii.

44. British Library, Add. MS 28533.

45. 1 Edward VI, c. 14, in *Statutes of the Realm*, vol. 4, pp. 24–33.

46. For the difficulties of one (admittedly conservative) parish priest, see the case of Christopher Trychay at Morebath in Devon. Duffy, *The Voices of Morebath*, pp. 115–20.

47. Queen Mary's Articles, 1554, in *Visitation Articles*, vol. 2, pp. 322–9; R. Houlbrooke, 'The Clergy, the Church Courts and the Marian Restoration in Norwich', Duffy and Loades (eds), *The Church of Mary Tudor*, pp. 124–48.

48. Loades, *The Reign of Mary Tudor*, pp. 299–302.

49. *Calendar of the Patent Rolls, Philip and Mary*, vol. 3, pp. 274–5.

50. *The Chronicle of Queen Jane and of the First Two Years of Mary*, ed. J. G. Nichols, Camden Society, 48 (London: Camden Society, 1850), p. 16.

51. *The Diary of Henry Machyn*, p. 42.

52. Loades, *The Reign of Mary Tudor*, p. 99.

53. Duffy, *The Stripping of the Altars*, p. 549. At Leverton in Lincolnshire the churchwardens had to travel to Lincoln to redeem their possessions. 'Churchwardens Accounts of Leverton in the County of Lincoln, 1492–1598', ed. E. Peacock, *Archaeologia*, 41 (1867), pp. 333–70.

54. Duffy, *The Stripping of the Altars*, p. 548.

55. R. Hutton, 'The Local Impact of the Tudor Reformations', in C. Haigh (ed.), *The English Reformation Revised* (Cambridge: Cambridge University Press, 1987), pp. 114–38.

56. 'Stanford Churchwardens' Accounts, 1552–1602', ed. W. Haines, *Antiquary*, 17 (1888), pp. 70–213, on pp. 70–2, 117–20, 168–72, 209–13.

57. Bishop Bonner's Articles for London Diocese, no. 48, in *Visitation Articles*, vol. 2, p. 342.

58. Duffy, *The Stripping of the Altars*, p. 551.

59. *Visitation Articles*, vol. 2, pp. 402–8.

60. *Testamenta Eboracensia: A Selection of Wills from the Registry at York, Vol. 4*, ed. J. Raine and J. W. Clay, Publications of the Surtees Society, 53 (Durham: Surtees Society, 1869), p. 170; J. Stow, *A Survey of London*, ed. C. L. Kingsford, 2 vols (Oxford: Clarendon Press, 1908) vol. 1, p. 114.

61. Guildhall Library, Journal MS XV, f. 325b.

62. *Four Supplications, 1529–1553*, ed. F. J. Furnivall and J. Meadows Cooper (London: Early English Text Society, 1871), pp. 93–102; E. Kerridge, *Agrarian Problems in the Sixteenth Century and After* (London: Allen & Unwin, 1969).

63. *Calendar of the Patent Rolls, Philip and Mary*, vol. 2, pp. 9, 323.

64. For example, the grant, on the petition of Sir Rowland Hyll, to found a grammar school at Drayton, Shropshire; or the schools founded at Thaxted, Essex and Bromgrove, Worcestershire. *Calendar of the Patent Rolls, Philip and Mary*, vol. 3, pp. 51, 156, 260.

65. J. Strype, *Ecclesiastical Memorials*, 3 vols (Oxford: Clarendon Press, 1820), vol. 3, ii, p. 484; Mayer, *Reginald Pole*, p. 138.

4 Religion and Daily Life

1. Duffy, *The Stripping of the Altars*, pp. 10–12.

2. Prologue to *The Canterbury Tales*, ll. 449–50: 'In the parisshe wif ne was ther noon, That to the offrynge bifore her sholde goon'.

3. N. Pevsner, *Buildings of England: North East Norfolk and Norwich* (Harmondsworth: Penguin, 1962), p. 112.

4. J. Brand, *Popular Antiquities of Great Britain*, ed. H. Carew Hazlitt, 3 vols (London: J. R. Smith, 1870), vol. 1, pp. 38–9; N. Tanner, *The Church in Late Medieval Norwich* (Toronto: Pontifical Institute of Medieval Studies, 1984).

5. For a discussion of the significance of Candlemas, see Duffy, *The Stripping of the Altars*, pp. 15–16.

6. *Missale ad usum Insignis et Praeclare Ecclesiae Sarum*, ed. F. H. Dickinson (Burntisland, 1861–83), col. 697.

7. D. M. Owen, *The Church and Society in Medieval Lincolnshire* (Lincoln: Lincoln Local History Society, 1971), p. 111. This story dates from the fourteenth century.

8. For example, *The Book of Margery Kempe*.
9. Convocation in July 1536 passed a measure for the abrogation of 'superfluous' holy days, which instructed that all feasts of dedication should be observed on the same day (1 October) and that no holy days should be observed during harvest (1 July–29 September). D. Wilkins, *Concilia Magna Brittaniae et Hiberniae*, 4 vols (London, 1737), vol. 3, p. 823. This was enforced by the Royal Supremacy without the intervention of parliament.
10. Duffy, *The Stripping of the Altars*, pp. 41–2.
11. *Dives and Pauper*, ed. P. H. Barnum, 2 vols (London: Early English Text Society, 1976–80), vol. 1, pp. 173–4.
12. As instructed by Convocation, see note 9 above.
13. Duffy, *The Stripping of the Altars*, pp. 37–52.
14. *Ordynarye of Chrystyantye or of Chrysten Men* (London: Wynkyn de Worde, 1502) [*RSTC* 5198], sig. xiv (v).
15. J. Fowler, 'On Medieval Representations of the Months and Seasons', *Archaeologia*, 44 (1873), pp. 137–224; *The Kalendar of Shepheredes*, ed. H. O. Sommer (London: K. Paul, Trench, Trübner & Co., 1892).
16. *The Kalendar of Shepheredes*, p. 19.
17. H. Kamen, *Philip of Spain* (New Haven, CT: Yale University Press, 1997), p. 189.
18. Duffy, *The Stripping of the Altars*, pp. 137–9.
19. Going back to the canons of Elfric in 957, and those of Westminster in 1200. J. Johnson, *English Canons*, 2 vols (Oxford: Parker, 1850–1).
20. *Visitation Articles*, vol. 2, p. 9.
21. E. Lipton, *Affections of the Mind: The Politics of Sacramental Marriage in Late Medieval English Literature* (Notre Dame, IN: University of Notre Dame Press, 2007), pp. 1–20.
22. Houlbrooke, *Church Courts*, pp. 56–62.
23. M. S. Luria and R. L. Hoffman (eds.), *Middle English Lyrics* (New York: Norton, 1974), no. 86.
24. Houlbrooke, *Church Courts*, pp. 78–9.
25. P. Heath, *The English Parish Clergy on the Eve of the Reformation* (London: Routledge & Kegan Paul, 1969).
26. 'The Commons Supplication against the Ordinaries' (1532), in *State Papers of King Henry VIII*, 11 vols (London: Record Commission, 1830–52), vol. 1, no. 22.
27. 26 Henry VIII, c. 6, in *Statutes of the Realm*, vol. 3, pp. 441–2.
28. Knowles, *The Religious Orders in England*, vol. 3: The Tudor Age.
29. P. Hughes, *The Reformation in England*, 3 vols (London: Hollis & Carter, 1954–6), vol. 1, pp. 56–7.
30. Ibid., vol. 1, pp. 57–8.
31. 27 Henry VIII, c. 28, in *Statutes of the Realm*, vol. 3, p. 575.
32. G. Baskerville, *English Monks and the Suppression of the Monasteries* (London: Cape, 1937), pp. 227–45.
33. A point made frequently in writings defending the Supremacy, notably *The Glasse of Truth* (London, 1532) [*RSTC* 11918]; Elton, *Policy and Police*, pp. 173–80.
34. Duffy, *The Stripping of the Altars*, pp. 424–47.
35. 'An Act for the Advancement of True Religion'; Dickens, *The English Reformation*, pp. 189–90.
36. Daniell, *The Bible in English*; Jenkins and Preston, *Biblical Scholarship and the Church*, pp. 231–3.

37. G. Burnet, *The History of the Reformation of the Church of England*, 3 vols (London, 1679–1715), vol. 1, p. 237.
38. Hughes, *The Reformation in England*, p. 363.
39. *Visitation Articles*, vol. 2, p. 115.
40. J. F. Davis, *Heresy and Reformation in the South East of England 1520–1559* (London: Royal Historical Society, 1983), pp. 98–149.
41. Duffy, *The Voices of Morebath*, p. 121.
42. For a full discussion of this resistance where it was greatest, see Whiting, *The Blind Devotion of the People*.
43. MacCulloch, *Tudor Church Militant*, pp. 57–104.
44. Jordan, *Edward VI: The Threshold of Power*, pp. 335–60.
45. Duffy, *The Stripping of the Altars*, pp. 463–73.
46. *Tudor Royal Proclamations*, vol. 2, p. 4; 1 Mary, st. 2, c. 2 (First Act of Repeal); *Visitation Articles*, vol. 2, pp. 322–9.
47. W. H. Frere, *The Marian Reaction in its Relation to the English Clergy* (London: SPCK, 1896), pp. 46–71; G. Baskerville, 'Married Clergy and Pensioned Religious in Norwich Diocese, 1555', *English Historical Review*, 48 (1933), pp. 43–64. In Essex 88 incumbents were deprived out of 319. H. Grieve, 'The Deprived Married Clergy in Essex, 1553–1561', *Transactions of the Royal Historical Society*, 4th series, 22 (1940), pp. 141–69.
48. 'Robert Parkyn's Narrative of the Reformation', ed. A. G. Dickens *English Historical Review*, 62 (1947), pp. 58–63, on p. 82.
49. *Visitation Articles*, vol. 2, p. 326.
50. Duffy, *The Stripping of the Altars*, pp. 556–7.
51. Loades, *Mary Tudor*.
52. Mayer, 'The Success of Cardinal Pole's Final Legation'.
53. Duffy, *The Stripping of the Altars*, pp. 521–3.
54. For two rather different answers to this question, see Dickens, *The English Reformation*, pp. 264–72; Duffy, *Fires of Faith*, pp. 171–87.
55. This can only be deduced, not demonstrated. For the status of the heretic as criminal, see Hughes, *The Reformation in England*, vol. 1, pp. 254–5.
56. D. Palliser 'Popular Reactions to the Reformation during the Years of Uncertainty, 1530–1570', in Haigh (ed.), *The English Reformation Revised*, pp. 94–114.
57. A. Ryrie, *The Age of Reformation* (Harlow: Pearson, 2009), pp. 195–204.
58. Foxe, *Actes and Monuments*, pp. 2005–7.
59. National Archives, SP11/5, no. 6, ff. 39–40.
60. J. S. Cockburn, *A History of the English Assizes, 1558–1714* (Cambridge: Cambridge University Press, 1972), p. 207, citing the *Acts of the Privy Council, 1577–8*, pp. 168–9.
61. Loades, *The Oxford Martyrs*, p. 198.
62. 'The Narrative of Edward Underhill' (British Library, Harley MS 425), in A. F. Pollard, *Tudor Tracts* (London: Constable, 1903), pp. 170–99, on p. 179.

5 Heresy and Dissent

1. A. Caracciolo, *Vita Pauli IV* (Cologne, 1612). For a discussion of Carafa's role as a leader of the *zelanti* in Rome in the 1540s, see D. Fenlon, *Heresy and Obedience in Tridentine Italy* (Cambridge: Cambridge University Press, 1972), pp. 55–6.
2. R. H. Bainton, *Erasmus of Christendom* (New York, Scribner, 1969), pp. 298–328.

3. J. I. Tellechea Idigoras, *Fray Bartolomé Carranza de Miranda: Investigaciones historicas*, Historia, 109 (Pamplona: Gobierno de Navarra, Departmento de Educacion y Cultura, 2002).

4. Zwingli's view of the Eucharist was that it was entirely commemorative, which has been dubbed the doctrine of the 'real absence'. G. R. Potter, *Zwingli* (Cambridge: Cambridge University Press, 1976); P. McNair, *Peter Martyr in Italy: An Anatomy of Apostasy* (Oxford: Oxford University Press, 1967), pp. 2–3.

5. R. Taverner, *A Catechisme or Institution of the Christen Religion* (London, 1539) [*RSTC* 23709]; N. Wyse, *A Consolacyon for Chrysten People to Repayre Agayn the Lordes Temple* (London, 1538) [*RSTC* 26063].

6. Thompson, *The Later Lollards*, discusses these variations of doctrine, as does Rex, *The Lollards*.

7. M. Deansley, *The Lollard Bible and other Medieval Biblical Versions* (Cambridge: Cambridge University Press, 1920), pp. 252–66.

8. Davis, *Heresy and Reformation*, pp. 26–41.

9. Ibid., p. 27; Rochester Diocesan Registry, Rochester Registers, iv (Fisher), f. 133r.

10. National Archives, STAC 2/34/28.

11. This desire for change is both elusive and controversial, but offerings at shrines such as Walsingham and Canterbury had shown a marked falling off in the ten years or so before Henry acted. This was probably due to a shift of fashion in piety within the traditional structure rather than to any early influence of Protestantism, but it certainly made the King's task easier. For different interpretations of this situation, see Dickens, *The English Reformation*; Duffy, *The Stripping of the Altars*; C. Haigh, *English Reformations* (Oxford: Oxford University Press, 1993).

12. *Opus Epistolarum Des. Erasmi Epistolae*, ed. P. S. Allen et al., 12 vols (Oxford: Oxford University Press, 1906–58), vol. 10, p. 259.

13. *The Correspondence of Sir Thomas More*, ed. E. F. Rogers (Princeton, NJ: Princeton University Press, 1947), p. 198.

14. Davis, *Heresy and Reformation*, p. 30.

15. Foxe, *Actes and Monuments*, p. 1013.

16. E. G. Rupp, *Studies in the Making of the English Protestant Tradition* (Cambridge: Cambridge University Press, 1947), pp. 23–8.

17. Diarmaid MacCulloch, personal communication.

18. For a detailed examination of Cranmer's position, see MacCulloch, *Thomas Cranmer*, and for a judicious reassessment of Cromwell's evangelism, D. Eppley, *Defending the Royal Supremacy and Discerning God's Will in Tudor England* (Aldershot: Ashgate, 2007).

19. G. R. Elton, *Thomas Cromwell*, 2nd edn, ed. D. Loades (Oxford: Davenant, 2008), pp. 19–22.

20. Foxe, *Actes and Monuments*, pp. 1029 (Bainham), 1100–24 (Lambert), 1234–8 (Askew).

21. These efforts were inspired by Henry VIII's own *Assertio Septem Sacramentorum* (London, 1521) [*RSTC* 13078]; Lutton, *Lollardy and Orthodox Religion*, pp. 149–95.

22. In November 1527 the Steelyard was raided by Sir Thomas More in a search for heretical writings and vernacular Bibles, several of which were found. British Library, Lansdowne MS 160, f. 312; J. A. Guy, *The Public Career of Sir Thomas More* (Brighton: Harvester, 1980), p. 13.

23. Thomas, *Religion and the Decline of Magic*. The insistence that a human body could only be in one place at a time became a trope with the reformers.

24. W. P. Stephens, *The Theology of Huldrych Zwingli* (Oxford: Oxford University Press, 1986); Newcombe, *John Hooper*, pp. 36–44.

25. K. G. Powell, 'The Social Background to the Reformation in Gloucestershire', *Transactions of the Bristol and Gloucestershire Archaeological Society*, 92 (1973), pp. 96–120, on p. 99.

26. Newcombe, *John Hooper*, p. 19.

27. Jordan, *Edward VI: The Young King*, pp. 206–24; MacCulloch, *Tudor Church Militant*; Loades, *Mary Tudor*, pp. 142–50, 157–70.

28. J. W. Martin, *Religious Radicals in Tudor England* (London: Hambledon, 1989).

29. 1 Edward VI, c. 1, '... a statute against those who do contemn, despise, or with unseemly and ungodly words deprave and revile the Holy Sacrament of the body and blood of our Lord, commonly called the Sacrament of the Altar', in *Statutes of the Realm*, vol. 4, p. 2.

30. The issue of vestments arose over the consecration of Bishop John Hooper to the see of Gloucester in 1551. Following the advice of Bullinger and Martyr, Hooper eventually conceded. The Prayer Book intervention came over the 'Black Rubric' which Knox (and others) insisted on inserting into the text to explain the requirement to receive the communion kneeling.

31. The universal contemporary condemnation of Bocher and Van Paris has served to conceal the fact that no law was in existence to justify their execution, the medieval statutes under which Henry VIII had operated having been repealed in 1547.

32. There had been significant opposition to attempts at ecclesiastical restoration in Mary's second parliament and many magistrates seem to have acted reluctantly against offenders after January 1555. Foxe, *Actes and Monuments*. For a recent appraisal of the role of the justices in the persecution, see Duffy, *Fires of Faith*, pp. 102–27.

33. Burnet, *The History of the Reformation*, vol. 2, pp. 45–6; *Acts of the Privy Council*, vol. 2, pp. 25–6.

34. Van der Delft to the Queen Dowager, 7 March 1547, in *Calendar of State Papers, Spanish*, vol. 9, p. 50.

35. Van der Delft to the Queen Dowager, 6 September 1547, in ibid., vol. 9, p. 148.

36. 23 October 1547, in *Acts of the Privy Council*, vol. 2, pp. 140–1.

37. *Victoria History of the County of Essex*, 8 vols (London: Constable, 1903–83), vol. 2, pp. 26–7; National Archives, SP10/5, no. 19.

38. W. K. Jordan, *Philanthropy in England, 1480–1660* (London: Allen & Unwin, 1959); Orme, *English Schools in the Middle Ages*.

39. P. Marshall, 'Papist as Heretic: The Burning of John Forest, 1538', *Historical Journal*, 41 (1998), pp. 351–74.

40. J. C. Spalding (ed.), *The Reformation of the Ecclesiastical Laws of England, 1552*, Sixteenth-Century Essays and Studies, 19 (Kirksville, MO: Northeast Missouri State University, 1992), pp. 64–5.

41. Greater London Record Office, Vicar General's Book, 1546–60, DL/C/331, f.110.

42. Davis, *Heresy and Reformation*, p. 101.

43. See, for example, their reactions to the Queen's intention to celebrate a requiem mass for her brother. Report of 2 August 1553, in *Calendar of State Papers, Spanish*, vol. 11, p. 156.

44. Renard to the Queen Dowager, in ibid., vol. 11, p. 175.

45. D. Loades, *Two Tudor Conspiracies* (Cambridge: Cambridge University Press, 1965), pp. 87–8.

46. 'Whist quod Wyatt, you may not so much as name religion, for that will withdraw from us the hearts of many ... And yet to thee be it said ... we mind only the restitution of God's Word'. Proctor, *The Historie of Wiatts Rebellion* (1554), in Pollard, *Tudor Tracts*, p. 210.

47. Newcombe, *John Hooper*, pp. 112–20.

48. Loades, *The Oxford Martyrs*, pp. 167–91; Duffy, *Fires of Faith*, p. 103.

49. Muller, *Stephen Gardiner and the Tudor Reaction*, pp. 222–35; Redworth, *In Defence of the Church Catholic*, pp. 311–29.

50. 1 & 2 Philip & Mary, c. 6, in *Statutes of the Realm*, vol. 4, p. 244.

51. Foxe, *Actes and Monuments*, pp. 1484–529; Duffy, *Fires of Faith*, pp. 97–9.

52. Professor Duffy argues this case forcefully in ibid, pp. 171–87.

53. Foxe, *Actes and Monuments*, pp. 2047–56.

54. John Philpot underwent fifteen examinations before a variety of inquisitors. Even the obscure William Tyms was examined three times. Ibid., pp. 1796–829, 1896–7.

55. G. Alexander, 'Bonner and the Marian Persecutions', in Haigh (ed.), *The English Reformation Revised*, pp. 157–75.

56. C. H. Garrett, *The Marian Exiles* (Cambridge: Cambridge University Press, 1938); D. G. Danner, *Pilgrimage to Puritanism: The History and Theology of the Marian Exiles at Geneva, 1555–1560* (New York: Peter Levey, 1999). For Francis Russell, second Earl of Bedford, see *ODNB*.

57. For the idea that many of these victims of persecution were radicals, see P. Collinson, 'The Persecution in Kent', in Duffy and Loades (eds), *The Church of Mary Tudor*, pp. 309–33; T. S. Freeman, 'Dissenters from a Dissenting Church: The Challenge of the Freewillers, 1550–1558', in Marshall and Ryrie (eds), *The Beginnings of English Protestantism*, pp. 129–56.

58. For example the case of the three men of Carleton Rood in Norfolk who neglected to creep to the cross at Easter 1554, or Ralph Gyfford of Stoke by Nayland, who produced a feeble excuse for not attending divine service. Norfolk Record Office, Act/7/8 (unfoliated); Davis, *Heresy and Reformation*, p. 108.

59. Foxe, *Actes and Monuments*, pp. 1556–9, 1562–5.

60. Houlbrooke, 'The Clergy, the Church Courts and the Marian Restoration'.

61. Ibid.

62. J. N. King, 'John Day, Master Printer of the English Reformation', in Marshall and Ryrie (eds), *The Beginnings of English Protestantism*, pp. 180–208, on pp. 186–8.

63. R. Lutton, 'Geographies and Materialities of Piety: Reconciling Competing Narratives of Religious Change in Pre-Reformation and Reformation England', in Lutton and Salter (eds), *Pieties in Transition*, pp. 11–40.

64. Ibid., p. 28.

65. Ibid., p. 35.

66. Donato Rullo to Cardinal Seripando, 1 December 1554, in C. de Frede, *La Restaurazione Cattolica in Inghilterra sotto Maria Tudor* (Naples: Libreria scientifica editrice, 1971), p. 57.

6 The Training of Clergy

1. Hughes, *The Reformation in England*, vol. 1, pp. 83–4.
2. It was quite normal for the bishop to delegate this work to one of his diocesan officials, whose diligence might leave a lot to be desired.
3. *Letters and Memorials of Cardinal Allen*, ed. T. F. Knox (London: D. Nutt, 1882), p. 32.
4. Wilkins, *Concilia*, vol. 3, pp. 717–26.
5. W. de Meltham, *Sermo Exhortatius Cancellarii Eborum hiis qui ad sacros ordines petunt promoveri* (London, 1510) [*RSTC* 17806]; Hughes, *The Reformation in England*, vol. 1, p. 85.
6. Heath, *The English Parish Clergy*.
7. Duffy, *The Stripping of the Altars*, p. 53.
8. R. M. Haines, *Ecclesia Anglicana: Studies in the English Church of the Later Middle Ages* (Toronto: University of Toronto Press, 1989), pp. 129–37.
9. W. A. Pantin, *The English Church in the Fourteenth Century* (Cambridge: Cambridge University Press, 1955), pp. 189–95, 211–12.
10. *Instructions for Parish Priests*, ed. E. Peacock (London: Early English Text Society, 1868); *Mirk's Festial*.
11. Guido de Monte Rocherii, *Manipulus Curatorum* (London, 1508) [*RSTC* 12474].
12. *Ordynarye of Crystyantye or of Chrysten Men*; *The Floure of the Commaundementes of God* (London: W. de Worde, 1510) [*RSTC* 23876]; *Exoneratorium Curatorum* (London, 1534) [*RSTC* 10634].
13. *The Book of Margery Kempe*.
14. Rose-Troup, *The Western Rebellion*, appendix K, p. 493, from a manuscript in Lambeth Palace Library.
15. Duffy, *The Stripping of the Altars*, p. 80. For a discussion of Bible readership before the reformation, see R. Rex, *Henry VIII and the English Reformation* (London: Macmillan, 1993).
16. T. More, *A Dialogue concerning Heresies*, Book III, cc. 11–13, in *The Complete Works of Sir Thomas More*.
17. Ibid., cc. 11, pp. 225–6.
18. *The Book of Margery Kempe*, p. 149.
19. This was not difficult, provided that the celebrant was prepared to ignore the rubric about reading 'with a clear and distinct voice'. The 1549 rite was mainly a translation of the Sarum Use, and if the service was muttered in the customary fashion, it did not matter much what language was being used. This was one of the main reasons for the changes introduced in 1552.
20. J. Bossy, *Christianity in the West, 1400–1700* (Oxford: Oxford University Press, 1985).
21. Newcombe, *John Hooper*, pp. 183–98.
22. Ibid., pp. 173–5.
23. Rose-Troup, *The Western Rebellion*, p. 262.
24. Ibid., pp. 156–7.
25. Duffy, *The Voices of Morebath*, pp. 175–7.
26. Foxe, *Actes and Monuments*, pp. 1519–27.
27. Whiting, *The Blind Devotion of the People*, pp. 152–4.
28. Ibid., p. 126; National Archives, STAC 2/2/267.
29. Newcombe, *John Hooper*, p. 175.

30. Cross, 'The English Universities', p. 60.
31. Ibid.
32. Mullinger, *The University of Cambridge*, vol. 2, pp. 145–6.
33. C. H. Smyth, *Cranmer and the Reformation under Edward VI* (London: SPCK, 1926), pp. 108–25.
34. MacCulloch, *Tudor Church Militant*, p. 119.
35. Mullinger, *The University of Cambridge*, pp. 147–8; Loades, *John Dudley*, pp. 263–4.
36. Cross, 'The English Universities', p. 63.
37. For a discussion of Pole's legacy in this respect, see Mayer, *Reginald Pole*.
38. Duffy, 'Cardinal Pole Preaching', pp. 184–5.
39. Garrett, 'The Legatine Register of Cardinal Pole'.
40. Foxe, *Actes and Monuments*, p. 1483.
41. Mayer, 'The Success of Cardinal Pole's Final Legation', p. 165; A. H. Thompson, 'Pluralism in the Medieval Church; with Notes on Pluralities in the Diocese of Lincoln, 1366', *Reports and Papers of the Associated Architectural Societies*, 33 (1915), pp. 43–72.
42. Mayer, 'The Success of Cardinal Pole's Final Legation', p. 166.
43. Ibid., p. 168.
44. G. Bray, *The Anglican Canons, 1529–1947*, Church of England Record Society, 6 (Woodbridge: Boydell, 1998), pp. 75–9.
45. Ibid., pp. 101–5.
46. Ibid., pp. 107–15.
47. Ibid., p. 127. The original decree reads 'Cum magna sit hoc tempore ecclesiasticarum personarum penuria, praesertim idonearum, quae ecclesisis seu ecclesiasticis muneribus vel praeficiantur, vel inserviant'.
48. Ibid.
49. 'Those who are in charge of schools, shall have their faith, their practice and their doctrine carefully examined, and if they be found to be such as we have required in this constitution, they shall be confirmed in their appointments ... But if not, we order their removal and the substitution in their place of other, suitable persons.' Ibid., p. 129.
50. Ibid.
51. That is, assuming an average of 10–12 boys in each age year of each seminary, and a full take-up of the scheme.
52. *Visitation Articles*, vol. 2, p. 361.
53. Burnet, *The History of the Reformation*, vol. 3, p. 257.
54. For a full discussion of this phenomenon, see P. Collinson, *The Elizabethan Puritan Movement* (London: Cape, 1967).
55. B. Gregory, *Salvation at Stake: Christian Martyrdom in Early Modern Europe* (Cambridge, MA: Harvard University Press, 1999), pp. 153–96.
56. Mayer, *Reginald Pole*.

7 The Face of Persecution

1. Foxe, *Actes and Monuments*, pp. 2111–12. This occurred at Smarden, in Kent, and the magistrate's name was Drayner.
2. Strype, *Ecclesiastical Memorials* (1721), vol. 3, i, pp. 338–9.
3. Taylor was a doctor both of the civil law and of the canon law, very unusual qualifications for a parish priest. Foxe, *Actes and Monuments*, pp. 1519–27.
4. Ibid., p. 1521.

5. J. Craig, 'Reformers, Conflict and Revisionism: The Reformation in Sixteenth-Century Hadleigh', *Historical Journal*, 42 (1999), pp. 1–23.

6. Gardiner was anxious to get as many heretics out of the country as he could, and regularly gave advance warning of summonses to encourage flight. The most conspicuous example was the six hours' warning given to Hugh Latimer which, Foxe concluded, meant 'that they would not have him appear, but rather to have fled out of the realm'. *Actes and Monuments*, p. 1730. On the whole, this worked for the foreign divines, but not for the natives. Redworth, *In Defence of the Church Catholic*, pp. 293–4.

7. This policy seems to have been pursued for as long as Gardiner was influential in the management of the campaign – roughly until the autumn of 1555. Foxe, *Actes and Monuments*, pp. 1525–7.

8. Ibid., p. 1525.

9. Ibid., p. 2045. This incumbent was 'Parson Newall', who was later responsible for the apprehension of Richard Yeomans, Taylor's curate, when he ventured to return to Hadleigh.

10. Houlbrooke, 'The Clergy, the Church Courts and the Marian Restoration'.

11. Such feats of memory were by no means uncommon among the illiterate, who were much given to swapping texts with their interrogators – to the latter's intense annoyance. Foxe, *Actes and Monuments*, p. 1556.

12. Ibid. White was 'one of good honour, well accounted among his neighbours'. It is hard to know how seriously to take all this virtue and discretion, because he is clearly being used as a model against which to measure other illiterate 'teachers'. Ibid.

13. This was also a trope among the Protestants. White had clearly been listening to godly sermons. Ibid., p. 1558.

14. Ibid.

15. For a discussion of crowd reactions to public executions, see J. G. Bellamy, *Crime and Public Order in England in the Later Middle Ages* (London: Routledge, 1973), pp. 185–90.

16. Foxe, *Actes and Monuments*, p. 1561. Exactly what position Barton occupied in the Earl's service is not known. He does not appear among those servants and others identified in E. Zevin, 'Noble Power and the Tudor Monarchy: The Life of Edward Stanley, Earl of Derby' (PhD thesis, City of New York University, 2009), pp. 211–14. According to Professor Zevin, Derby did his best to let Marsh off, which probably accounts for the intervention of the bishop.

17. Ibid.

18. Hooper, for instance, was recognized as a priest, but not as a bishop, because his priestly orders had been conferred under the traditional rite. Newcombe, *John Hooper*.

19. Foxe, *Actes and Monuments*, p. 1565.

20. Ibid., p. 1594. He changed back again under Elizabeth; hence the saying 'better a poor man at ease than Lord Rich of Leighs'. *ODNB*.

21. Foxe, *Actes and Monuments*, p. 1595.

22. So described by Foxe, but the only commission of Oyer and Terminer which included Lord Rich had been issued on 2 May 1554. *Calendar of the Patent Rolls, Philip and Mary*, vol. 1, p. 27.

23. For Thomas Whittle and Edward Arblaster, see Foxe, *Actes and Monuments*, p. 1844.

24. 'The Narrative of Edward Underhill', in Pollard (ed.), *Tudor Tracts*, p. 186.

25. 'Then took I a little house in a secret corner, at the nether end of Wood Street; where I might better shift the matter'. Ibid.

26. Heresy was classed as a felony by the statutes of Henry IV and Henry V, and all felons' goods were forfeited to the Crown. Bellamy, *Crime and Public Order*, p. 190.

27. Foxe, *Actes and Monuments*, pp. 1943–50. For a discussion of the implications of these cases, see D. M. Ogier, *Reformation and Society in Guernsey* (Woodbridge: Boydell, 1996), pp. 57–8. The Elizabethan Commissioners' report is among the Salisbury manuscripts at Hatfield House (Cecil 207/12).

28. Foxe, *Actes and Monuments*, p. 1945.

29. Ogier, *Reformation and Society*, p. 57.

30. Foxe refuted Harding's attack on Perotine at considerable length in the 1583 edition of the *Actes and Monuments*.

31. Bartlett Green and Thomas Hawkes were both examined several times, and treated with consideration by Bonner. Ibid., pp. 1851–6, 1585–94.

32. For example the six who were burned together at Colchester on 28 April 1556, and who are briefly recorded in Bonner's register. Ibid., p. 1909.

33. Ibid., p. 1954. For a discussion of the role of families and friends in supporting prisoners, see Bellamy, *Crime and Public Order*, pp. 162–98.

34. For example, Thomas Hawkes refused to have his child baptized. Foxe, *Actes and Monuments*, p. 1585.

35. This seems to have been a gesture more often used by women. See the stories of Elizabeth Cooper and Joyce Lewes. Ibid., pp. 2005, 2012.

36. As in the case of John Denley, burned at Uxbridge on 8 August 1555. Duffy, *Fires of Faith*, p. 123.

37. Foxe, *Actes and Monuments*, p. 2023.

38. Ibid., p. 2012. Joyce Lewes had been denounced by her husband, who refused to be bound for her. She was clearly a lady of independent mind.

39. Ibid., pp. 2048–9.

40. Notably Sir Anthony Kingston, with whom he had frequently clashed, and an unnamed woman 'who had frequently railed upon him' in the days of his power. Ibid., pp. 1510–12.

41. Duffy, *Fires of Faith*, p. 129. Bonner to Pole, July 1558. Petyt MS 538, xlvii, f.3. *Second Report of the Historical Manuscripts Commission, Appendix* (London, 1841), p. 152.

42. Julins Palmer was ostensibly converted to Protestantism by this performance, but, as Professor Duffy points out, he was almost certainly a Protestant before. *Fires of Faith*, pp. 155–6.

43. *All the Submyssyons and Recantations of Thomas Cranmer* (London, 1556) [*RSTC* 5990], pp. 96–7.

44. Duffy, *Fires of Faith*, pp. 155–8.

45. *Acts of the Privy Council*, vol. 5, p. 224.

46. Duffy, *Fires of Faith*, p. 129.

47. Loades, *The Reign of Mary Tudor*, pp. 100–4; *Calendar of State Papers, Spanish*, vol. 11, p. 322.

48. *Calendar of State Papers, Spanish*, vol. 13, pp. 366, 370; Duffy, *Fires of Faith*, pp. 29–30.

49. 'The Count of Feria's Dispatch to Philip II of 14 November 1558', ed. and trans. M.-J. Rodriguez Salgado and S. Adams, *Camden Miscellany*, 28 (1984), pp. 302–44.

50. *Calendar of State Papers, Venetian*, vol. 6, pp. 93–4.

51. Huggarde, *The Displaying of the Protestantes*, p. 127. For a further discussion of Huggarde and his role in the controversy, see J. W. Martin, 'Miles Hogarde, Artisan and Aspiring Author in Sixteenth-Century England', *Renaissance Quarterly*, 34 (1981), pp. 83–105.

52. Huggarde, *The Displaying of the Protestantes*, p. 64.
53. *A Plaine and Godlye Treatise concernynge the Masse*, cited in Duffy, *Fires of Faith*, pp. 76–7.
54. Loades, *The Oxford Martyrs*, pp. 186–8.
55. John Bradford, for example, kept notes of all his prison conversations with those sent to convert him and left letters to the Citizens of London as well as to the City and University of Cambridge. Foxe, *Actes and Monuments*, pp. 1625–30.
56. Ibid.
57. Bellamy, *Crime and Public Order*, pp. 162–98.
58. *The Works of Bishop Ridley*, ed. H. Christmas (Cambridge: Parker Society 1841), pp. 391–2; Loades, *The Oxford Martyrs*, p. 169.
59. Duffy, *Fires of Faith*, pp. 171–88.
60. Mayer, 'The Success of Cardinal Pole's Final Legation'; Duffy, *Fires of Faith*, pp. 155–70.
61. Ferdinand and Isabella had succeeded in blending Catholic orthodoxy with Spanish pride and xenophobia to produce a uniquely aggressive identity, in which all heresy was thought to be the work of subversive outsiders. H. Kamen, *The Spanish Inquisition: An Historical Revision* (London: Weidenfeld & Nicholson, 1997).
62. Loades, *The Reign of Mary Tudor*, pp. 319–20.
63. Wizeman, *The Theology and Spirituality*, pp. 148–57.

8 The Imagery of John Foxe

1. 'I had well hoped, that these my travailes in this kind of writing had been well at an ende, whereby I might have resumed my studies agayne to other purposes', but a further effort was clearly needed. Foxe, *Actes and Monuments* (1570), p. *i.
2. Foxe, *Actes and Monuments* (1563), p. 1654.
3. T. Brice, *A Compendious Register in Metre* (London, 1559) [*RSTC* 3726], reprinted in Pollard, *Tudor Tracts*, pp. 259–88; J. Aylmer, *An Harborowe for Faithfull and True Subjects* (London, 1559) [*RSTC* 1005].
4. For example the story of the escape of Catherine, the Dowager Duchess of Suffolk, which was further elaborated in the 1576 edition. Foxe, *Actes and Monuments* (1576), sig. 5Q4v.
5. Ogier, *Reformation and Society*, pp. 57–8.
6. Foxe, *Actes and Monuments* (1583), p. 1597.
7. Ibid., p. 1769.
8. Duffy, *Fires of Faith*, p. 155.
9. G. Parry, 'John Foxe, "Father of Lyes", and the Papists', in D. Loades (ed.), *John Foxe and the English Reformation* (Aldershot: Ashgate, 1997), pp. 295–305.
10. N[icholas] D[oleman] [Robert Parsons], *A Treatise of Three Conversions of England from Paganisme to Christian Religion* (St Omer, 1603) [*RSTC* 19416].
11. Foxe, *Actes and Monuments*, pp. 2051–2.
12. Ibid., pp. 1101–23.
13. D. Loades, 'John Foxe and Henry VIII', *John Foxe Bulletin*, 1:1 (2002), pp. 1–12.
14. 'The Story of Thomas Hawkes', in Foxe, *Actes and Monuments*, pp. 1591–2.
15. Ibid., p. 1769.
16. Ibid., p. 1493.
17. See Chapter 7 above, pp. 123–4, for the opinion of Giovanni Michieli.

18. Duffy, *Fires of Faith*, pp. 155–70.
19. Foxe, *Actes and Monuments*, p. 2098.
20. Huggarde, *The Displaying of the Protestantes*, p. 127.
21. S. Felch, 'Shaping the Reader in the *Acts and Monuments*', in Loades (ed.), *John Foxe and the English Reformation*, pp. 52–65.
22. R. Smith, *A Bouclier of the Catholike Fayth of Christes Church* (London, 1554) [*RSTC* 22816].
23. See, for example, John Knox's letter to Anne Lock, 6 April 1559, 'God [will] grant you his Holie Spirit rightlie to judge', in *The Works of John Knox*, ed. D. Laing, 6 vols (Edinburgh: Wodrow Society, 1846–64), vol. 6, p. 14.
24. Wizeman, *The Theology and Spirituality*, pp. 64–78.
25. Collinson, 'The Persecution in Kent', p. 316.
26. 46 were burned at Smithfield, out of 112 in London diocese.
27. Collinson, 'The Persecution in Kent'.
28. See J. Bale, *The Image of Bothe Churches* (Antwerp, 1545) [*RSTC* 1296.5].
29. Collinson, 'The Persecution in Kent', p. 317. She had, allegedly, been 'a busy proselytizer at court'.
30. H. Hart, *A Godly newe short Treatyse Instructyng every Parson, howe they shulde Trade theyr Lyves in the Imytacyon of Vertu, and Shewying of Vyce* (London, 1548) [*RSTC* 12887].
31. Freeman, 'Dissenters from a Dissenting Church'.
32. Foxe, *Actes and Monuments*, pp. 1679–80.
33. Ibid.
34. P. Collinson, *Godly People: Essays in Protestantism and Puritanism* (London: Hambledon, 1983), 'Cranbrook and the Fletchers, Popular and Unpopular Religion in the Kentish Weald', pp. 420–2.
35. Foxe, *Actes and Monuments*, pp. 1665–76.
36. Ibid., p. 1980.
37. Ibid. As Patrick Collinson points out, the cross reference is in fact incorrect. It should be to p. 1672.
38. British Library, Harley MS 416, ff. 123–4; T. S. Freeman, 'Notes on a Source for John Foxe's Account of the Marian Persecution in Kent and Sussex', *Historical Research*, 67 (1994), pp. 203–11, on p. 204.
39. British Library, Harley MS 421, ff. 92–3, 94–5, 101–3; Collinson, 'Persecution in Kent', p. 328.
40. Ibid., pp. 329–30. Fishcocke had been in trouble before, in the days of Henry VIII. *Letters and Papers*, vol. 18, ii, no. 311.
41. Huggarde, *The Displaying of the Protestantes*, p. 121.
42. M. S. Robinson, 'Doctors, Silly Poor Women and Rebel Whores; The Gendering of Conscience in Foxe's Acts and Monuments', in C. Highley and J. N. King (eds), *John Foxe and His World* (Aldershot: Ashgate, 2002), pp. 235–48.
43. Ibid., pp. 235–6. John Careless wrote 'Blessed be the Lord our God, which of his great mercie hath so beautified in these our dayes, that even unto many godly women he hath given most excellent giftes of knowledge and understanding of his truth'. Foxe, *Actes and Monuments* (1596), p. 1748.
44. Foxe, *Actes and Monuments* (1596), p. 1796.
45. Collinson, 'The Persecution in Kent', p. 317.

46. R. Hooker, *Of the Laws of Ecclesiastical Polity*, Everyman's Library, 201–2, 2 vols (London: J. M. Dent & Co., 1907), vol. 1, pp. 103–4.

47. Foxe, *Actes and Monuments* (1596), p. 1873; Robinson, 'Doctors, Silly Poor Women and Rebel Whores', p. 242.

48. Foxe, *Actes and Monuments*, p. 2006.

49. Foxe, *Actes and Monuments* (1596), p. 1876; Robinson, 'Doctors, Silly Poor Women and Rebel Whores', p. 244.

50. Bale, *The Image of Bothe Churches*; J. N. King, 'The Godly Woman in Elizabethan Iconography', *Renaissance Quarterly*, 38 (1985), pp. 43–7.

51. E. Macek, 'The Emergence of a Female Spirituality in the *Book of Martyrs*', *Sixteenth-Century Journal*, 19 (1988), pp. 63–80.

52. *Commentarii rerum in Ecclesia Gestarum* (Strasburg: Rihelius, 1554) and *Rerum in Ecclesia Gestarum* (Basle: Oporinus, 1559). The latter contained a brief summary of recent events.

53. D. Loades, 'Afterword', in Highley and King (eds), *John Foxe and His World*, pp. 277–90.

54. Felch, 'Shaping the Reader'.

55. Foxe, *Actes and Monuments*, pp. 557–67; Thompson, *The Later Lollards*.

56. For Wycliffe, see Foxe, *Actes and Monuments*, p. 447.

57. Foxe later gave a vivid description of Bonner's 'death and filthy end'. *Actes and Monuments*, p. 2114.

58. J. Roberts, 'Bibliographical Aspects of John Foxe', in Loades (ed.), *John Foxe and the English Reformation*, pp. 36–51.

59. For a discussion of the implications of this bull, see Hughes, *The Reformation in England*, vol. 3, pp. 272–3; D. Loades, *Elizabeth I* (London: Hambledon, 2003), p. 194.

60. 'Foure considerations geven out to Christian Protestantes, professors of the Gospell, with a brief exhortation to reformation of life'. A preface to the 1583 edition of Foxe, *Actes and Monuments*.

61. J. Foxe, *The First (and Second) Volumes of the Ecclesiastical History*, 2 vols (London, 1570) [*RSTC* 11223].

62. F. Heal, 'What can King Lucius do for You? The Reformation and the Early British Church', *English Historical Review*, 120 (2005), pp. 593–614.

63. Ibid.

64. 'Foure considerations ...' and the other prefaces to the 1583 edition.

65. *RSTC* 11229; *RSTC* 11226; *RSTC* 11227; *RSTC* 11228. For the agenda of the 1632 edition, see D. Nussbaum, 'Appropriating Martyrdom; Fears of Renewed Persecution and the 1632 Edition of the *Acts and Monuments*', in Loades (ed.), *John Foxe and the English Reformation*, pp. 178–91.

66. Preface to the 1563 edition.

67. Foxe, *Actes and Monuments*, p. 2101.

68. Foxe, *Actes and Monuments* (1563), p. 1619; Duffy, *Fires of Faith*, pp. 165–6.

Postscript

1. For a full discussion of Elizabeth's preparations – as far as they were known to him – see 'The Count of Feria's Despatch to Philip II'.

2. *The Diary of Henry Machyn*, p. 178.

3. Ibid.

4. J. C. Cox, *The Parish Registers of England* (London: Methuen, 1910), pp. 32–5; Duffy, *The Voices of Morebath*, pp. 169–70.

5. Machyn misdates his death to 19 November, but adds 'there [at Lambeth] he lay tyll the consell sett the tyme he shuld be bered, and when and wher'. *The Diary of Henry Machyn*, p. 178.

6. For a full discussion of the circumstances surrounding the passage of these Acts, see N. Jones, *Faith by Statute* (London: Royal Historical Society, 1982). The bishops fought tenaciously against the bill of Uniformity, and were outvoted only after the Queen had removed two of them by arrest for contempt following the disputation which was held during the Easter recess.

7. Turberville was deprived on 10 August 1559, and died on the 1 November following.

8. Duffy, *The Voices of Morebath*, pp. 170–1.

9. *The Zurich Letters*, ed. H. Robinson (London: Parker Society, 1845), pp. 44–5.

10. C. Haigh, 'The Continuity of Catholicism in the English Reformation', *Past and Present*, 93 (1983), pp. 37–69.

11. Royal Injunctions of Queen Elizabeth, 1559, in *Visitation Articles*, vol. 3, pp. 8–29; W. P. Haugaard, *Elizabeth and the English Reformation* (Cambridge: Cambridge University Press, 1968).

12. The average duration of a vacancy occurring between 1557 and 1559 was about fifteen months; excluding Llandaff, where there was no vacancy, and Oxford, which was held open for nine and a half years.

13. Hughes, *The Reformation in England*, vol. 3, pp. 22–3.

14. Duffy, *The Voices of Morebath*, pp. 119–23, 152–5.

15. Ibid., p. 172.

16. Whiting, *The Blind Devotion of the People*, pp. 231–5; Houlbrooke, *Church Courts*, pp. 48–50.

17. Duffy, *The Voices of Morebath*, pp. 175–6.

18. A practice which was never officially condemned, but was contrary to tradition. It was occasionally used as a 'concession' in negotiating with dissidents, as had been the case in Bohemia and in the Imperial Interim of 1548.

19. Jordan, *Philanthropy in England*; Sweetinburgh, 'The Poor, Hospitals and Charity'; N. Orme, *Education and Society in Medieval and Renaissance England* (London: Hambledon Press, 1989); D. Cressy, *Education in Tudor and Stuart England* (London: Arnold, 1975).

20. Duffy, *The Voices of Morebath*, p. 178, n. 84; *The Accounts of the Wardens of Morebath, Devon, 1515–1573*, ed. J. E. Binney (Exeter: J. G. Commin, 1904), pp. 241, 252.

21. Local studies have made it clear that this happened throughout the country. See, for example, M. C. Skeeters, *Community and Clergy: Bristol and the Reformation, 1530–1570* (Oxford: Oxford University Press, 1993); J. Freeman, 'The Parish Ministry in the Diocese of Durham, c. 1570–1640' (PhD thesis, University of Durham, 1979).

22. Duffy, *The Voices of Morebath*, pp. 175–7.

23. Ibid., p. 177.

24. 'Robert Parkyn's Narrative of the Reformation'.

25. M. S. Byford, 'The Price of Protestantism: Assessing the Impact of Religious Change on Elizabethan Essex, the Cases of Heydon and Colchester 1558–1594' (DPhil thesis, University of Oxford, 1988), p. 42.

26. Ibid.

27. Duffy, *The Voices of Morebath*, p. 179; A. Fletcher and D. MacCulloch, *Tudor Rebellions* (Harlow: Longmans, 1997).

28. Fletcher and MacCulloch, *Tudor Rebellions*; C. Sharp, *The Rising in the North: The 1569 Rebellion, being a reprint of the 'Memorials of the Rebellion of the Earls of Northumberland and Westmoreland'* (Durham: Shotton, 1975), pp. 74–90.

29. *The Accounts of the Wardens of Morebath*, p. 252.

30. Haigh, *English Reformations*, pp. 285–95; C. J. Sommerville, *The Secularisation of Early Modern England: From Religious Culture to Religious Faith* (Oxford: Oxford University Press, 1992).

31. Kumin, *The Shaping of a Community*, pp. 204–21.

32. Collinson, *The Elizabethan Puritan Movement*; R. O'Day, *The English Clergy: the Emergence and Consolidation of a Profession, 1558–1642* (Leicester: Leicester University Press, 1979), pp. 86–104; W. R. D. Jones, *William Turner: Tudor Naturalist, Physician, and Divine* (London: Routledge, 1988), pp. 40–54.

33. Jordan, *Philanthropy in England*.

34. *Archdeacon Harpsfield's Visitation of 1557*, ed. L. E. Whatmore, Catholic Records Society, 45–6 (London: Catholic Records Society, 1950–1).

35. P. Collinson, *The Religion of Protestants: The Church in English Society, 1559–1625* (Oxford: Clarendon Press, 1982), pp. 136–40.

36. Collinson, 'The Persecution in Kent', p. 331

37. *Visitation Articles*, vol. 3, pp. 8–29, 59–73.

38. W. Cecil, *The Execution of Justice in England* (London, 1583) [*RSTC* 4902], ed. R. Kingdon, Folger Documents of Tudor and Stuart Civilization (Ithaca, NY: Folger Shakespeare Library, 1965), p. 8.

39. See J. J. Larocca, 'Papacy and Pounds: The Effect of the Jesuit Mission on Penal Legislation', in T. M. McCoog (ed.), *The Reckoned Expense: Edmund Campion and the Early English Jesuits* (Woodbridge: Boydell, 1996), pp. 249–64.

40. Ibid.

41. A. Walsham, *Church Papists: Catholicism, Conformity and Confessional Polemic in Early Modern England* (Woodbridge: Boydell/Royal Historical Society, 1993); A. Dillon, *The Construction of Martyrdom in the English Catholic Community, 1535–1603* (Aldershot: Ashgate, 2002).

42. Dillon, *The Construction of Martyrdom*, pp. 1–17.

43. Walsham, *Church Papists*; J. Bossy, *The English Catholic Community, 1570–1850* (London: Darton, Longman & Todd, 1975).

44. At the examination of Thomas Wattes, a Billericay linen draper, the defendant was asked by Sir Anthony Browne where he learned his heresies, to which he responded 'even of you Sir ... For in King Edward dayes in open sessions you spake against this Religion now uses ... you then said the masse was abhominable'. Browne, of course, denied the charge. Duffy, *Fires of Faith*, p. 119.

45. Loades, *Mary Tudor*, p. 244; Duffy, 'Cardinal Pole Preaching', pp. 176–200.

46. See, for example, the story of the Colchester martyrs. Foxe, *Actes and Monuments*, pp. 1971–4.

47. Duffy, *Fires of Faith, passim*. Sometimes, however, conscience caught up with these evasions, as was the case with Richard Sharpe of Bristol. Foxe, *Actes and Monuments*, p. 2052.

48. The Royal Articles of 1559 were entirely concerned with behaviour and, although aimed at the clergy, were not at all doctrinal, except by implication. *Visitation Articles*, vol. 3, pp. 1–7.
49. Even Foxe's account of Elizabeth's sufferings recognizes this point. *Actes and Monuments*, pp. 2091–2, 2094–7.
50. W. P. Haugaard, 'Elizabeth Tudor's Book of Devotions: A Neglected Clue to the Queen's Life and Character', *Sixteenth-Century Journal*, 12 (1981), pp. 79–105.
51. Verstegen wrote the majority of his works in Latin or French. Only after 1590 did he begin to publish in English, and by then his market was very largely confined to the recusant community. Dillon, *The Construction of Martyrdom*, pp. 229–42.

WORKS CITED

Manuscripts

British Library

    Add. MS 28533.

    Egerton MS 2886.

    Harley MS 416, 421, 425, 444.

    Lansdowne MS 160.

National Archives

    KB8.

    SP1, SP10, SP11, SP69.

    STAC 2.

    HCA/13/9.

Guildhall Library, Journal MS XV.

Greater London Record Office, DL/C/331.

Norfolk Record Office, Act/7/8.

Rochester Diocesan Registry, Rochester Registers, iv.

Calendars

Calendar of the Patent Rolls, Edward VI., 6 vols (London: HMSO, 1924–9).

Calendar of the Patent Rolls, Philip and Mary, 4 vols (London: HMSO, 1936–9).

Calendar of the Patent Rolls, Elizabeth, 9 vols (London: HMSO, 1939–86).

Calendar of State Papers, Domestic, Edward VI, ed. C. S. Knighton (London: HMSO, 1992).

Calendar of State Papers, Domestic, Mary, ed. C. S. Knighton (London: HMSO, 1998).

Calendar of State Papers, Spanish, ed. R. Tyler et al., 13 vols in 20 (London: Longman, Green, Longman & Roberts, 1862–1964).

Calendar of State Papers, Venetian, ed. R. Brown et al., 38 vols (London: Longman, Green, Longman & Roberts, 1864–1947).

Second Report of the Historical Manuscripts Commission, Appendix (London, 1841).

Primary Sources

The Accounts of the Wardens of Morebath, Devon, 1515–1573, ed. J. E. Binney (Exeter: J. G. Commin, 1904).

Acts of the Privy Council, ed. J. R. Dasent, 32 vols (London: HMSO, 1880–1907).

Allen, W., *Letters and Memorials of Cardinal Allen*, ed. T. F. Knox (London: D. Nutt, 1882).

Ars Moriendi (London: Wynkyn de Worde, 1506) [*RSTC* 788].

Aylmer, J., *An Harborowe for Faithfull and True Subjects* (London, 1559) [*RSTC* 1005].

Bale, J., *The Image of Bothe Churches* (Antwerp, 1545) [*RSTC* 1296.5].

Bede, *Bede's Ecclesiastical History of the English People*, ed. B. Colgrave and R. A. B. Mynors, corrected edn (Oxford: Oxford University Press, 1991).

Bonner, E., *A Profitable and Necessarye Doctryne, with certayne Homelies* (London, 1555) [*RSTC* 3283].

—, *An Honest Godlye Instruction: And Information for the Tranynge, and Bringinge up of Children* (London, 1556) [*RSTC* 3281].

Brice, T., *A Compendious Register in Metre* (London, 1559) [*RSTC* 3726], reprinted in Pollard, *Tudor Tracts*, pp. 259–88.

Cecil, W., *The Execution of Justice in England* (London, 1583) [*RSTC* 4902], ed. R. Kingdon, Folger Documents of Tudor and Stuart Civilization (Ithaca, NY: Folger Shakespeare Library, 1965).

Christopherson, J., *An Exhortation to all Menne to Take Hede and Beware of Rebellion* (London, 1554) [*RSTC* 5207].

The Chronicle of Queen Jane and of the First Two Years of Mary, ed. J. G. Nichols, Camden Society, 48 (London: Camden Society, 1850).

'Churchwarden's Accounts of Levendon in the County of Lincoln, 1492–1598', ed. E. Peacock, *Archaelogia*, 41 (1867), pp. 333–70.

Commentarii rerum in Ecclesia Gestarum (Strasburg: Rihelius, 1554).

Consilium ... de emendanda ecclesia (1537), reprinted in B. J. Kidd, *Documents Illustrative of the Continental Reformation* (Oxford: Oxford University Press, 1911), pp. 307–18.

Cranmer, T., *All the Submyssions and Recantations of Thomas Cranmer* (London, 1556) [*RSTC* 5990].

—, *The Works of Thomas Cranmer*, ed. J. E. Cox, 2 vols (London: Parker Society, 1844–6).

Davis, N. (ed.), *Non-Cycle Plays and Fragments* (London: Early English Text Society, 1970).

Diaz-Plaja, F. (ed.), *La Historia de Espana en sus Documentos* (Madrid: Instituto de Estudios Políticos, 1958).

Dives and Pauper, ed. P. H. Barnum, 2 vols (London: Early English Text Society, 1976–80).

D[oleman], N. [R. Parsons], *A Treatise of Three Conversions of England from Paganisme to Chrsytian Religion* (St Omer, 1603) [*RSTC* 19416].

Erasmus, D., *Opus Epistolarum Des. Erasmi Roterdami*, ed. P. S. Allen et al., 12 vols (Oxford: Oxford University Press, 1906–58).

An Exclamation upon the Erronious and Fantasticall Sprite of Heresy (London, [1553?]) [*RSTC* 10615].

Exoneratorium Curatorum (London, 1534) [*RSTC* 10634]

Figueroa, G. S., Count of Feria, 'The Count of Feria's Despatch to Philip II of 14 November 1558', ed. M.-J. Rodriguez Salgado and S. Adams, *Camden Miscellany*, 28 (1984) pp. 302–44.

Fisher, J., *A Sermon very Notable Fruicteful, and Godlie* (London, 1554) [*RSTC* 10896].

—, *The English Works of John Fisher*, ed. J. E. B. Mayor (London: Early English Text Society, 1876).

The Floure of the Commaundementes of God (London: W. de Worde, 1510) [*RSTC* 23876].

Four Supplications, 1529–1553, ed. F. J. Furnivall and J. Meadows Cooper (London: Early English Text Society, 1871).

Foxe, J., *The First (and Second) Volumes of the Ecclesiastical History*, 2 vols (London, 1570) [*RSTC* 11223].

—, *The Acts and Monuments of the English Martyrs* (1583 edn, available at http://www.hrion-line.ac.uk/johnfoxe/) [editions 1563, 1570, 1576 available at same site; and there were also editions in 1596, 1610, 1632].

—, *Foxe's Book of Martyrs: Selected Nar*ratives, ed. J. N. King (Oxford: Oxford University Press, 2009).

Furnivall, F. J. (ed.), *Political, Religious and Love Poems from the Archbishop of Canterbury's Lambeth MS no. 306* (London: Early English Text Society, 1866).

Gardiner, S., *The Letters of Stephen Gardiner*, ed. J. A. Muller (Cambridge: Cambridge University Press, 1933).

The Glasse of Truth (London, 1532) [*RSTC* 11918].

Guido de Monte Rocherii, *Manipulus Curatorum* (London, 1508) [*RSTC* 12474].

Gwynneth, J., *A Brief Declaration of the Notable Victory geven of God* (London, 1554) [*RSTC* 12556.7].

Harpesfield, N., *Archdeacon Harpsfield's Visitation*, ed. L. E. Whatmore, Publications of the Catholic Records Society, 45–6 (London: Catholic Records Society, 1950–1).

Hart, H., *A Godly newe short Treatyse Instructyng every Parson, howe they shulde Trade theyr Lyves in the Imytacyon of Vertu, and Shewying of Vyce* (London, 1548) [*RSTC* 12887].

Henry VIII, *Assertio Septem Sacramentorum* (London, 1521) [*RSTC* 13078].

Hooker, R., *The Laws of Ecclesiastical Polity*, Everyman's Library, 201–2, 2 vols (London: J. M. Dent & Co., 1907).

Horstmann, C. (ed.), *The Minor Poems of the Vernon Manuscript*, 2 vols (London: Early English Text Society, 1892–1901).

Huggarde, M., *The Displaying of the Protestantes* (London, 1556) [*RSTC* 13557–8].

Instructions for Parish Priests, ed. E. Peacock (London: Early English Text Society, 1868).

Jaffe, P. (ed.), *Regesta pontificum romanorum annum 1198*, 2nd edn, ed. S. Loewenfeld et al., 2 vols (Leipzig: Veit, 1885–8).

The Kalendar of Shepherdes, ed. H. O. Sommer (London: K. Paul, Trench, Trübner & Co., 1892).

Kempe, M., *The Booke of Margery Kempe*, ed. S. B. Meech and H. E. Allen (London: Early English Text Society, 1940).

The King's Book, ed. T. A. Lacey (London: SPCK, 1932).

Kitching, C. J. (ed.), *The London and Middlesex Chantry Certificates, 1548*, London Record Society Publications, 16 (London: London Record Society, 1980).

Knox, J., *The Works of John Knox*, ed. D. Laing, 6 vols (Edinburgh: Wodrow Society, 1846–64).

Lamb, J. (ed.), *A Collection of Letters, Statutes and other Documents, from the MS Library of Corp. Christ. Coll.* (London: J. W. Parker, 1838).

Letters and Papers, Foreign and Domestic, of the Reign of Henry VIII, ed. J. Gairdner et al., 23 vols in 35 (London: Longman, Green, Longman, Roberts & Green, 1862–1910).

Luria, M. S., and R. L. Hoffman (eds.), *Middle English Lyrics* (New York: Norton, 1974).

Machyn, H., *The Diary of Henry Machyn*, ed. J. G. Nichols, Camden Society, 42 (London: Camden Society, 1848).

The Manual of Prayers, or the Primer in Englysh and Laten ... set forth by John [Hilsey], Bishop of Rochester (London, 1539) [RSTC 16009.5].

Meltham, W. de, *Sermo Exhortatius Cancellarii Eborum hiis qui ad sacros ordines petunt promoveri* (London, 1510) [*RSTC* 17806].

Mirkus, J., *Mirk's Festial: A Collection of Homilies by Johannes Mirkus*, ed. T. Erbe (London: Early English Text Society, 1905).

Missale ad usum Insignis et Praeclare Ecclesiae Sarum, ed. F. H. Dickinson (Burntisland, 1861–83).

More, T., *A Dialog of Comfort against Tribulacion, made by Syr Thomas More Knyght* (London, 1553) [*RSTC* 18082].

—, *The Workes of Sir Thomas More Knyght, sometime Lorde Chauncellour of England* (London, 1557) [*RSTC* 18076].

—, *The Correspondence of Sir Thomas More*, ed. E. R. Rogers (Princeton, NJ: Princeton University Press, 1947).

Nichols, J. G. (ed.), *Narratives of the Days of the Reformation* (London: Camden Society, 1859).

Ordynarye of Chrystyantye or of Chrysten Men (London: Wynkyn de Worde, 1502) [*RSTC* 5198]

Parkyn, R., 'Robert Parkyn's Narrative of the Reformation', *English Historical Review*, 62 (1947), pp. 58–63.

A Plaine and Godlye Treatise, concernynge the Masse (London, 1555) [*RSTC* 17629].

Pole, R., *Epistolarum Reginaldi Poli, SRE Cardinalis et aliorum ad ipsum*, ed. A. M. Quirini, 5 vols (Brescia: Rizzardi, 1744–57).

—, *The Correspondence of Reginald Pole. 3. A Calendar 1553–1558: Restoring the English Church*, ed. T. F. Mayer (Aldershot: Ashgate, 2004).

Pollard, A. F. (ed.) *Tudor Tracts* (London: Constable, 1903).

Pollard, L., *Fyve Homilies* (London: 1556) [*RSTC* 20091].

Proctor, J., *The Historie of Wiatts Rebellion* (London, 1554) [*RSTC* 20407], reprinted in Pollard, *Tudor Tracts*, pp. 199–259.

Public Record Office, *Fourth Report of the Deputy Keeper of the Public Records* (London: HMSO, 1843).

Rerum in Ecclesia Gestarum (Basle: Oporinus, 1559).

Ridley, N., *The Works of Bishop Ridley*, ed. H. Christmas (Cambridge: Parker Society, 1841).

Roye, G. de, *Thus Endeth the Doctrinal of Sapyence*, ed. W. Caxton (London, 1489) [*RSTC* 21431].

Rymer, T., et al. (eds), *Foedera, Conventiones, Litterae, etc.*, 20 vols (London: A. & J. Churchill, 1704–35).

Smith, R., *A Bouclier of the Catholike Fayth of Christes Church* (London, 1554) [*RSTC* 22816].

Standish, J., *The Triall of the Supremacie* (London, 1556) [*RSTC* 23211].

'Stanford Churchwarden's Accounts, 1552–1602', ed. W. Haines, *Antiquary*, 17 (1888), pp. 70–213.

State Papers of King Henry VIII, 11 vols (London: Record Commission, 1830–52).

Statutes of the Realm, ed. A Luders, T. E. Tomlins, J. Raithby et al., 11 vols (London, 1810–28).

Stopes, L., *An Ave Maria in Commendation of our Most Vertuous Quene* (London, 1553) [*RSTC* 23292].

Stow, J., *A Survey of London by John Stow*, ed. C. L. Kingsford, 2 vols (Oxford: Clarendon Press, 1908).

Strype, J., *Ecclesiastical Memorials*, 3 vols (London, 1721; Oxford: Clarendon Press, 1820).

Taverner, R., *A Catechisme or Institution of the Christen Religion* (London, 1539) [*RSTC* 23709].

Testamenta Eboracensia: A Selection of Wills from the Registry at York, Vol. 4, ed. J. Raine and J. W. Clay, Publications of the Surtees Society, 53 (Durham: Surtees Society, 1869).

Tres Cartas de lo sucedido en el viaje de su Alteza a Inglaterra (Madrid: La Sociedad de Bibliofilos Espanoles, 1877).

Tudor Royal Proclamations, ed. P. L. Hughes and J. F. Larkin, 3 vols (New Haven, CT: Yale University Press, 1964–9).

Tunstall, C., *De Veritatis Corporis Domini* (London, 1554) [*RSTC* 24633.5].

Two Sermons Preached by the Boy Bishop; one at St. Pauls, temp. Henry VII, the other at Glouces-ter, temp. Mary, ed. J. G. Nichols, Camden Miscellany, 7 (London: Camden Society, 1875).

Tyndale, W., *The Practice of Prelates* (Antwerp, 1530).

Udall, N., *The First Tome or Volume of the Paraphrases of Erasmus upon the New Testament* (London, 1548) [*RSTC* 2854].

Underhill, E., 'The Narrative of Edward Underhill', in Pollard, *Tudor Tracts*, pp. 170–99.

Visitation Articles and Injunctions of the Period of the Reformation, ed. W. H. Frere and W. M. Kennedy, Alcuin Club Collections, 14–16, 3 vols (London: Longmans, Green, 1910).

Watson, T., *Holsome and Catholyke Doctryne concerninge the Seven Sacraments* (London, 1558) [*RSTC* 25112].

Wilkins, D., *Concilia Magna Brittaniae et Hiberniae*, 4 vols (London, 1737).

Wingfield, R., 'The Vita Mariae Angliae Reginae of Robert Wingfield of Brantham', ed. D. MacCulloch, *Camden Miscellany*, 28 (1984), pp. 181–301.

Wyse, N., *A Consolacyon for Chrysten People to Repayre Agayn the Lordes Temple* (London, 1538) [*RSTC* 26063].

The Zurich Letters, ed. H. Robinson (London: Parker Society, 1845).

Secondary Sources

Adair, J., *The Pilgrims Way: Shrines and Saints in Britain and Ireland* (London: Thames & Hudson, 1978).

Alexander, G., 'Bonner and the Marian Persecution', in Haigh (ed.), *The English Reformation Revised*, pp. 157–75.

Alsop, J. D., 'A Regime at Sea: The Navy and the Succession Crisis of 1553', *Albion*, 24 (1992), pp. 577–90.

Aries, P., *The Hour of our Death*, trans. H. Weaver (London: Allen Lane, 1981).

Aston, M., *Lollards and Reformers: Images and Literacy in Late Medieval Religion* (London: Hambledon, 1984).

Bainton, R. H., *Erasmus of Christendom* (New York: Scribner, 1969).

Baldwin, D., *The Chapel Royal: Ancient and Modern* (London: Duckworth, 1990).

Baskerville, G., 'Married Clergy and Pensioned Religious in Norwich Diocese, 1555', *English Historical Review*, 48 (1933), pp. 43–64.

—, *English Monks and the Suppression of the Monasteries* (London: Cape, 1937).

Bellamy, J. G., *Crime and Public Order in England in the Later Middle Ages* (Routledge, 1973).

Bennett, M., *Richard II and the Revolution of 1399* (Stroud: Sutton, 1999).

Binski, P., *Medieval Death: Ritual and Representation* (New Haven, CT: Yale University Press, 1996).

Blair, J., 'From Minster to Parish', in J. Blair (ed.), *Minsters and Parish Churches: The Local Church in Transition, 950–1200* (Oxford: Oxford Committee for Archaeology, 1988), pp. 1–19.

Bossy, J., *The English Catholic Community, 1570–1850* (London: Darton, Longman & Todd, 1975).

—, *Christianity in the West, 1400–1700* (Oxford: Oxford University Press, 1985).

— (ed.), *Disputes and Settlements: Law and Human Relations in the West* (Cambridge: Cambridge University Press, 1993).

Brand, J., *Popular Antiquities of Great Britain*, ed. H. Carew Hazlett, 3 vols (London: J. R. Smith, 1870).

Bray, G. (ed.), *The Anglican Canons, 1529–1947*, Church of England Records Society, 6 (Woodbridge: Boydell, 1998).

Brigden, S., *London and the Reformation* (Oxford: Clarendon Press, 1989).

Burnet, G., *The History of the Reformation of the Church of England*, 3 vols (London, 1679–1715).

Bush, M. L., *The Government Policy of Protestor Somerset* (Manchester: Manchester University Press, 1975).

Burckhardt, J., *The Age of Constantine the Great*, trans. M. Hadas (London: Routledge & Kegan Paul, 1949).

Byford, M. S., 'The Price of Protestantism: Assessing the Impact of Religious Change in Elizabethan Essex, the Cases of Heydon and Colchester, 1558–1594' (DPhil thesis, University of Oxford, 1988).

Cameron, E., *The Reformation of the Heretics: The Waldenses of the Alps, 1480–1580* (Oxford: Oxford University Press, 1984).

Caracciolo, A., *Vita Pauli IV* (Cologne, 1612).

Cockburn, J. S., *A History of the English Assizes, 1558–1714* (Cambridge: Cambridge University Press, 1972).

Collinson, P., *The Elizabethan Puritan Movement* (London: Cape, 1967).

—, *The Religion of Protestants: The Church in English Society, 1559–1625* (Oxford: Clarendon Press, 1982).

—, *Godly People: Essays in Protestantism and Puritanism* (London: Hambledon, 1985).

—, 'The Persecution in Kent', in Duffy and Loades (eds), *The Church of Mary Tudor*, pp. 309–33.

Cox, J. C. *The Parish Registers of England* (London: Methuen, 1910).

Cornwall, J., *The Revolt of the Peasantry, 1549* (London: Routledge, 1977).

Craig, J., 'Reformers, Conflict and Revisionism: The Reformation in Sixteenth-Century Hadleigh', *Historical Journal*, 42 (1999), pp. 1–23.

Cressy, D., *Education in Tudor and Stuart England* (London: Arnold, 1975).

—, *Literacy and the Social Order: Reading and Writing in Tudor and Stuart England* (Cambridge: Cambridge University Press, 1980).

Cross, C., 'The English Universities, 1553–1558', in Duffy and Loades (eds), *The Church of Mary Tudor*, pp. 57–76.

Danner, D. G., *Pilgrimage to Puritanism: The History and Theology of the Marian Exiles at Geneva, 1555–1560* (New York: Peter Levey, 1999).

Daniell, D., *The Bible in English: Its History and Influence* (New Haven, CT: Yale University Press, 2003).

Davies, J. C., *The Baronial Opposition to Edward II* (Cambridge: Cambridge University Press, 1918).

Davies, N., *Europe: A History* (London: Pimlico, 1997).

Davis, J. F., *Heresy and Reformation in the South East of England 1520–1559* (London: Royal Historical Society, 1983).

Deansley, M., *The Lollard Bible and other Medieval Biblical Versions* (Cambridge: Cambridge University Press, 1920).

Dickens, A. G., *Robert Holgate*, St Anthony's Hall Publications, 8 (London: St Anthony's Press, 1955).

—, *The English Reformation* (London: Batsford, 1964).

Dillon, A., *The Construction of Martyrdom in the English Catholic Community, 1535–1603* (Aldershot: Ashgate, 2002).

Dockray, K., *Henry V* (Stroud: Tempus, 2004).

Duffy, E., *The Stripping of the Altars* (New Haven, CT: Yale University Press, 1992).

—, *The Voices of Morebath* (New Haven, CT: Yale University Press, 2001).

—, 'Cardinal Pole Preaching: St. Andrew's Day 1557', in Duffy and Loades (eds), *The Church of Mary Tudor*, pp. 176–200.

—, *Fires of Faith: Catholic England under Mary Tudor* (New Haven, CT: Yale University Press, 2009).

Duffy, E., and D. Loades (eds), *The Church of Mary Tudor* (Aldershot: Ashgate, 2006).

Dyer, A. D., *Decline and Growth in English Towns, 1400–1640* (London: Macmillan, 1991).

Dyer, C., *Standards of Living in the Later Middle Ages: Social Change in England, c. 1200–1520* (Cambridge: Cambridge University Press, 1989).

Edwards, J., 'Corpus Christi at Kingston upon Thames: Bartolomé Carranza and the Eucharist in Marian England', in Edwards and Truman (eds), *Reforming Catholicism*, pp. 139–53.

—, 'Spanish Influence in Marian England', in Duffy and Loades (eds), *The Church of Mary Tudor*, pp. 201–26.

Edwards, J., and R. Truman (eds), *Reforming Catholicism in the England of Mary Tudor: The Achievement of Fray Bartolomé Carranza* (Aldershot: Ashgate, 2005).

Elton, G. R., *Policy and Police* (Cambridge: Cambridge University Press, 1972).

—, *The Tudor Constitution* (Cambridge: Cambridge University Press, 1982).

—, *Thomas Cromwell*, 2nd edn, ed. D. Loades (Oxford: Davenant, 2008).

Eppley, D., *Defending the Royal Supremacy and Discerning God's Will in Tudor England* (Aldershot: Ashgate, 2007).

Farmer. H., *The Oxford Dictionary of the Saints* (Oxford: Oxford University Press, 1978).

Felch, S., 'Shaping the Reader in the *Acts and Monuments*', in Loades (ed.), *John Foxe and the English Reformation*, pp. 52–65.

Fenlon, D., *Heresy and Obedience in Tridentine Italy* (Cambridge: Cambridge University Press, 1972).

Finucane, R., *Miracles and Pilgrims: Popular Beliefs in Medieval England* (London: Dent, 1977).

Fletcher, A., and D. MacCulloch, *Tudor Rebellions* (Harlow: Longmans, 1997).

Fowler, J., 'On Medieval Representations of the Months and Seasons', *Archaelogia*, 44 (1873), pp. 137–224.

Frede, C. de, *La Restaurazione Cattolica in Inghilterra sotto Maria Tudor* (Naples: Libreria scientifica editrice, 1971).

Freeman, J., 'The Parish Ministry in the Diocese of Durham, c. 1570–1640' (PhD thesis, University of Durham, 1979).

Freeman, T. S., 'Notes on a Source for John Foxe's Account of the Marian Persecution in Kent and Sussex', *Historical Research*, 67 (1994), pp. 203–11.

—, 'Dissenters from a Dissenting Church: The Challenge of the Freewillers, 1550–1558', in Marshall and Ryrie (eds), *The Beginnings of English Protestantism*, pp. 129–56.

Frere, W. H., *The Marian Reaction in its Relation to the English Clergy* (London: SPCK, 1896).

Garrett, C. H., *The Marian Exiles* (Cambridge: Cambridge University Press, 1938).

—, 'The Legatine Register of Cardinal Pole, 1554–7', *Journal of Modern History*, 13 (1941), pp. 189–94.

Gibbs, G., '"Marking the Days": Henry Machyn's Manuscript and the Mid-Tudor Era', in Duffy and Loades (eds), *The Church of Mary Tudor*, pp. 281–308.

Green, I., *Print and Protestantism in Early Modern England* (Oxford: Oxford University Press, 2000).

Gregory, B., *Salvation at Stake: Christian Martyrdom in Early Modern Europe* (Cambridge, MA: Harvard University Press, 1999).

Grieve, H., 'The Deprived Married Clergy in Essex, 1553–1561', *Transactions of the Royal Historical Society*, 4th series, 22 (1940), pp. 141–69.

Guy, J. A., *The Public Career of Sir Thomas More* (Brighton: Harvester, 1980).

Gwyn, P., *The King's Cardinal: The Rise and Fall of Thomas Wolsey* (London: Barrie & Jenkins, 1990).

Haigh, C., 'The Continuity of Catholicism in the English Reformation', *Past and Present*, 93 (1983), pp. 37–69.

— (ed.), *The English Reformation Revised* (Cambridge: Cambridge University Press, 1987).

—, *English Reformations* (Oxford: Oxford University Press, 1993).

Haines, R. M., *Ecclesia Anglicana: Studies in the English Church of the Later Middle Ages* (Toronto: University of Toronto Press, 1989).

Harvey, B. E., *Living and Dying in England, 1100–1540: The Monastic Experience* (Oxford: Oxford University Press, 1993).

Haugaard, W. P., *Elizabeth and the English Reformation* (Cambridge: Cambridge University Press, 1968).

—, 'Elizabeth Tudor's Book of Devotions: A Neglected Clue to the Queen's Life and Character', *Sixteenth-Century Journal*, 12 (1981), pp. 79–105.

Heal, F., 'What can King Lucius do for You? The Reformation and the Early British Church', *English Historical Review*, 120 (2005), pp. 593–614.

Heath, P., *The English Parish Clergy on the Eve of the Reformation* (London: Routledge & Kegan Paul, 1969).

Hegarty, A., 'Carranza and the English Universities', in Edwards and Truman (eds), *Reforming Catholicism*, pp. 153–72.

Highley, C., and J. N. King (eds), *John Foxe and His World* (Aldershot: Ashgate, 2002).

Hoak, D., 'The Coronations of Edward VI, Mary and Elizabeth I', in Knighton and Mortimer (eds), *Westminster Abbey Reformed*, pp. 114–52.

Holt, J. C., *Magna Carta and Medieval Government* (London: Hambledon, 1985).

Hope, A., 'Martyrs of the Marsh: Elizabeth Barton, Joan Bocher and Trajectories of Martyrdom in Reformation Kent', in Lutton and Salter (eds), *Pieties in Transition*, pp. 41–58.

Houlbrooke, R., *Church Courts and the People during the English Reformation* (Oxford: Oxford University Press, 1979).

—, *Death, Religion and the Family in England 1480–1750* (Oxford: Oxford University Press, 1998).

—, 'The Clergy, the Church Courts and the Marian Restoration in Norwich', in Duffy and Loades (eds), *The Church of Mary Tudor*, pp. 124–48.

Hoyle, R. W., *The Pilgrimage of Grace and the Politics of the 1530s* (Oxford: Oxford University Press, 2001).

Hudson, A., *The Premature Reformation: Wycliffite Texts and Lollard History* (Oxford: Oxford University Press, 1988).

Hughes, P., *The Reformation in England*, 3 vols (London: Hollis & Carter, 1954–6).

Hutton, R., 'The Local Impact of the Tudor Reformation', in Haigh (ed.). *The English Reformation Revised*, pp. 114–38.

Ives, E., *Lady Jane Grey: A Tudor Mystery* (Oxford: Wiley/Blackwell, 2009).

James, S., *Katheryn Parr: The Making of a Queen* (Stroud: Sutton, 1999).

Jedin, H., *A History of the Council of Trent*, trans. E. Graf, 2 vols (London: T. Nelson, 1958).

Jenkins, A., and P. Preston, *Biblical Scholarship and the Church: A Sixteenth-Century Crisis of Authority* (Aldershot: Ashgate, 2007).

Johnson, J., *English Canons*, 2 vols (Oxford: Parker, 1850–1).

Jones, N. L., *Faith by Statute* (London: Royal Historical Society, 1982).

Jones, W. R. D., *William Turner: Tudor Naturalist, Physician and Divine* (London: Routledge, 1988).

Jordan, W. K., *Philanthropy in England, 1480–1660* (London: Allen & Unwin, 1959).

—, *Edward VI: The Young King* (London: Allen & Unwin, 1968).

—, *Edward VI: The Threshold of Power* (London: Allen & Unwin, 1970).

Kamen, H., *Philip of Spain* (New Haven, CT: Yale University Press, 1997).

—, *The Spanish Inquisition: An Historical Revision* (London: Weidenfeld & Nicholson, 1997).

Kearney, H., *Scholars and Gentlemen: University and Society in Pre-Industrial Britain* (London: Faber, 1970).

Kerridge, E., *Agrarian Problems in the Sixteenth Century and After* (London: Allen & Unwin, 1969).

King, J. N., *English Reformation Literature: The Tudor Origins of the Protestant Tradition* (Princeton, NJ: Princeton University Press, 1982).

—, 'The Godly Woman in Elizabethan Iconography', *Renaissance Quarterly*, 38 (1985), pp.43–7.

—, 'John Day, Master Printer of the English Reformation', in Marshall and Ryrie (eds), *The Beginnings of English Protestantism*, pp. 180–208.

Knighton, C. S., and R. Mortimer (eds), *Westminster Abbey Reformed, 1540–1640* (Aldershot: Ashgate, 2003).

Knowles, D., *The Religious Orders in England*, 3 vols (Cambridge: Cambridge University Press, 1955–9).

—, *Bare Ruined Choirs: The Dissolution of the English Monasteries* (Cambridge: Cambridge University Press, 1976).

Kumin, B., *The Shaping of a Community: The Rise and Reformation of the English Parish, c. 1400–1560* (Aldershot: Ashgate, 1996).

Ladurie, E. Le Roy, *Montaillou: Cathars and Catholics in a French Village, 1294–1324*, trans. B. Bray (Harmondsworth: Penguin, 1980).

Lampe, G. W. H. (ed.), *The Cambridge History of the Bible, Vol. 2: The West, from the Fathers to the Reformation* (Cambridge: Cambridge University Press, 1969).

Larocca, J. J., 'Papacy and Pounds: The Effect of the Jesuit Mission on Penal Legislation', in T. M. McCoog (ed.), *The Reckoned Expense: Edmund Campion and the Early English Jesuits* (Woodbridge: Boydell, 1996), pp. 249–64.

Lehmberg, S. E., 'Supremacy and Viceregency: A Re-Examination', *English Historical Review*, 81 (1966), pp. 225–35.

Lipton, E., *Affections of the Mind: The Politics of Sacramental Marriage in Late Medieval English Literature* (Notre Dame, IN: University of Notre Dame Press, 2007).

Loach, J., 'The Marian Establishment and the Printing Press', *English Historical Review*, 100 (1986), pp. 138–51.

—, *Edward VI* (New Haven, CT: Yale University Press, 1999).

Loades, D., *Two Tudor Conspiracies* (Cambridge: Cambridge University Press, 1965).

—, *The Oxford Martyrs* (London: Batsford, 1970).

—, *Mary Tudor: A Life* (Oxford: Blackwell, 1989).

—, *The Reign of Mary Tudor* (London: Longmans, 1991).

—, *John Dudley, Duke of Northumberland* (Oxford: Oxford University Press, 1996).

— (ed.), *John Foxe and the English Reformation* (Aldershot: Ashgate, 1997).

—, *Tudor Government* (Oxford: Blackwell, 1997).

—, 'Anticlericalism in the Church of England before 1558; An "Eating Canker"?', in N. Aston and M. Cragoe (eds), *Anticlericalism* (Stroud: Sutton, 2000), pp. 18–41.

—, 'Afterword', in Highley and King (eds), *John Foxe and His World*, pp. 277–90.

—, 'John Foxe and Henry VIII', *John Foxe Bulletin*, 1:1 (2002), pp. 1–12.

—, 'The Sanctuary', in Knighton and Mortimer (eds), *Westminster Abbey Reformed*, pp. 75–93.

—, *Elizabeth I* (London: Hambledon, 2003).

—, *Intrigue and Treason, the Tudor Court 1547–1558* (London: Pearson, 2004).

—, 'The Personal Religion of Mary I', in Duffy and Loades (eds), *The Church of Mary Tudor*, pp. 1–29.

—, *Henry VIII: Court, Church and Conflict* (London: National Archives, 2009).

—, *The Six Wives of Henry VIII* (Stroud: Amberley, 2009).

Lot, F., *The End of the Ancient World* (London: Routledge, 1966).

Lutton, R., *Lollardy and Orthodox Religion in Pre-Reformation England* (London: Royal Historical Society, 2006).

—, 'Geographies and Materialities of Piety: Reconciling Competing Narratives of Religious Change in Pre-Reformation and Reformation England', in Lutton and Salter (eds), *Pieties in Transition*, pp. 11–40.

Lutton, R., and E. Salter (eds), *Pieties in Transition: Religious Practices and Experiences, c. 1400–1640* (Aldershot: Ashgate, 2007).

MacCulloch, D., *Thomas Cranmer* (New Haven, CT: Yale University Press, 1996).

—, *Tudor Church Militant: Edward VI and the Protestant Reformation* (London: Allen Lane, 1999).

Macek, E., 'The Emergence of a Female Spirituality in the Book of Martyrs', *Sixteenth-Century Journal*, 19 (1988), p. 63–80.

McGrath, A., *Christian Theology: An Introduction* (Oxford: Blackwell, 1994).

McNair, P., *Peter Martyr in Italy: An Anatomy of Apostasy* (Oxford: Oxford University Press, 1967).

Makower, F., *The Constitutional History of the Church of England* (London: Swan Sonnenschein, 1895).

Marshall, P., 'Papist as Heretic: The Burning of John Forrest, 1538', *Historical Journal*, 41 (1998), pp. 351–74.

—, *Beliefs and the Dead in Reformation England* (Oxford: Oxford University Press, 2002).

Marshall, P., and A. Ryrie (eds), *The Beginnings of English Protestantism* (Cambridge: Cambridge University Press, 2002).

Martin, J. W., 'Miles Hogarde, Artisan and Aspiring Author in Sixteenth-Century England', *Renaissance Quarterly*, 34 (1981), pp. 83–105.

—, *Religious Radicals in Tudor England* (London: Hambledon, 1989).

Mayer, T. F., *Reginald Pole: Prince and Prophet* (Cambridge: Cambridge University Press, 2000).

—, 'The Success of Cardinal Pole's Final Legation', in Duffy and Loades (eds), *The Church of Mary Tudor*, pp. 149–75.

Mayr-Harting, H., *The Coming of Christianity to Anglo-Saxon England* (London: Batsford, 1972).

Muller, J. A., *Stephen Gardiner and the Tudor Reaction* (1926; London: Octagon, 1970).

Mullinger, J. B., *The University of Cambridge*, 3 vols (Cambridge: Cambridge University Press, 1873–1911).

Newcombe, D. G., *John Hooper: Tudor Bishop and Martyr* (Oxford: Davenant, 2009).

Nussbaum, D., 'Appropriating Martyrdom: Fears of Renewed Persecution and the 1632 Edition of the *Acts and Monuments*', in Loades (ed.), *John Foxe and the English Reformation*, pp. 178–91.

O'Day, R., *The English Clergy: The Emergence and Consolidation of a Profession, 1558–1642* (Leicester: Leicester University Press, 1979).

Ogier, D. M., *Reformation and Society in Guernsey* (Woodbridge: Boydell, 1996).

Oldenbourg, Z., *Massacre at Montsegur: A History of the Albigensian Crusade* (1961; London: Phoenix, 2000).

Oman, C., *The Dark Ages, ad 476–918*, 6th edn (London: Rivington, 1919).

Orme, N., *English Schools in the Middle Ages* (London: Methuen, 1973).

—, *Education and Society in Medieval and Renaissance England* (London: Hambledon Press, 1989).

Owen, D. M., *The Church and Society in Medieval Lincolnshire* (Lincoln: Lincoln Local History Society, 1971).

The Oxford Dictionary of National Biography (Oxford: Oxford University Press, 2004) [*ODNB*].

Palliser, D., 'Popular Reactions to the Reformation during the Years of Uncertainty, 1530–1570', in Haigh (ed.), *The English Reformation Revised*, pp. 94–114.

Pantin, W. A., *The English Church in the Fourteenth Century* (Cambridge: Cambridge University Press, 1955).

Parry, G., 'John Foxe, "Father of Lyes", and the Papists', in Loades (ed.), *John Foxe and the English Reformation*, pp. 295–305.

Pevsner, N., *Buildings of England: North East Norfolk and Norwich* (Harmondsworth: Penguin, 1962).

Potter, G. R., *Zwingli* (Cambridge: Cambridge University Press, 1976).

Powell, K. G., 'The Social Background to the Reformation in Gloucestershire', *Transactions of the Bristol and Gloucestershire Archaeological Society*, 92 (1973), pp. 96–120.

Redworth, G., *In Defence of the Church Catholic: The Life of Stephen Gardiner* (Oxford: Blackwell, 1990).

Rex, R., *Henry VIII and the English Reformation* (London: Macmillan, 1993).

—, 'The Friars in the English Reformation', in Marshall and Ryrie (eds), *The Beginnings of English Protestantism*, pp. 38–59.

—, *The Lollards* (Basingstoke: Macmillan, 2002).

Richardson, W. C., *A History of the Court of Augmentations, 1536–1554* (Baton Rouge, LA: University of Louisiana Press, 1961).

Roberts, J., 'Bibliographical Aspects of John Foxe', in Loades (ed.), *John Foxe and the English Reformation*, pp. 36–51.

Robinson, M. S., 'Doctors, Silly Poor Women and Rebel Whores: The Gendering of Conscience in Foxe's Acts and Monuments', in Highley and King (eds), *John Foxe and His World*, pp. 235–48.

Rose-Troup, F., *The Western Rebellion of 1549* (London: Smith, Elder, 1913).

Rupp, E. G., *Studies in the Making of the English Protestant Tradition* (Cambridge: Cambridge University Press, 1947).

Ryrie, A., *The Age of Reformation* (Harlow: Pearson, 2009).

Scarisbrick. J. J., *Henry VIII* (London: Eyre & Spotiswoode, 1968).

—, *The Reformation and the English People* (Oxford: Blackwell, 1984).

Sharp, C., *The Rising in the North: The 1569 Rebellion, being a reprint of the 'Memorials of the Rebellion of the Earls of Northumberland and Westmoreland'* (Durham: Shotton, 1975).

Simon, J., *Education and Society in Tudor England* (Cambridge: Cambridge University Press, 1979).

Skeeters, M. C., *Community and Clergy: Bristol and the Reformation, 1530–1570* (Oxford: Oxford University Press, 1993).

Smyth, C. H., *Cranmer and the Reformation under Edward VI* (London: SPCK, 1926).

Sommerville, C. J., *The Secularisation of Early Modern England: From Religious Culture to Religious Faith* (Oxford: Oxford University Press, 1992).

Spalding, J. C. (ed.), *The Reformation of the Ecclesiastical Laws of England, 1552*, Sixteenth-Century Essays and Studies, 19 (Kirksville, MO: Northeast Missouri State University, 1992).

Squibb, G. D., *Doctors Commons: A History of the College of Advocates and Doctors of Law* (Oxford: Clarendon Press, 1977).

Stephens, W. P., *The Theology of Huldrych Zwingli* (Oxford: Oxford University Press, 1986).

Sumption, J., *The Albigensian Crusade* (London: Faber, 1999).

Sweetinburgh, S., 'The Poor, Hospitals and Charity in Sixteenth Century Canterbury', in Lutton and Salter (eds), *Pieties in Transition*, pp. 59–73.

Tanner, N., *The Church in Late Medieval Norwich* (Toronto: Pontifical Institute of Medieval Studies, 1984).

Tellechea Idigoras, J. I., *Fray Bartolomé Carranza y el Cardenal Pole* (Pamplona: Diputación Foral de Navarra, Institución Príncipe de Viana, Consejo Superior de Investigaciones Científicas, 1977).

—, *Fray Bartolomé Carranza de Miranda: Investigaciones historicas*, Historia, 109 (Pamplona: Gobierna de Navarra, Departmento de Educacion y Cultura, 2002).

—, 'Fray Bartolomé Carranza: A Spanish Dominican in the England of Mary Tudor', trans. R. Truman, in Edwards and Truman (eds), *Reforming Catholicism*, pp. 21–33.

Thomas, K., *Religion and the Decline of Magic* (London: Weidenfeld & Nicholson, 1971).

Thompson, A. H., 'Pluralism in the Medieval Church; with Notes on Pluralities in the Diocese of Lincoln, 1366', *Reports and Papers of the Associated Architectural Societies*, 33 (1915), pp. 43–72.

Thompson, J. A. F., *The Later Lollards, 1414–1520* (Oxford: Oxford University Press, 1965).

Turner, R., *King John* (London: Longmans, 1994).

Victoria History of the County of Essex, 8 vols (London: Constable, 1903–83).

Victoria History of the County of Shropshire, 7 vols (London: Constable, 1908–98).

Wabuda, S., *Preaching during the English Reformation* (Cambridge: Cambridge University Press, 2002).

Walker, G. *Persuasive Fictions: Faction, Faith and Political Culture in the Reign of Henry VIII* (Aldershot: Scolar, 1996).

Walsham, A., *Church Papists: Catholicism, Conformity and Confessional Polemic in Early Modern England* (Woodbridge: Boydell/Royal Historical Society, 1993).

Westlake, H. F., *The Parish Gilds of Mediaeval England* (London: SPCK, 1919).

Whiting, R., *The Blind Devotion of the People: Popular Religion and the English Reformation* (Cambridge: Cambridge University Press, 1989).

Wizeman, W., 'The Sermons of Thomas Watson', in Duffy and Loades (eds), *The Church of Mary Tudor*, pp. 258–80.

—, *The Theology and Spirituality of Mary Tudor's Church* (Aldershot: Ashgate, 2006).

Wood, A., *The History and Antiquities of the University of Oxford*, 2 vols (Oxford, 1792–6).

Woodcock, B. L., *Medieval Ecclesiastical Courts in the Diocese of Canterbury* (Oxford: Oxford University Press, 1952).

Wood Legh, K. L., *Perpetual Chantries in Britain* (Oxford: Oxford University Press, 1965).

Youings, J., *The Dissolution of the Monasteries* (London: Penguin, 1971).

Zevin, E., 'Noble Power and the Tudor Monarchy: The Life of Edward Stanley, Earl of Derby' (PhD thesis, City of New York University, 2009).

INDEX